Bloom's Modern Critical Views

African-American
  Poets: Volume I
African-American
  Poets: Volume II
Aldous Huxley
Alfred, Lord Tennyson
Alice Walker
American Women
  Poets: 1650–1950
Amy Tan
Arthur Miller
Asian-American
  Writers
The Bible
The Brontës
Carson McCullers
Charles Dickens
Christopher Marlowe
C.S. Lewis
Dante Aligheri
David Mamet
Derek Walcott
Don DeLillo
Doris Lessing
Edgar Allan Poe
Émile Zola
Emily Dickinson
Ernest Hemingway
Eudora Welty
Eugene O'Neill
F. Scott Fitzgerald
Flannery O'Connor
Franz Kafka
Gabriel García
  Márquez
Geoffrey Chaucer

George Orwell
G.K. Chesterton
Gwendolyn Brooks
Hans Christian
  Andersen
Henry David Thoreau
Herman Melville
Hermann Hesse
H.G. Wells
Hispanic-American
  Writers
Homer
Honoré de Balzac
Jamaica Kincaid
James Joyce
Jane Austen
Jay Wright
J.D. Salinger
Jean-Paul Sartre
John Irving
John Keats
John Milton
John Steinbeck
José Saramago
J.R.R. Tolkien
Julio Cortázar
Kate Chopin
Kurt Vonnegut
Langston Hughes
Leo Tolstoy
Marcel Proust
Margaret Atwood
Mark Twain
Mary Wollstonecraft
  Shelley
Maya Angelou

Miguel de Cervantes
Milan Kundera
Nathaniel Hawthorne
Norman Mailer
Octavio Paz
Paul Auster
Philip Roth
Ralph Waldo Emerson
Ray Bradbury
Richard Wright
Robert Browning
Robert Frost
Robert Hayden
Robert Louis
  Stevenson
Salman Rushdie
Stephen Crane
Stephen King
Sylvia Plath
Tennessee Williams
Thomas Hardy
Thomas Pynchon
Tom Wolfe
Toni Morrison
Tony Kushner
Truman Capote
Walt Whitman
W.E.B. Du Bois
William Blake
William Faulkner
William Gaddis
William Shakespeare
William Wordsworth
Zora Neale Hurston

Bloom's Modern Critical Views

AMY TAN
New Edition

Edited and with an introduction by
Harold Bloom
Sterling Professor of the Humanities
Yale University

BLOOM'S
LITERARY CRITICISM
An imprint of Infobase Publishing

Editorial Consultant, Laurie Champion

Bloom's Modern Critical Views:
Amy Tan—New Edition
Copyright ©2009 by Infobase Publishing

Introduction ©2009 by Harold Bloom

Bloom's Literary Criticism
An imprint of Infobase Publishing
132 West 31st Street
New York NY 10001

Library of Congress Cataloging-in-Publication Data

Amy Tan / edited and with an introduction by Harold Bloom. — New ed.
     p. cm. — (Blooms's modern critical views)
Includes bibliographical references and index.
ISBN 978-1-60413-179-6 ((hardcover: alk. paper) : alk. paper) 1. Tan, Amy—Criticism
and interpretation. 2. Women and literature—United States—History—20th century.
3. Women and literature—United States—History—21st century. 4. Chinese American
women in literature. 5. Chinese Americans in literature. I. Bloom, Harold.

PS3570.A48Z525 2008
813'.54—dc22
                                    2008028039

Cover design by Ben Peterson

Printed in the United States of America
Bang BCL 10 9 8 7 6 5 4 3 2 1

This book is printed on acid-free paper.

All links and Web addresses were checked and verified to be correct at the time of
publication. Because of the dynamic nature of the Web, some addresses and links may
have changed since publication and may no longer be valid.

Contents

Editor's Note

My introduction admires what still seems to me the best of Amy Tan: "Two Kinds" in *The Joy Luck Club*.

Melanie McAlister attempts to provide political contexts for *The Joy Luck Club*, while Marina Heung invokes mother-daughter relationships.

The Kitchen God's Wife provokes Judith Caesar to meditation on imperialism, after which Sau-Ling Cynthia Wong locates Tan in her readership's situation.

Myth in Tan is Wenying Xu's subject, while M. Marie Booth Foster brings us back to the mother-daughter agon.

The burden of Americanization in *The Hundred Secret Senses* is taken up by Lina Unali, after which Patricia L. Hamilton discourses on astrology in Amy Tan.

Yuan Yuan contrasts Tan and Maxine Hong Kingston, while Shen-Mei Ma finds new age imagery relevant to Tan.

Shadows of the canonical are elaborated by Lisa M. S. Dunick in regard to all of Tan to date.

HAROLD BLOOM

Introduction

AMY TAN (1952–)

I have written about Amy Tan's "Two Kinds" before and return to it in this rather brief introduction because it is a kind of paradigm-passage in what is still a very early phase of an emerging Chinese-American literature. The passage haunts me because it could fit equally well into the early Jewish American literature of my youth, two-thirds of a century ago.

> She yanked me by the arm, pulled me off the floor, snapped off the TV. She was frighteningly strong, half pulling, half carrying me toward the piano as I kicked the throw rugs under my feet. She lifted me up and onto the hard bench. I was sobbing by now, looking at her bitterly. Her chest was heaving even more and her mouth was open, smiling crazily as if she were pleased I was crying.
>
> "You want me to be someone I'm not!" I sobbed. "I'll never be the kind of daughter you want me to be!"
>
> "Only two kinds of daughters," she shouted in Chinese. "Those who are obedient and those who follow their own mind! Only one kind of daughter can live in this house. Obedient daughter!"
>
> "Then I wish I wasn't your daughter. I wish you weren't my mother," I shouted. As I said these things I got scared. I felt like worms and toads and slimy things were crawling out of my chest, but it also felt good, as if this awful side of me had surfaced, at last.
>
> "Too late to change this," said my mother shrilly.

And I could sense her anger rising to its breaking point. I wanted to see it spill over. And that's when I remembered the babies she had lost in China, the ones we never talked about.

"Then I wish I'd never been born!" I shouted. "I wish I were dead! Like them."

It was if I had said the magic words, Alakazam!—and her face went blank, her mouth closed, her arms went slack, and she backed out of the room, stunned, as if she were blowing away like a small brown leaf, thin, brittle, lifeless.

This has the power of simplicity and of universality, though its style is a touch inadequate to its anguish. "Two Kinds" has the irony, as a title, of meaning also two worlds, China and the United States. The daughter, understandably in flight from a love so possessive that it could destroy, is also obsessed by an unwarranted yet inevitable guilt. And yet she must rebel, since the musical genius that her mother demands is simply not there. I remember acquaintances of my own childhood, in the later 1930s in the east Bronx, who suffered agonies of enforced violin lessons, as though each one of them could revive the musical tradition of Jewish Odessa. I still bless my long-dead mother for letting me alone, so that I could sit on the floor in a corner to read endlessly, which is all that I have ever wanted to do.

Tan's mother backs away "like a small brown leaf, thin, brittle, lifeless," more a ghost than a person. The image again is universal, being as much Homeric and Virgilian as Chinese. Amy Tan is still young enough to get beyond *The Joy Luck Club*, though she has not yet done so. Whatever the future course of her work will be, she at least has joined Maxine Hong Kingston in breaking a new road, doubtless at considerable inner cost.

MELANIE MCALISTER

(Mis) Reading The Joy Luck Club

"Everyone loves Amy Tan. She's the flavor of the month, the hot young thing, the exotic new voice that is giving hope to a publishing industry weary of the old trends."

Washington Post, 8 October 1989

"You don't really want black folks, you are just looking for yourself with a little color to it."

Bernice Johnson Reagon, in *Home Girls: A Black Feminist Anthology*

In 1989, Amy Tan's first novel, *The Joy Luck Club*, hit the best-seller list, where it stayed for nine months.[1] The hardcover edition was reprinted twenty-seven times, with more than 220,000 copies in print.[2] In addition, *The Joy Luck Club* was selected by two major book clubs as a featured alternative selection and was serialized in four magazines. The novel was nominated for the prestigious American Book Award. Four months after its initial publication, paperback rights to *The Joy Luck Club* sold to Vintage publishers for $1.2 million.[3] The mass paperback edition, issued in June of 1990, had a first run of two million copies. As the 1980s came to a close, Chinese American writer Amy Tan became an overnight celebrity.

The reviews of *The Joy Luck Club* in the major media have mirrored its popular success. Reviewers in the *LA Times*, *The New York Times*, and *The*

Asian America: Journal of Culture and the Arts, Volume 1 (1992): pp. 102–118. Copyright © 1992 Melanie McAlister.

Christian Science Monitor, among others, have praised Tan's control of language and her ability to tell a story. They have also consistently pointed out that Tan's novel offers a "universal" narrative, despite its seemingly exotic content. As Julie Lew tells us in *The New York Times:* "Unlike the eccentric characters in *Tripmaster Monkey,* . . . the women in *The Joy Luck Club* could belong to any immigrant group" (Lew 1989). We might also note the enthusiasm of *Esquire:* "How often do we get a voice this haunting? About a subject so universal?" (*Esquire* 1989). Or the assurances offered in a *Washington Post* story on Tan's success: "The four mothers and four daughters in *The Joy Luck Club* may seem interchangeable as they recount their experiences in China (arranged marriages, arranged lives, evil men) and America (fights with mother, growing up Chinese, evil men), but the emotions are raw and powerful, and peculiarly universal" (Streitfield 1989). Thus, the reviewers have sung the praises of *The Joy Luck Club,* insisting that Amy Tan has written a story which, underneath its Chinese ornamentation, is the same for all of us.

The combination of accolades and appropriations that have greeted *The Joy Luck Club* invites immediate comparisons with Maxine Hong Kingston, who was lionized by feminists and by the literati, but who also was criticized in some Asian American political and literary circles. Kingston's critics argued that she played into exotic images of Chinese by returning to a mythologized homeland rather than looking to the Asian experience in America. Kingston, they insisted, only energized the dominant Orientalist discourse in the United States (Chin 1985). Kingston's enormous popularity with non-Asian readers only compounded the pressure: the opinion-makers were finally paying attention to an Asian American writer, and their insistence on seeing her as the first and representative voice of "the" Asian experience in America led many Asian Americans to argue that Kingston had failed to properly represent the community.[4]

A similar reception has greeted Tan, who is being heralded as the definitive voice of the new Asian immigrants. Orville Schell's review of *The Joy Luck Club* in *The New York Times Book Review* presents the novel as a product of the coming-of-age of a younger generation of Chinese Americans. Unlike their parents, Schell argues, these second-generation immigrants have wanted nothing to do with a China "besmirched by Communism." After the political barriers began to fall in the 1970s, however, these younger Chinese Americans have had to come to terms with the "dormant Chinese side of themselves." With Tan's novel, Schell announces, "we feel as if a deep wound in the Chinese American experience is finally being sutured back together again" (Schell 1989).

What Schell does *not* say, but which is perhaps more salient, is that Tan's novels come at a time when intellectuals and ruling-class Americans are themselves coming to terms with the "new" capitalist-road China of the post-Mao period, as well as with the increasing world-wide economic dominance of Japan. The relationship of the United States to Asia is, of necessity, being revamped. At the same time, and not coincidentally, the position of Asians and Asian-Americans in the United States is rapidly evolving. The last 15 to 20 years have brought significant numbers of Asian Americans—now defined as the model minority—into the middle class, and into increasingly visible positions in the intellectual and economic elite. (We could note, as one example, the appointment of an Asian American, Chang-Lin Tien, as the new president of the University of California at Berkeley in February 1990.)

Of course, Asian Americans are still virtually excluded from the main centers of political power, but the older racial formations that cast Asians as "unassimilable" were broken down in the 1970s and 80s by new social and economic forces. The new Orientalist/Assimilationist paradigm that arose in response simultaneously insists on the exotic "otherness" of Asian culture *and* on the necessity—for Asian Americans—of putting aside all but the most superficial elements of that culture in order to be assimilated into America. In the late 1980s, there have even been occasional examples of Asian Americans being classed as "white," as the racial discourses in the United States increasingly polarizes blacks, particularly black youth, against the law-abiding, middle-class citizens of the rest of the country.[4] Thus, what it means to be Asian in America is reduced to mere ornamentation—sushi, Chinatown shops, and the Karate kid—a series of colorful add-ins that work to sustain the myth of a pluralist society without fundamentally challenging its categories.[5]

Pluralism, as I am using it here, is something much more (or maybe much less) than a generalized tolerance and appreciation of diversity. It involves the assumption, within that general tolerance, that diversity does *not* mark stark differences in interests and power among groups. Ellen Rooney analyzes this assumption of universality in her discussion of pluralism in literary theory: in that construct, all readers are assumed to share a certain commonality, that is, their potential to be persuaded by an argument. The possibility that readers might have interests that stand as a theoretical limit to their persuasion is never considered. "These assumptions make an irreconcilable divergence of interests *within* the critical community an unthinkable form of discontinuity" (Rooney 5). Politically, pluralism, as it is most often articulated, assumes that each person can be "brought in" to the mainstream paradigm: there are no exclusions because there are understood to be no genuinely competing interests.

In this environment of the appropriation and containment of Asian American history, serious questions are being raised about who or what Tan represents, and about the impact of her like-it-or-not role as the new spokesperson for Asian Americans. Since Tan has been elevated to the role of a representative Asian American voice, and she has to some degree apparently accepted this role, it is understandable that she is being critiqued for the skewed representation of Asian Americans she offers. *The Joy Luck Club* is, after all, a novel centered on economically successful families, most of whom were of the upper class in China and, who manage, despite language barriers and hardships, to become financially secure in the United States. The inexorable string of professional daughters in Tan's story—an architect, a tax accountant, a graphic designer married to a dermatologist, and, at the bottom of the scale, a copy-writer for a small ad agency—hardly represents a cross-section of the Chinese-American community. At a time when Chinese and Japanese "success" is being used as a weapon against other racial and ethnic groups (as well as against the white working class), Tan's depictions of Asian Americans whose entry into the middle class is assumed and unproblematic can appear as yet another version of the model minority myths of the dominant class.[6]

However, while it is absolutely vital that the "model minority" myth be countered, I would argue that critiques that focus on Tan's failure to properly represent the Chinese American (or the Asian American) community are misdirected. The issue of representation is a tricky one. To which community is Tan responsible? The Chinese American community? Chinese Americans who have become professionals? Asian American women? All Asian Americans? At the most basic level, who or what Tan (or any other writer) represents will be inevitably altered by the context in which her work is viewed. As literature, *The Joy Luck Club* is not inherently more (or less) Asian American literature than it is women's literature, immigrant literature, mother-daughter literature, people-of-color literature, post-modern literature, American literature. In fact, the novel fits all these categories, and innumerable others. Attempts to analyze literature in terms of how well it represents a fixed category of people almost inevitably leads to an "information retrieval approach" to literature—literature becomes ethnography; its function is to fill in the gaps of society's, particularly white society's, knowledge about the culture at hand. The literary nature of the text is minimal; what is reinforced is a simplistic and ultimately condescending attitude toward "ethnic art," one that requires that representations of, and by, "the Other" be contained and presented as information, rather than as any challenge to the categories of the aesthetic of the mainstream.

This is not to imply that literature cannot also be cultural information or representation. Certain literature (and I am thinking particularly of the local color realist schools in the United States) takes as part of its project the representation of a certain way of life: Kate Chopin offered insights into Creole society in the late 1800s, Edith Wharton documented in detail the disintegration of the Anglo-Saxon leisure class at the turn of the century; Toshio Mori's *Yokohama, California* provided a "slice of life" of the Japanese community in the 1920s, 30s, and early 40s. But literature is always also representation, creation, text. It is important to realize that this tendency to view literature primarily in terms its function as a "window on the world" seems strongest in reference to "ethnic" writers. The approach largely bypasses canonical texts: *Huck Finn* is rarely studied in history classes as a novelistic representation of what life was like in the South before the Civil War; Hemingway's evocative descriptions are not generally understood as an accurate representation or description of the life of white men in the mid 20th century (although granted, such approaches might offer fascinating insights). The *literariness* of these texts is assumed: their interest is supposed to lie in both their formal, stylistic qualities and their themes and content, but not primarily in their usefulness as information about a sociological group. Of course, literature can be, and often is, a representation of and a statement about real conditions. But we must at the same time remember that the tendency to read literature simply as ethnography, or history, is charged, and sometimes dangerous.[7]

I am not arguing that literature cannot be critiqued politically, or that "art" is a realm separate from "life" or "politics." What I do believe is that it is far more fruitful to read literature in terms of its politics than to examine it for its representativeness in terms of a particular group. What are the effects of the text? In what ways can it be read? How does it answer the (various) questions we as readers might bring to it? What does it say about the world it depicts? The challenge at hand, then, is to examine *The Joy Luck Club,* not for its accuracy of representation of the new generation of Asian Americans, nor for its use of "universal" themes, but instead for its (potential) intervention as cultural product. In particular, I am interested in the question of whether Tan's novel is complicit with, or is counter to, the Orientalism assimilationist discourse that has so enthusiastically adopted it.

Lyrical Dreams v. Strategic Reading

To read *The Joy Luck Club* as anti-Orientalist and anti-assimilationist demands, it seems to me, a strategic reading. It is a reading I am particularly drawn to, in part because the text lends itself to such a strategy, and in part as a response to the casual racism so prevalent in the mainstream reviews. It is clear to me from an examination of several of the reviews of *The Joy Luck Club* that the critical embrace of Tan's novel has required some very selective (mis)readings on the part of the reviewers. The major media has insisted on interpreting Tan's text lyrically, passing over the individuality of the characters in order to more easily assimilate a uniform version of "the Chinese American experience" into a vision of American inclusionism.

In this light, it is worth examining Orville Schell's review in more detail, since his is the most blatant (but by no means unique) example of the ways in which Tan is misread by reviewers. Schell's mistakes are instructive, and point the way to a strategy of resistance-reading.

Schell begins his review by misreading the novel's opening scene. It is worth noting the particular nature of the reading Schell offers, since he erases the exact distinctions between past and present that are being drawn by the narrator, Jing-mei (June) Woo. Schell's mistakes are indicative of his determined Orientalization of the four older women (the mothers) of the novel: in his formulation, the mothers are artifacts, whose irrelevance to the modern world of the United States makes it easier and more imperative to assimilate their daughters, who are "like us." Here, then, is the description of the opening story from Schell's review: "The members of the Joy Luck Club are four aging 'aunties' who gather regularly in San Francisco. . . . When one of the women dies, her daughter, Jing-mei (June) Woo, is drafted to sit in for her at the game. But she feels uncomfortably out of place in this unassimilated environment among older women who still wear 'funny Chinese dresses with stiff stand-up collars, and blooming branches of embroidered silk sewn over their breasts,' who meet in one another's houses, where 'too many once fragrant smells' from Chinese cooking have been 'compressed onto a thin layer of invisible grease.' The all-too Chinese ritual of the Joy Luck Club has always impressed her as little more than a 'shameful Chinese custom, like the secret gatherings of the Ku Klux Klan or the tom-tom dances of TV Indians preparing for war'" (Schell 3). She is made uncomfortable by the older generation's insistence on maintaining old customs and parochial habits, which she views as an impediment to breaking loose from her parents' cultural gravity.

In fact, in this scene, Jing-mei, at the age of thirty-six, has walked into the meeting of the Joy Luck Club, and is struck by how different things are from the old days. As a child, Jing-mei used to come with her mother to that same house. Back then (presumably 25 or so years earlier),—the aunts were wearing "funny Chinese dresses with stiff stand-up collars," back then, Jing-mei used to imagine that Joy Luck "was a shameful Chinese custom. . . . But tonight," she says, "there's no mystery. The Joy Luck aunties are all wearing slacks, bright print blouses, and different versions of sturdy walking shoes" (28). Before the game starts, the aunties and their husbands take a vote on what stocks to buy with the accumulated winnings from the mah-jong game. (They settle on Canadian gold stocks.)

Although *The Joy Luck Club* does articulate tensions between Chineseness and Americanness, between mothers and daughters, it is a tension fraught by complexity, not by the kind of simplistic binaries Schell is trying to draw. Schell's reading fits in well with a view of an exoticized Chinese population frozen in time, but the point of this opening scene is that the aunties are certainly *not* still wearing old-style Chinese clothes, and the adult Jing-mei is a long way from comparing Joy Luck to the Ku Klux Klan. Those changes, in herself and in her parents' generation, are part of what Jing-mei is struggling with, and part of what make the characters in the novel more than cardboard cutouts in an assimilationist morality play.

Schell also has serious difficulty actually telling the characters apart. *The Joy Luck Club* is told as a series of sets of stories: first, as a set of four stories, one for each of the four mothers (Jing-mei tells her recently deceased mother's story), followed by two sets narrated by the daughters, and it finally ends with the mother's narratives again. Since the mothers' and daughters' stories are not in the same order every time, and since the mothers' stories tend to be set in their childhoods in China while their daughters' are set in the recent past in the United States, an initial reading demands some attention to the inter-relationships between mother and daughter stories. In fact, for a reader unfamiliar with Chinese names, it takes a concentrated effort to keep clear which mothers' stories are related to which daughters' stories. Schell's review points out this fact, arguing that the abrupt transitions from China to the United States and back again often make it difficult to know just who is related to whom in the novel. For Schell, apparently, the difficulty is insurmountable. In one instance, he quotes a long passage that he attributes to June's mother; in fact, June's mother is dead at the beginning of the novel and is rarely quoted in the first person. The statement is made by Rose's mother, An-mei Hsu. Schell also refers to June's friend Lena as her sister, a seemingly trivial mistake, but a problematic one to make given the centrality of the two characters.

I imagine, however, that these seemingly small inconsistencies do not bother Schell a great deal. Similarly, his advice to the reader is not to bother too much over the specifics of who's who and what their particular histories are. If we try to keep up with the web of relationships and stories that characterize the novel, Schell argues, "we may readily feel bewildered and lost. . . . But these recherches to old China are so beautifully written that one should just allow oneself to be borne along as if in a dream."

If this type of lyrical reading of *The Joy Luck Club* relieves the exhausted and confused non-Chinese reader, it also, in Schell's vision, allows us to see the particular function of the disjointed nature of the stories: through our confusion, "we are ironically being reminded . . . of the enormity of the confusing mental journey Chinese emigrants had to make. And, most ironic, we are also reminded by these literary disjunctions that it is precisely this mental chasm that members of the younger generation must now recross in reverse in order to resolve themselves as whole Chinese Americans; in *The Joy Luck Club* we get a suggestion of the attendant confusion they must expect to endure in order to get to the other side."

In fact, *The Joy Luck Club* is impoverished terribly if the reader does not understand its interconnections. If the individuality of the mothers and their daughters is lost in a lyricism that confuses them all, the power of each story—of the particular set of relations between mother and daughter is destroyed. By refusing to read attentively, Schell rewrites Tan's novel as an Orientalist dream world.

I would suggest that the disjointed narrative structure of *The Joy Luck Club* has a very different function. Tan's novel requires an attentive reading strategy, one that forces the reader *not* to see all the aunties or all the daughters as interchangeable. *The Joy Luck Club* demands that the non-Chinese reader counter her tendency to see "one" Chinese American voice; she must instead see differences among the characters, and their stories. Otherwise, the book just will not make sense. The silent and depressed Ying-Ying St. Clair is a very different woman than the courageous and domineering Lindo Wong. Their life stories tell something about how they came to be the women they are: Ying-Ying was a very wealthy and pampered child who was later abandoned at a young age by her husband; Lindo came from a poor family, was sold off as a wife/servant to a mere boy and his family, and managed to get out of the marriage by wit and determination. Not surprisingly, each of these women develops a unique relationship with her daughter: Ying-Ying moves from passivity to intervention in her daughter's life, while Lindo's daughter Waverly must come to see that her mother's strength will not destroy her.

Thus, it is possible to understand the very structure of the novel as a strategy against the discourse of Orientalism. By having each of her characters tell her story, in her own words, of who she is and how she has come into her own, Tan confronts an Orientalist discourse that depends on the sameness of Chinese difference.

Subjectivity: Telling the Stories; Constructing the Self

> "Yet so many of the stories that I write, that we all write, are my mother's stories. Only recently did I fully realize this: that through years of listening to my mother's stories of her life, I have absorbed not only something of the stories themselves, but something of the manner in which she spoke, something of the urgency that involves the knowledge that her stories—like her life—must be recorded."
>
> Alice Walker, *In Search of Our Mothers' Gardens*

A reading of the mother-daughter stories as a counter to Orientalist assimilationism can be sustained at the level of content as well as form. In *The Joy Luck Club,* the silence of Asian and Asian American women is broken: stories are told, subjectivity is constructed. Tan attempts a collective story—a narration that moves into the voice of the mothers, which allows them to speak for and recontextualize themselves. In the United States, the mothers have been silenced by the language barrier, by the cultural prejudices and the racism that render them "outside," and ineffective. Through the telling of these stories, the subaltern speaks. And in speaking, she rewrites herself, in all her specificity and individuality, into a new position vis-à-vis both her daughters and the dominant discourse around her.

The story of Ying-Ying St. Clair and her daughter Lena is perhaps the most evocative example of the power of telling the stories. Ying-Ying exists, in her American context, in perhaps the most Orientalized position imaginable: she does not speak English; her husband does not understand Chinese; their marital interactions are a series of gestures, silences, and (on the husband's part) mis-assumptions and appropriations. The husband, St. Clair, speaks for Ying-Ying, and over her. And the power of his speech is considerable. When Ying-Ying arrived in the United States, St. Clair gave her an American name, Betty. At the same time, he wrote the wrong birthdate on her documents: "So, with the sweep of a pen," Lena tells us, "my mother lost her name and became a Dragon instead of a Tiger" (104). The relationship between Ying-Ying and her husband is characterized by a failure of communication so complete it has an almost comic absurdity: "We're moving up in the world," my father proudly announced, this being the occasion of his promotion to sales supervisor of a clothing manufacturer. "Your mother is thrilled" (107).

The Irish-American St. Clair draws his power of speech from both his gender and racial positions vis-à-vis Ying-Ying. But it is Lena's task to recognize her own complicity in the silencing of her mother. Lena understands Chinese, and her mother often speaks to her, "saying things my father could not possibly imagine." However, Lena is also limited by a profound failure of understanding. After Ying-Ying gives birth to a stillborn child, St. Clair asks his daughter to translate his wife's rapid speech, since, for once, the husband had no words to put in his wife's mouth. But Lena, though she can translate the words, does not. "[The baby] looked right through me," Ying-Ying cries. "I knew he could see everything inside me. How I had given no thought to killing my other son? How I had given no thought to having this baby!" (112) Lena, however, does not understand; since she has no idea of her mother's past, Ying-Ying's reference to her abortion at the age of eighteen just seems like nonsense to her daughter. And since Lena feels she can't tell her father that her mother is "crazy," she simply rewrites her mother's pain into banality. Lena "translates": "She says we must all think very hard about having another baby. She says she hopes this baby is very happy on the other side. And she thinks we should leave now and go have dinner" (112).

It is this failure of communication through language—the daughter understands the words but not the meanings—that makes a clear sense of the relationships in the stories of *The Joy Luck Club* necessary. The second generation has participated in the rewriting of their mothers; they have been part of the dominant ideology that silences and exoticizes the first generation. Ying-Ying in particular recognizes the destructive nature of that silence:

> For all these years I kept my mouth closed so selfish desires would not fall out. And because I remained quiet for so long now my daughter does not hear me. . . . All these years I kept my true nature hidden. . . . And because I moved so secretly now my daughter does not see me. . . . We are lost, she and I, unseen and not seeing, unheard and not hearing, unknown by others. (67)

For both mothers and daughters, then, these interacting tales are the response, the insistence that silence be replaced by the battle for subjectivity. Once the stories of the past are told, the younger generation can no longer see their mothers as artifacts, as misfits, whose unaccountable "craziness" makes their young American lives miserable. The breaking of the silence through stories positions the mothers as subjects of their own histories; in so doing, it restructures the relationship between mother and daughter. "Now," Ying-Ying insists, "I must tell my daughter everything" (252). For Ying-Ying and Lena, the re-visioning of history through telling its stories is also an intervention in the present. Ying-Ying's determination to tell her daughter everything is also a determination to give Lena strength, to "cut her tiger spirit loose." With the recovery of her past in China, Ying-Ying: finds her voice in the present and is thus able to move into the future with her daughter. The recovery of the past is not a retreat, but a promise.

The Complicity of Silence

> "Ideas about color, like ideas about anything else, derive their importance, indeed their very definition, from their context. . . . It is the ideological context that tells people which details to notice, which to ignore, and which to take for granted in translating the world around them into ideas about the world."
>
> Barbara Fields, "Ideology and Race in American History"

The Joy Luck Club is a mother-daughter story: it stands firmly in a rich and multi-vocal literary tradition that takes the tortuous, life-giving relations between female generations as a central theme. But the resolution of the generational conflicts in the novel is revealing. Tan describes the mother-daughter relationships as they are inscribed at the intersection of racial and class ideology in the United States. Ultimately, however, the challenge she poses to racism is class-bound, not because her characters are middle-class, but because the text reinforces the daughters' middle class assumptions.

The embarrassed and angry responses the daughters have to their mothers are often class- as well as racially-based. Jing-mei's fear of becoming like her mother, for example, should be understood as more than the "universal" tension between generations.

> So there was no doubt in her mind, whether I agreed or not: Once you are born Chinese, you cannot help but feel and think Chinese.
> "Someday you will see," said my mother. "It is in your blood, waiting to be let go."
> And when she said this, I saw myself transforming like a werewolf, a mutant tag of DNA suddenly triggered, replicating itself insidiously into a syndrome, a cluster of telltale Chinese behaviors, all those things my mother did to embarrass me—haggling with store owners, pecking her mouth with a toothpick in public, being color-blind to the fact that lemon yellow and pale pink are not good combinations for winter clothes. (267)

Jing-mei's fear of exhibiting "telltale Chinese behaviors" is tellingly articulated here in class terms. It is the white middle and upper-middle class that defines the cultural and economic context that declares toothpicks aren't to be used in public, that makes it "obvious" that lemon yellow and pale pink don't match. June's embarrassment about her mother's dressing habits could as easily have been expressed by an upwardly mobile white working class woman about the clothes her mother buys at Wal-Mart. And although June thinks her mother is being too Chinese by chewing toothpicks in public, the fact is that plenty of assimilated and/or native-born Americans exhibit the same behavior. The alternative June posits to her mothers Chineseness is a very particular kind of white, middle-class Americanness—if there is something distinctively Chinese about toothpicks in your teeth, there is at the same time something suspiciously lower class about it.

Fortunately for June, she goes to China, discovers the Chineseness that was always inside her and realizes that, *she* (unlike her mother) can be Chinese American without falling into the trap of being declasse.

What is unfortunate for the reader is the silence that surrounds June's self-discovery; the text simply mirrors June's new sense of self. The complex relationship between assimilation and upward mobility is unproblematic in the novel. Since ideas about racial and ethnic distinctiveness are never unmarked by class dynamics, Tan's coding as "Chinese" certain behaviors, which in the dominant discourse signify "lower class," is ideologically significant.

As Barbara Fields argues in her watershed essay, "Ideology and Race in American History," there is a tendency to position racial ideology as something that exists outside history, beyond social relations. Fields instead argues for an understanding of race as ideology—an ideology whose material base must be located, not in the inevitable consequences produced by physical differences, but in relations of power. Her argument about the development of a racialist ideology to justify slavery is also applicable to an understanding of other social relations coded along the lines of race: "Race became the ideological medium through which people posed and apprehended basic questions of power and dominance, sovereignty and citizenship, justice and right" (Fields 162). The effect of that discourse has been to deflect conflicts over social and economic power, toward a tendency to view racism as a "tragic flaw" of the American character rather than as a result of concrete struggles and identifiable social relations. *The Joy Luck Club* follows June's positioning her conflicts with her mother as solely issues of Chineseness and Americanness, thus eliding the complex intersections of class dynamics and racialist ideology that situate the daughters' relations to their less assimilated mothers.

What is not said at the resolution of the novel is that June's embarrassment reflects the ways in which she has been interpellated by the dominant Orientalist and middle-class discourse. It is this discourse that firmly declares that Asian women are only acceptable in one of two ways: when they are safe in an exoticized Asian past, or when they have acquired the graceful manners and subtly-matched tweeds of the white middle class. The text counters June to the extent that her embarrassment about her mother is Orientalist, but Tan's silence in relation to the second, class-based assumption reverberates through the text.

Conclusion

In *The Joy Luck Club,* Tan writes, and writes powerfully, against the Orientalism that has silenced the mothers. She breaks that silence, insisting, both through her narrative form and in the nature of the stories she tells, on the subjectivity and agency of the very different women who make up the cast of the Joy Luck Club. At the same time, however, *The Joy Luck Club*'s strategic disjuncture and highly developed characterizations are interwoven with problematically unresolved silences. Tan's allegiance to the class myths of American culture means that, while she opens the door to a critique of the Orientalism assimilationist paradigm, she never quite walks through it. We are left with a partial intervention, one that is powerful as far as it goes, but disappointing in its inability to take the next step.

As readers, we can and should develop a strategic counter to the crass Orientalism of the mainstream press; we can use the novel to read against the drive to construct exotic Asian women uniform in their difference. But we will quickly run into the class-based limits of Tan's text, and the silences thus engendered. Strategic reading will not, then, make *The Joy Luck Club* something is it not, but it might help to construct a very different novel than the one described in *The New York Times* book review.

Notes

1. Amy Tan. *The Joy Luck Club.* (New York. G. P. Putnam's Sons, 1989). Future references will given in the text.

2. Figures are from the press kit provided by Ballantine publishers.

3. "'Joy Luck Club' Rights Acquired by Vintage," *The New York Times,* April 15, 1989. The mass market paperback edition of the novel was eventually published by Ivy Books, an imprint of Ballantine Books. Both Ballantine and Vintage are owned by Random House.

4. For an analysis of the debates on Kingston and a defense of her writing, see Robert Lee, "The Woman Warrior as an Intervention in Asian-American Historiography," in Shirley G. Lim, ed. *Approaches to Teaching The Woman Warrior* (New York Modern Language Association, 1991).

5. At my home institution, Brown University, the student newspaper, the *Brown Daily Herald,* initially covered a series of attacks on students in the fall of 1989 as being black-on-white attacks, classing the Asian and Asian American students who were attacked as "white." Later, the BDH changed its policy and began referring to "white and Asian" students.

6. The boycotts started in the spring of 1990 against two Korean-owned grocery stores in the Flatbush section of Brooklyn only highlight the rising tensions and the complexities of this new dynamic.

7. Of course, the debates about the constructed natures of the representations of both ethnography and history are relevant here. But the argument that literature should not be treated simply as information can be sustained both within and outside of the poststructuralist theories of discourse.

Works Cited

Chin, Frank. "This is Not An Autobiography," *Genre.* XVIII (Summer 1985): 109–130.

Clifford, James and George Marcus, eds. *Writing Culture: The Poetics and Politics of Ethnography.* Berkeley: University of California Press, 1986.

Fields, Barbara. "Ideology and Race in American History." In *Race, Region, and Reconstruction: Essays in Honor of C. Van Woodward,* ed. J. Morgan Kousser and James M. McPherson. New York: Oxford University Press, 1982.

"*Joy Luck Club*' Rights Acquired by Vintage." *New York Times* (April 15, 1989): C15.

Lee, Robert. "The Woman Warrior as an Intervention in Asian American Historiography." In *Approaches to Teaching The Woman Warrior.* ed. Shirley Geok-lin Lim. New York: Modern Language Association, 1991. 52–63.

Lew, Julie. *The New York Times.* July 4, 1989.

Reagon, Bernice Johnson. "Coalition Politics: Turning the Century." In *Home Girls: A Black Feminist Anthology,* ed. Barbara Smith. New York: Kitchen Table/Women of Color Press, 1983.

Rooney, Ellen. *Seductive Reasoning: Pluralism as the Problematic of Contemporary Literary Theory.* Ithaca: Cornell University Press, 1989.

Schell, Orville. "Your Mother is In Your Bones." *The New York Times Book Review*. (19 March
     1989): 3ff.
Scott, Joan. *Gender and the Politics of History*. New York: Columbia University Press, 1988.
Streitfield, David. "The 'Luck' of Amy Tan. . . . " *Washington Post*, October 8, 1989.
Tan, Amy. *The Joy Luck Club*. New York: G. P. Putnam's Sons, 1989.
Walker, Alice. "In Search of Our Mothers' Gardens." In *In Search of Our Mothers' Gardens*.
     San Diego: Harcourt, Brace, Jovanovich, 1989.
Weed, Elizabeth. ed., *Coming to Terms: Feminism, Theory, Politics*. New York. Routledge,
     1989.

MARINA HEUNG

Daughter-Text/Mother-Text: Matrilineage in Amy Tan's Joy Luck Club

The critical literature on matrilineage in women's writings has already achieved the status of a rich and evolving canon.[1] At the same time, in recognizing race, class, and gender as crucial determinants in writings by women of color, some critics have indicated the need to develop a distinct framework for understanding these works. For example, Dianne F. Sadoff has examined the literature by African American women to note that "race and class oppression intensify the black woman writer's need to discover an untroubled matrilineal heritage." Referring to Alice Walker's adoption of Zora Neale Hurston as a literary foremother, Sadoff shows how "in celebrating her literary foremothers . . . the contemporary black woman writer covers over more profoundly than does the white writer her ambivalence about matrilineage, her own misreadings of precursors, and her link to an oral as well as written tradition."[2] Readers like Sadoff [3] suggest that, although matrilineage remains a consistent and powerful concern in the female literary tradition, the recognition of culturally and historically specific conditions in women's lives requires that we appropriately contextualize, and thereby refine, our readings of individual texts.

In the realm of writings by Asian Americans, this work has begun. Although it does not focus explicitly on the idea of matrilineage, Amy Ling's *Between Worlds: Women Writers of Chinese Ancestry* is the first book to outline

Feminist Studies, Volume 19, Number 3 (Fall 1993): pp. 597–616. © 1993 Feminist Studies, Inc.

17

the literary tradition of one group of Asian American women. Her effort, Ling says, is inspired by Walker's "search for our mothers' gardens."[4] Similarly, in a recent essay, Shirley Geok-lin Lim identifies Monica Sone's *Nisei Daughter* as a "mother text" for Joyce Kogawa's *Obasan*. In discussing these authors, Lim enumerates literary characteristics shared by Asian American and Asian Canadian women writers, such as "multiple presences, ambivalent stories, and circular and fluid narratives."[5] Lim's analysis points toward a commonality between Sone and Kogawa and two other writers, Maxine Hong Kingston and Chuang Hua.[6] In Kingston's *Woman Warrior* and Hua's *Crossings*, anti-realistic narrative strategies and a provisional authorial stance correlate with experiences of cultural dislocation and of destabilized and fluid identities.[7] Thus, the works of Sone, Kogawa, Kingston, and Hua collectively define an emerging canon cohering around concerns with racial, gender, and familial identity and the concomitant rejection of monolithic literary techniques.

In *Nisei Daughter, Obasan, The Woman Warrior,* and *Crossings,* the theme of matrilineage revolves around the figure of the daughter. With the exception of *Crossings* (which focuses on a daughter-father relationship), each of these works depicts how a daughter struggles toward self-definition by working through the mother-daughter dyad. The daughter's centrality thus places these writings firmly in the tradition delineated by Marianne Hirsch in *The Mother/Daughter Plot: Narrative, Psychoanalysis, Feminism.* Examining women's fiction from the eighteenth century through postmodernism, Hirsch notes the predominance of the daughter's voice and the silencing of the mother. This inscription of the "romance of the daughter" forms part of the feminist revision of the Freudian family plot.

> It is the woman as *daughter* who occupies the center of the global reconstruction of subjectivity and subject-object relation. The woman as *mother* remains in the position of other, and the emergence of feminine-daughterly subjectivity rests and depends on that continued and repressed process of *othering* the mother. . . . Daughter and mother are separated and forever trapped by the institution, the function of motherhood. They are forever kept apart by the text's daughterly perspective and signature: the mother is excluded from the discourse by the daughter who owns it.

Interestingly, Hirsch's few examples of departures from this pattern are drawn only from the writings of African American women. As she suggests, the scantiness of this sampling of "corrective" family romances, incorporating rather than repressing maternal discourse, reinforces the argument that feminist writers need to construct a new family romance to move the mother "from object to subject."[8]

Published in 1989, Amy Tan's novel, *The Joy Luck Club,* is about four Chinese American daughters and their mothers.[9] Like *The Woman Warrior* and *Crossings,* the novel contains autobiographical elements. In an interview, Tan describes how she was moved to establish a dialogue with her mother: "When I was writing, it was so much for my mother and myself . . . I wanted her to know what I thought about China and what I thought about growing up in this country. And I wanted those words to almost fall off the page so that she could just see the story, that the language would be simple enough, almost like a little curtain that would fall away."[10] But despite Tan's explicit embrace of a daughter's perspective, *The Joy Luck Club* is remarkable for foregrounding the voices of mothers as well as of daughters. In the opening chapter of the novel, Jing-Mei Woo (also known as June) stands in for her recently deceased mother at an evening of mah-jong held by the Joy Luck Club, a group of elderly aunts and uncles. On this evening, three of her "Joy Luck aunties" give her money to fly to China to meet two half-sisters, twins who were abandoned by her mother during the war. In the last chapter of the novel, June makes this trip with her father. Her story (taking up four chapters) is told in her voice. The rest of the chapters are similarly narrated in the first person by three of June's coevals (Waverly Jong, Rose Jordan Hsu, and Lena St. Clair) and their mothers (Lindo Jong, An-Mei Hsu, and Ying-Ying St. Clair). Thus, totaling sixteen chapters in all, the novel interweaves seven voices, four of daughters, and three of mothers. In the way that it foregrounds maternal discourse, *The Joy Luck Club* materializes Marianne Hirsch's vision of a mother/daughter plot "written in the voice of mothers, as well as those of daughters . . . [and] in combining both voices [finds] a double voice that would yield a multiple female consciousness."[11] But because the maternal voices in the novel bespeak differences derived from the mothers' unique positioning in culture and history, the subjectivities they inscribe, in counterpointing those of the daughters, also radically realign the mother/daughter plot itself.

In the chapter, "Double Face," in *The Joy Luck Club,* a scene implicitly illustrates the incompleteness of a model of the mother/daughter dyad defined only from the daughter's perspective. Here, the central motif is a mirror reflecting a mother and a daughter. Interweaving the themes of vision, recognition, and reflection, this scene shows the limits of viewing identification as an issue problematic for the daughter alone. The scene is set after Waverly has persuaded her mother to get her hair cut. Lindo is seated before a mirror as Waverly and Mr. Rory (the hairdresser) scrutinize her hairstyle. Sitting silently, Lindo listens to the two discuss her "as if [she] were not there." Her daughter translates Mr. Rory's questions for her, even though Lindo can understand English perfectly well. When Waverly speaks directly to her, she does so loudly, "as if [Lindo has] lost [her] hearing." But because this scene is narrated from Lindo's perspective, her vision and subjectivity are in fact in control. Even as her daughter seems determined to nullify her presence, Lindo sees the superficial social ease between Waverly and Mr. Rory as typical of how "Americans don't really look at one another when talking." Despite her silence and apparent acquiescence, she interposes herself nonverbally through her smiles and her alternation between her "Chinese face" and her "American face" ("the face Americans think is Chinese, the one they cannot understand") (p. 255).

The scene turns on Mr. Rory's sudden exclamation at seeing the uncanny resemblance between mother and daughter reflected in the mirror. Lindo notes Waverly's discomfiture: "'The same cheeks.' [Waverly] says. She points to mine and then pokes her cheeks. She sucks them outside in to look like a starved person" (p. 256). Waverly's response exhibits her "matrophobia," defined by Adrienne Rich as the daughter's fear of "becoming one's mother."[12] Feminists have analyzed the daughter's ambivalence toward identification with the mother,[13] but Lindo's response in this scene allows us to consider identification from a maternal perspective. Much as Lindo possesses a "double face," she also has access to a "double vision." Seeing herself mirrored in her daughter, she recalls her own mother in China.

> And now I have to fight back my feelings. These two faces, I think, so much the same! The same happiness, the same sadness, the same good fortune, the same faults.
> I am seeing myself and my mother, back in China, when I was a young girl. (p. 256)

With her "double vision," Lindo is not threatened by her daughter's attempted erasure of her; in fact, she is moved by her daughter's resemblance to her, even as she registers Waverly's response. Lindo's perspective is informed by her personal history and by her ability to bridge time and cultures. At the same time, Lindo's knowledge of family history provides one key to her sense of ethnic identity. As critics have noted, in writings by Asian American women, issues of matrilineage are closely bound with those of acculturation and race. Thus, Shirley Lim writes: "The essential thematics of maternality is also the story of race . . . [The mother] is the figure not only of maternality but also of racial consciousness."[14] But in presenting the mother as the potent symbol of ethnic identity, Lim implicitly adopts the perspective of the daughter. In her scheme, the mother's primary role is to set into motion the daughter's working through toward a separate selfhood and a new racial identity. Yet this elevation of the daughter as the figure around whom the "dangers of rupture and displaced selves" converge[15] marginalizes maternal subjectivity and voicing. But surely the issues of identification, differentiation, and ethnic identity have meaning for mothers as well, and this meaning must to a significant degree devolve from their relationships with their own mothers. As exemplified in this episode in "Double Face," *The Joy Luck Club* moves maternality to the center. It locates subjectivity in the maternal and uses it as a pivot between the past and the present. In so doing, it reclaims maternal difference and reframes our understanding of daughterly difference as well.

Recent feminist revisions of the Freudian Oedipal family romance assume a culturally and historically specific model of the nuclear family. In her influential book, *The Reproduction of Mothering: Psychoanalysis and the Sociology of Gender*, Nancy Chodorow shows how the institution of motherhood based on childcare provided by women sustains the central problematics of separation and differentiation for daughters.[16] Using a paradigm that is white, middle-class, and Western, Chodorow's analysis is not universally applicable. In this vein, Dianne F. Sadoff and Ruth Perry and Martine Watson Brownley show how the Black family, distorted through the history of slavery in particular, needs to be understood through alternative models.[17] Such a culturally specific critique needs to be applied to the traditional Chinese family as well. Because of their historical devaluation, women in the Chinese family are regarded as disposable property or detachable appendages despite their crucial role in maintaining the family line through childbearing. Regarded as expendable "objects to be invested in or bartered," the marginal status of Chinese women shows itself in their forced transfer from natal families to other families through the practice of arranged marriage, concubinage, adoption, and pawning.[18] The position of women—as daughters, wives, and mothers—in Chinese society is therefore markedly provisional, with their status and expendability fluctuating according to their families' economic circumstances, their ability to bear male heirs, and the proclivities of authority figures in their lives.

This pattern of radical rupture within families is illustrated by the family histories of An-Mei, Lindo, and Ying-Ying in *The Joy Luck Club*. As a child, An-Mei is raised by her grandmother; she has only confused memories of her mother. One day, when her grandmother is dying, her mother appears and removes her to Shanghai; An-Mei is then adopted into a new family where her mother is the fourth concubine of a wealthy merchant.

In contrast to An-Mei, Lindo is removed from her natal family through marriage, not adoption. At age two, Lindo is engaged to a young boy who is a stranger to her. A bride in an arranged marriage at sixteen, Lindo finally succeeds in freeing herself through a ruse by which she convinces her husband's family to find a concubine for him.

Like Lindo, Ying-Ying is chosen as a bride by a stranger, a man who associates deflowering her with the act of *kai gwa* ("open the watermelon"). A "wild and stubborn" girl in her youth, Ying-Ying's spirit is destroyed in this brutal marriage. Later, when she is pregnant, her husband leaves her for another woman; she decides to get an abortion.

In *The Joy Luck Club*, family allegiances are complicated and disrupted within a kinship system in which blood ties are replaced by a network of alternate affiliations. When Lindo is engaged to the son of the Huang family, for instance, her family relationships are immediately reconfigured. Her mother starts treating her "as if [she] belonged to someone else," and she begins to be referred to as her future mother-in-law's daughter.

For An-Mei, the breakage and realignment of relationships involving parents and siblings are even more radical and arbitrary. When her mother removes her from her grandmother's household, her brother—her mother's first son—is left behind because patrilineal claims on male children cannot be challenged. After her adoption into her new family, An-Mei is introduced to three other wives in the family—each a potential surrogate mother. For instance, her mother tells her to call the Second Wife "Big Mother." She also acquires a new brother, Syaudi, who now becomes her "littlest brother" (p. 230). But An-Mei has to undergo one final upheaval when she finds out that Syaudi is truly her brother by blood and not adoption. This happens when her mother's attendant tells her how An-Mei's mother was forced into concubinage and bore a son; this son was then adopted by the Second Wife as her own. In this way, An-Mei makes a shocking discovery: "That was how I learned that the baby Syaudi was really my mother's son, my littlest brother" (p. 237).

Unlike Lindo and An-Mei, Suyuan Woo (June's mother) sees her family dispersed as a result of cataclysmic historical events. During the Japanese bombardment of Kweilin during the war, she is forced to flee south without her husband; discarding her possessions along the way and desperate for food, she finally abandons her twin daughters on the road. Later in America, her new daughter, June, grows up with the knowledge of a truncated family, haunted by her mother's words: "Your father is not my first husband. You are not those babies" (p. 26).

These stories of disrupted family connections, of divided, multiplied, and constantly realigned perceptions of kinship, constitute a pattern clearly diverging from the monolithic paradigm of the nuclear family. In *The Joy Luck Club*, their experiences of broken and fluctuating family bonds inspire Lindo, An-Mei, and Ying-Ying to construct stories of bonding with the mother precisely in answer to their memories of profound rupture and abandonment. Speaking from their experiences of mother loss, these immigrant mothers offer altered versions of the "romance of the daughter." Whereas typical versions of this romance highlight generational conflict and the repression of the mother, An-Mei, Lindo, and Ying-Ying construct consoling tales enacting a fantasy of symbiosis with the maternal. Recalling her first sight of her mother after a long separation, An-Mei describes how their exchange of gazes locks them into instant identification: "[My mother] looked up. And when she did, I saw my own face looking back at me" (p. 45). An-Mei also privileges her mother's story about two turtles joined through suffering; from this parable of shared grief, An-Mei derives a message connecting her to her mother: "That was our fate, to live like two turtles seeing the watery world together from the bottom of the little pond" (p. 217). In this way, An-Mei transforms common experiences of pain and victimization into testimonials of mother/daughter bonding. Similarly, instead of feeling outrage at her mother's collaboration in her arranged betrothal and marriage, Lindo actually chooses collusion with her mother, behaving as the proper daughter-in-law so that her mother will not lose face (p. 55).

However, years later, in America, Lindo's assertion of instinctive bonding with her mother is contested by new realities. She comes to regret how her mother "did not see how [her] face changed over the years. How [her] mouth began to droop. How [she] began to worry but still did not lose [her] hair . . ." (p. 257). Acknowledging these inevitable changes in herself, Lindo implicitly admits the loss of symbiosis. Her transplantation into American culture and her advancing age have made her face no longer a perfect match of her mother's. Quite simply, her new "double face" reflects her changed cultural identity: "I think about our two faces. I think about my intentions. Which one is American? Which one is Chinese? Which one is better? If you show one, you must also sacrifice the other" (p. 266).

At the same time, Lindo's recognition of her own doubled identity has implications for how she understands her relationship with her daughter. Like her, Waverly is the product of two cultures, but Lindo sees that Waverly's experience of cultural mixing is different from her own: "Only her skin and hair are Chinese. Inside—she is all American-made" (p. 254). The otherness of her daughter's hybridized self for Lindo makes it unlikely that mother and daughter can achieve perfect identification: the burden of differences in personal history and cultural conditioning is too great. Yet, in *The Joy Luck Club,* the mothers' ability to accept their own loss of the maternal image also enables them to separate from their daughters. As Ying-Ying says: "I think this to myself even though I love my daughter. She and I have shared the same body. There is part of her mind that is part of mine. But when she was born, she sprang from me like a slippery fish, and has been swimming away from me since" (p. 242). Thus, in Tan's novel, the maternal experience of generational conflict and differentiation takes into account the realities of cultural difference; through this awareness, the Joy Luck mothers can negotiate their ambivalences about their daughters' desires for cultural assimilation and autonomous selfhood.

•••

As the essential medium of subjectivity, language is the ground for playing out cultural differences. Gloria Anzaldúa has written about her language use as an insignia of her "borderlands" identity situated between Mexico and America: "Ethnic identity is twin skin to linguistic identity—I am my language. Until I can accept as legitimate Chicano Texas Spanish, Tex Mex and all the other languages I speak, I cannot accept the legitimacy of myself." The speaker of this "language of Borderlands," Anzaldúa suggests, has the freedom to "switch codes" at will; it is a "bastard" language located at the "juncture of culture [where] languages cross-pollinate and are revitalized."[19] In *The Joy Luck Club*, the language of the mothers—their border language—marks their positioning between two cultures. However, in exposing linguistic limits, the novel also argues for reclaiming language as an instrument of intersubjectivity and dialogue, and as a medium of transmission from mothers to daughters.

In the novel, the daughters understand Chinese, but they speak English exclusively. The mothers, in contrast, speak a version of Anzaldúa's "language of the Borderlands," a *patois* of Chinese and English that often confuses their daughters. Observing her aunties, June thinks: "The Joy Luck aunties begin to make small talk, not really listening to each other. They speak in their special language, half in broken English, half in their own Chinese dialect" (p. 34). Embarrassing at times to the daughters, this language is a form of self-inscription in an alien culture, a way of preserving significance in the new reality of America. For one, the nuggets of foreign words incorporated into this speech duplicate aspects of self-identity that have no equivalent in another language. Words like *lihai, chuming,* and *nengkan* must remain in their original Chinese in order to retain their power and meaning. For Ying-Ying, the essence of her youthful character before she became a lost soul, a "ghost," is contained in the word *lihai:* "When I was a young girl in Wushi, I was *lihai*. Wild and stubborn. I wore a smirk on my face. Too good to listen" (p. 243). Her confidence in her special knowledge is expressed by *chuming*, referring to her "inside knowledge of things" (p. 248). For Rose, *nengkan* expresses her mother's ability to act on pure will and determination, as shown in An-Mei's summoning of her son's spirit after he has drowned at the beach (pp. 121–131). On another occasion, An-Mei's command of this hybrid language enables her to articulate, on her daughter's behalf, Rose's disorientation during her divorce. When An-Mei complains that Rose's psychiatrist is making her *hulihudu* and *heimongmong*, Rose ponders: "It was true. And everything around me seemed to be *heimongmong*. These were words I have never thought about in English terms. I suppose the closest in meaning would be 'confused' and 'dark fog'" (p. 188).

In discussing the use of "multilanguedness" in women's writings, Patricia Yaeger suggests that the "incorporation of a second language can function

. . . as a subversive gesture representing an alternative form of speech which can both disrupt the repressions of authoritative discourse and still welcome or shelter themes that have not yet found a voice in the . . . primary language."[20] Although Yaeger is concerned with specific narrative strategies used in women's texts, her analysis has resonance for the significance of maternal speech in *The Joy Luck Club*. Without being overtly political or subversive, the mothers' bilingualism in the novel is nonetheless strategic. Switching from English to Chinese can express rejection and anger, as when June's mother berates her for not trying hard enough at her piano playing: "'So ungrateful,' I heard her mutter in Chinese. 'If she had as much talent as she has temper, she would be famous now'" (p. 136). Or, the switching of codes may initiate a shift into a different register of intimacy, as when the same mother speaks in Chinese when making her daughter a gift of a jade pendant (p. 208). To express her resentment against an American husband who persistently puts English words in her mouth, Ying-Ying uses Chinese exclusively with her daughter (p. 106). Deliberate deformations of language, too, are used to convey veiled criticisms, as when Ying-Ying snidely refers to her daughter's profession as an architect as "arty-tecky" (p. 242), and An-Mei dismisses Rose's psychiatrist as "psyche-tricks" (p. 188). Finally, the use of Chinese is a form of resistance to a hegemonic culture. In the following exchange, initiated when Waverly slyly asks about the difference between Jewish and Chinese mah-jong, Lindo's use of Chinese is self-reflexive; her switch from English to Chinese in itself expresses her sense of cultural difference and superiority.

> "Entirely different kind of playing," she said in her English explanation voice. "Jewish mah jong, they watch only for their own tile, play only with their eyes."
> Then she switched to Chinese: "Chinese mah jong, you must play using your head, very tricky. You must watch what everybody else throws away and keep that in your head as well. And if nobody plays well, then the game becomes like Jewish mah jong. Why play? There's no strategy. You're just watching people make mistakes." (p. 33)

In *The Joy Luck Club*, "multilanguedness" bears the imprint of their speakers' unique cultural positioning, but this assertion of difference is also vexed by its potential to confuse and exclude. For the daughters, the special meaning of maternal language requires translation. After her mother's death, June thinks: "My mother and I never really understood each other. We translated each other's meanings and I seemed to hear less than what was said, while my mother heard more" (p. 37). Another question is how effectively maternal language functions as a medium of transmission between generations. The mothers in the novel worry that the family history and knowledge preserved in their hybrid language will be elided after their deaths. At one point, June comes to understand how important it is for her aunties to preserve the meaning of "joy luck": "They see that joy and luck do not mean the same to their daughters, that to these closed American-born minds 'joy luck' is not a word, it does not exist. They see daughters who will bear grandchildren born without any connecting hope from generation to generation" (pp. 40–41).

Hybrid in its origins, maternal language in *The Joy Luck Club* possesses multiple, even contradictory, meanings. As an assertion of cultural identity, it both communicates and obfuscates. At the same time, it stands in counterpoint to maternal silence. To the daughters, maternal silence hints at "unspeakable tragedies" (p. 20), and the maternal injunction to "bite back your tongue" (p. 89) binds daughters and mothers in a cycle of self-perpetuating denial. Yet both daughters and mothers resist this bind. The Joy Luck aunties, after all, plead frantically with June to tell her mother's—and, by implication, their own—history ("Tell them, tell them"). Similarly, Lena is aware of the power of the unspoken: "I always thought it mattered, to know what is the worst possible thing that can happen to you, to know how you can avoid it, to not be drawn by the magic of the unspeakable" (p. 103). Finally, it is the incomprehension enforced by silence that keeps mothers "othered" in the eyes of their daughters. An-Mei, for instance, is dismissed by Suyuan as a woman with "no spine" who "never thought about what she was doing" (p. 30), and Ying-Ying is seen by June as the "weird aunt, someone lost in her own world" (p. 35). As for Lindo, her special insight allows her to understand why her daughter and her friends see her as a "backward Chinese woman" (p. 255).

In the tradition of breaking silence that has become one of the shaping myths in the writings of women of color,[21] maternal silence in the novel is transformed from a medium of self-inscription and subjectivity into an instrument of intersubjectivity and dialogue. For the mothers, storytelling heals past experiences of loss and separation; it is also a medium for rewriting stories of oppression and victimization into parables of self-affirmation and individual empowerment. For the Joy Luck mothers, the construction of a self in identification with a maternal figure thus parallels, finally, a revisioning of the self through a reinterpretation of the past.

In Lindo's case, the brutality of a forced marriage is transformed, through its retelling, into a celebration of courage and resistance. She recalls looking into a mirror on the day of her wedding and being surprised at seeing her own purity and strength: "Underneath the scarf I still knew who I was. I made a promise to myself: I would always remember my parents' wishes, but I would never forget myself"(p. 58). Through a clever scheme, Lindo escapes from her marriage. After arriving in America, she chooses her second husband, getting him to propose by inserting a message inside a fortune cookie. Because all her jewelry was taken from her during her first marriage, she makes sure that she receives genuine gold jewelry from her husband and as gifts that she buys for herself: "And every few years, when I have a little extra money, I buy another bracelet. I know what I'm worth. They're always twenty-four carats, all genuine" (p. 66).

For An-Mei and Ying-Ying, self-articulation remedies early teachings in silence and self-denial. Both begin to recall painful memories when they see how their speech can save their daughters. Ying-Ying is stirred to speak directly to Lena when she sees her daughter's unhappy marriage. At one time a "tiger girl" who gave up her *chi* ("breath" or "life-force") in an unhappy marriage, Ying-Ying now recognizes that her daughter has "become like a ghost, disappear" (p. 163). The emptiness of Lena's life—with her fancy swimming pool, her Sony Walkman, and cordless phone—is apparent to her. Watching Rose go through a difficult divorce, An-Mei recalls her own mother's dying words, that "she would rather kill her own weak spirit so she could give me a stronger one" (p. 240). In the end, An-Mei and Ying-Ying find their voices: Ying-Ying to "wake up" Rose (p. 240) and Lena to "penetrate her skin and pull her to where she can be saved" (p. 242).

The stories of their lives are the mothers' gifts to their daughter in the spirit with which the Joy Luck Club was originally founded. Years ago, June's mother formed the club in Kweilin in order to transmute the painful history of women like herself into a communal expression of defiance and hope, so that "each week [they] could forget past wrongs done to us . . . hope to be lucky" (p. 25). In breaking silence, these mothers reproduce the past as tales of "joy" and "luck." Like the scar on An-Mei's neck that her mother rubs in order to bring back a painful memory (p. 48), these narrations effect a passage from pain to catharsis, moving their tellers from inward knowledge to intersubjective dialogue. Significantly, each of the mother's stories suspends its mode of address between "I" and "you."[22] Thus, the closing sentence in Lindo's story is: "I will ask my daughter what she thinks" (p. 266). In inviting the daughters' interjections, the shift from interior monologue to dialogue enables the mothers to discover how they will mediate between the past and the present for their daughters. Their choices take them on the path, described by Kim Chernin, by which mothers can become "co-conspirator[s]" with their daughters to stand "outside the oppressive system, united in some common effort." Chernin suggests that a mother must ally herself with her daughter's struggle by first acknowledging that she too has passed "knowingly through a similar time of urgency and [has] been able to develop beyond it." She concludes that a mother's entry into collaboration with her daughter involves a commitment to speech. She must be willing to "admit her conflict and ambivalence, acknowledge the nearness or actuality of breakdown, become fully conscious of her discontent, the hushed, unspoken sense of her life's failure."[23] After all, as Adrienne Rich proposes, "the quality of the mother's life—however embattled and unprotected—is her primary bequest to her daughter." Thus, the determination to provide models of "courageous mothering," as envisioned by Rich,[24] is finally the subtext of the stories told by stories in *The Joy Luck Club*. Not the least of this maternal courage is the mothers' reclaiming of storytelling as an act of self-creation, one by which they enact, with a full complement of ambivalence and doubt, their passage from loss and dispossession to hope and affirmation.

• • •

In the opening story of the novel, June represents her recently deceased mother at a meeting of the Joy Luck Club. Feeling out of place, she imagines that the three Joy Luck aunties "must wonder now how someone like me can take my mother's place" (p. 27). The three aunties give her $1,200 to travel to China to meet her twin half-sisters, saying, "You must see your sisters and tell them about your mother's death. . . . But most important, you must tell them about her life" (p. 40). But until the moment of the meeting, June asks herself. "How can I describe to them in Chinese about our mother's life?" (p. 287).

The four stories told from June's point of view constitute pure family romance, in which family members are separated, lost, and reunited. The guiding spirit of this myth is June's mother, Suyuan. However, as told by June, the story is unmistakably the daughter's version of the family romance, in which a mother's death opens up the space for a daughter's recuperation of a lost maternal image.[25] Even while protesting that she doesn't know enough to tell her mother's story, June nevertheless proves correct her aunties' insistence: "Your mother is in your bones! . . . her mind . . . has become your mind" (p. 40). She starts cooking the same dishes for her father as her mother did; one evening she finds herself standing at the kitchen window, in imitation of her mother, rapping at a neighborhood cat (p. 209). Arriving in Shenzhen, China, just over the border from Hong Kong, she starts to feel different: "I can feel the skin on my forehead tingling, my blood rushing through a new course, my bones aching with a familiar old pain. And I think, My mother was right. I am becoming Chinese" (p. 267). Earlier she imagines that by dying her mother has left her, "gone back to China to get these babies" (p. 39). But as it turns out, it is she who is returning to China as her mother's emissary. Arriving in China with her father, she hears the final episode of her mother's story: how her mother was forced to abandon her twin babies and continued her search for them through the years. Turning to her father for this history, June urges him to tell it in Chinese: "No, tell me in Chinese. . . . Really, I can understand" (p. 281).

During the scene of June's reunion with her sisters, the rebounding of mirror images enacts a climactic moment, binding mother to daughter and sister to sister.

> Somebody shouts, "She's arrived!" And then I see her. Her short hair. Her small body. And that same look on her face. She has the back of her hand pressed hard against her mouth. She is crying as though she had gone through a terrible ordeal and were happy it is over.
>
> And I know it's not my mother, yet it is the same look she had when I was five and had disappeared all afternoon, for such a long time, that she was convinced that I was dead. And when I miraculously appeared, sleepy-eyed, crawling from underneath my bed, she wept and laughed, biting the back of her hand to make sure it was true.
>
> And now I see her again, two of her, waving, and in one hand is a photo, the Polaroid I sent them. As soon as I get beyond the gate, we run toward each other, all three of us embracing, all hesitations and expectations gone. (p. 287)

In this encounter, sisterly and maternal identifies are blurred, and through the recovery of lost sisters, the foundling myth is conflated with the romance of the daughter. Looking into her sisters' faces, June also sees mirrored in them part of her own ethnic identity: "And now I also see what part of me is Chinese. It is so obvious. It is my family. It is in our blood. After all these years, it can finally be let go" (p. 288).

At the beginning of the novel, while representing her mother at the Joy Luck Club, June muses: "And I am fitting at my mother's place at the mah-jong table, on the East, where things begin" (p. 41). June's story ends with her further east still in China, where there is yet another beginning. The meeting of the three sisters makes their generation whole again; resembling their mother as well as each other, the sisters' mutual identification recuperates maternal loss. Now June remembers her mother's remark to her: "Our whole family is gone. It is just you and I" (p. 272). With June's reunion with her sisters, however, the continuity of the family—but through the female line of descent—is reestablished. And finally, since the word the sisters speak upon recognizing each other—"Mama, Mama"—has common currency across cultures, matrilineage here signifies not only the possibility of a nurturing sisterhood but also the melding of cross-cultural linkages.

Although June's story matches the pattern of the idealized family romance, the overall structure of the novel offers such closure as a provisional possibility only. As we have seen, although maternal speech in the novel turns in the direction of intersubjectivity, this movement is tentative and incomplete. The narratives by Lindo, An-Mei, and Waverly shift from "I" to "you," but the absence of a reciprocal progression in their daughters' stories (from a daughter-ly "I" to the maternal "you") suggests the truncation of a truly dialogic process. Further, the novel's overall structure consciously resists any attempt to shape it definitively. As Valerie Miner has noted, the novel is "narrated horizontally as well as vertically."[26] Thus, June's symbolically complete and symmetrical story is contained within an overarching framework wrapping around a grouping of other stories whose arrangement is neither causal nor linear. Thus, although June's story offers closure in its progression from loss to recuperation, the other narratives are grouped in loose juxtaposition with each other. The mothers' stories are included in the first and last of the four main units in the novel and recount incidents in China; the daughters' stories appear in the middle two sections and are set in the immediate past or proximate present.

On closer reading, even the autonomy of each story as a clear-cut unit begins to dissolve, giving way to a subterranean pattern of resonances and mo-tifs erasing the definite boundaries between individual narratives. Under this scrutiny, actions and motifs mirror each other from story to story, undermining absolute distinctions of character and voice. Thus, the formative moment of Lindo's story, when she looks into the mirror on her wedding day and pledges "never to forget" herself, is duplicated by June's standing in front of a mirror as a teenager, contemplating her self-worth under the assault of her mother's expectations: "The girl staring back at me was angry, powerful. This girl and I were the same. I had new thoughts, willful thoughts, or rather thoughts filled with lots of won'ts. I won't let her change me, I promised myself. I won't be what I'm not" (p. 134). Similarly, Ying-Ying learns from the Moon Lady that the woman is "yin [from] the darkness within" and the man is "yang, bright with lighting our minds" (p. 81). Ying-Ying's lesson about the yin and the yang is echoed in Rose's description of her marriage: "We became inseparable, two halves creating the whole: yin and yang. I was victim to his hero. I was always in danger and he was always rescuing me." Or, to cite a final example of how the novel converges particular motifs: just before Rose's divorce, An-Mei tells her daughter that her husband is probably "doing monkey business with someone else" (p. 188); Rose scoffs at her mother's intuition, but a later discovery proves her mother right. Elsewhere, Lena similarly remarks on her own mother's "mysterious ability to see things before they happen"; in her case, Ying-Ying's uncanny foresight, like An-Mei's, predicts the collapse of Lena's marriage.

Signaling the author's intent to undermine the independence of indi-vidual narrative units, even the chapter titles, by connecting motifs between disparate stories, seem interchangeable. The title of Rose's story, "Half and Half," is echoed at the end of a story narrated by June when, turning to the

piano she has abandoned for many years, she plays two old tunes and realizes that they are "two halves of the same song" (p. 144). The theme of "half
and half" is continued in the story told by Waverly, in which her mother
tells her that she has inherited half of her character traits from each parent:
"half of everything inside you is from me, your mother's side, from the Sun
clan in Taiyuan" (p. 182). In another illustration of how thematic echoes
proliferate in the novel, this same story, entitled "Four Directions," encourages us to trace its various motifs elsewhere. Waverly's "good stuff" that she
has inherited from her mother reiterates the theme of "best quality" that is
continued in another story told by June: in "Best Quality," June's mother
chides her for not wanting the best for herself. Meanwhile, the theme of
"Four Directions" takes us back to the first story in the novel, where we find
June and her aunties seated at the mah-jong table, each occupying one of its
four directions.

Obviously, the notion of "four directions" is emblematic of the novel's
centrifugal structure. At one point, Lena asks: "How can the world in all its
chaos come up with so many coincidences, so many similarities and exact
opposites?" (p. 154). Or, as June intones, in a more complaining mood, "It's
the same old thing, everyone talking in circles" (p. 21). With its mirrored
motifs and interchangeable characterizations, *The Joy Luck Club* demands
a reading that is simultaneously diachronic and synchronic. Aligning itself with the modernist tradition of spatial form in narrative,[27] the novel
defeats any effort to read it according to linear chronology alone. Instead,
the reader's construction of interconnections between motif, character, and
incident finally dissolves individualized character and plot and instead col-
lectivizes them into an aggregate meaning existing outside the individual
stories themselves.

The multivalent structure of *The Joy Luck Club* resists reduction to
simple geometric designs; nevertheless, two figures—the rectangle and the
circle—help to chart Tan's play on the theme of maternity. As the novel
begins, June takes her place with three Joy Luck aunties around the mah-
jong table. Her position at one of the table's cardinal points determines the
direction of her journey east which ends in China. At the end point of June's
story, the trope of the rectangle merges with that of the circle: June's arrival in China brings her full circle to the place where her mother's story
began, and her meeting with her half-sisters sets into motion a circulation
of mirrored relationships blurring identities, generations, and languages. Because it repudiates linearity and symmetry, the circle is a privileged motif
in feminist writings, one that suggests the possibility of reconfiguring traditional familial dynamics and dismantling the hierarchical arrangements
of the Oedipal triangle and the patriarchal family. For instance, in her book
on the reclamation of the pre-Oedipal in women's novels, Jean Wyatt envi-

sions "the possibility . . . of imagining alternative family relations based on preoedipal patterns—family circles whose fluidity of interchange challenges the rigid gender and generational hierarchies of the patriarchal family." In Wyatt's analysis, there persists, in women's writings, the fantasy of a nurturant family where "family members come forward to share the work of fostering others' development [so that] the responsibility for nurturing [is extended] to a whole circle of 'mothering' people."[28]

In *The Joy Luck Club*, the discrete identities of familial members are woven into a collectivized interchangeability through the novel's parataxis—its use of contiguous juxtapositions of voices, narratives, and motifs.[29] Through the novel's interweaving of time frames and voices, three generations of women are included within a relational network linking grandmothers, mothers, daughters, aunts, and sisters. For these women, however, mutual nurturance does not arise from biological or generational connections alone; rather, it is an act affirming consciously chosen allegiances. As Wyatt suggests, mothering as a "reciprocal activity" generally presupposes "a strong mother figure who has a central position in the family," but even "when the mother is not there, the circle remains, its diffuse bonds extends to a circle of equals who take turns nurturing each other."[30] In *The Joy Luck Club*, the death of June's mother, Suyuan, invites the Joy Luck aunties to step into the circle of "mothering reciprocity"; indeed, it is Suyuan's absence that inaugurates the meeting between June and her half-sisters, when they confirm their mutual identification as each other's sisters and mothers.

As we have seen, the maternal voices in *The Joy Luck Club* begin to shift from "I" to "you" to engage the discrete subjectivities of mother and daughter in a tentative exchange of recognitions and identifications. In the same way, the novel's resonant structure and its use of parataxis effectively write the reader into the text as a crucial participant in the making of meaning.[31] The reader of *The Joy Luck Club* is a weaver of intricate interconnections who must, like Suyuan's unraveling of an old sweater, randomly "pull out a kinky thread of yarn, anchoring it to a piece of cardboard, [roll] with a sweeping rhythm, [and] start [a] story" (p. 21). This way of engaging the reader as an active constructor of meaning allows the feminist novel to project a community of sisterly readers.[32] In tracing a family history that blurs the demarcations between the roles of mothers, daughters, and sisters, *The Joy Luck Club* breaks down the boundary between text and reader in order to proffer the notions of sisterhood as a literary construction and as a community constituted through the act of reading. At once disintegrative and constructive in its operations, the novel holds its dual impulses in unresolved suspension and fulfills its fundamentally transformative project—a mutation from daughter-text to mother-text to sister-text.

NOTES

1. See Sandra M. Gilbert and Susan Gubar, eds., *The Norton Anthology of Literature by Women: The Tradition in English* (New York: W. W. Norton, 1985). For a useful survey of the critical literature on this subject, see Marianne Hirsch, "Mothers and Daughters," *Signs* 7 (Autumn 1981): 200–222.

2. Dianne F. Sadoff, "Black Matrilineage: The Case of Alice Walker and Zora Neale Hurston," in *Black Women in America: Social Science Perspectives,* ed. Micheline R. Malson, Elisabeth Mudimbe-Boyi, Jean O'Barr, and Mary Wyer (Chicago: University of Chicago Press, 1988), 198.

3. Marianne Hirsch reminds us of the need for "Western" frameworks to be "modified, reconstructed, and transformed" in considering the works of African American women writers. See Marianne Hirsch, *The Mother/Daughter Plot: Narrative, Psychoanalysis, Feminism* (Bloomington: Indiana University Press, 1989). See also Ruth Perry and Martine Watson Brownley, *Mothering the Mind: Twelve Studies of Writers and Their Silent Partners* (New York: Holmes Meier, 1984), 144–163; Natalie M. Rosinsky, "Mothers and Daughters: Another Minority Group," in *The Lost Tradition: Mothers and Daughters in Literature,* ed. Cathy N. Davidson and E. M. Broner (New York: Frederick Ungar, 1980), 280–290.

4. Amy Ling, *Between Worlds: Women Writers of Chinese Ancestry* (New York: Pergamon Press, 1990), xi. See also Elizabeth J. Ordoñez, "Narrative Texts by Ethnic Women: Rereading the Past, Reshaping the Future," *MELUS* 9 (Winter 1982): 19–28.

5. Shirley Geok-lin Lim, "Japanese American Women's Life Stories: Maternality in Monica Sone's *Nisei Daughter* and Joy Kogawa's *Obasan*," *Feminist Studies* 16 (Summer 1990): 290–291.

6. Maxine Hong Kingston, *The Woman Warrior: Memoirs of a Girlhood among Ghosts* (New York: Alfred A. Knopf, 1977), originally published in 1975; Chuang Hua, *Crossings* (Boston: Northeastern University Press, 1986), originally published in 1968.

7. See Malini Schueller, "Questioning Race and Gender Definitions: Dialogic Subversions in *The Woman Warrior,*" *Criticism* 31 (Fall 1989): 421–437; Amy Ling, "A Rumble in the Silence: *Crossings* by Hua," *MELUS* 9 (Winter 1982): 29–36.

8. Hirsch, 136–137, 6–8, 11, 178–191 (Hirsch's examples are *Sula* and *Beloved* by Toni Morrison and Alice Walkers "Everyday Use"), 12. The emphasis on daughters' narratives in writings by Asian American women is reflected in Helen M. Bannan's essay, "Warrior Women: Immigrant Mothers in the Works of Their Daughters," *Women's Studies* 6 (1979): 165–177.

9. Amy Tan, *The Joy Luck Club* (New York: G. P. Putnam's Sons, 1989). All references are to this edition; subsequent citations appear in parentheses in the text.

10. Amy Tan, "How Stories Written for Mother Became Amy Tan's Best Seller," interview by Julie Lew, *New York Times,* 4 July 1989, 19(N).

11. Hirsch, 161.

12. Adrienne Rich, *Of Woman Born: Motherhood as Experience and Institution* (New York: Bantam Books, 1977), 237.

13. See Nancy Chodorow, *The Reproduction of Mothering: Psychoanalysis and the Sociology of Gender* (Berkeley: University of California Press, 1978); Jane

Flax, "The Conflict between Nurturance and Autonomy in Mother-Daughter Relationships and within Feminism," *Feminist Studies* 4 (June 1978): 171–189; Christine Olivier, *Jocasta's Children: The Imprint of the Mother,* trans. George Craig (New York: Routledge, 1989); Rich, 218–258.

14. Lim, 293. Rosinsky (p. 280) writes: "Members of racial, ethnic, sexual, and economic minority groups, in particular, have delineated their apprehension of the social forces which intervene between mother and daughter. Perhaps because the added oppression of minority group membership exacerbates this often painful relationship, these writers seem particularly aware of its tragic destructiveness." Mary Dearborn has also written about how generational conflict is felt by many historians of ethnicity to be the most striking feature of ethnic American identity. See Mary V. Dearborn, *Pocahontas's Daughters: Gender and Ethnicity in American Culture* (New York: Oxford University Press, 1986), 72–73.

15. Elise Miller, "Kingston's *The Woman Warrior*: The Object of Autobiographical Relations," in *Compromise Formations: Current Directions in Psychoanalysis Criticism,* ed. Vera J. Camden (Kent: Kent State University Press, 1989), 148.

16. See Chodorow.

17. See Sadoff, 203; Perry and Brownley, 160. Hirsch similarly warns (p. 10) against the "androcentric and ethnocentric" biases inherent in the Freudian model of the family. For two critiques of Chodorow's analysis, see Elizabeth V. Spelman, *Inessential Woman: Problems of Exclusion in Feminist Thought* (Boston: Beacon Press, 1988), 83–113; Elizabeth Abel, "Race, Class, and Psychoanalysis? Opening Questions," in *Conflicts in Feminism,* ed. Marianne Hirsch and Evelyn Fox Keller (New York: Routledge, 1990), 185–204.

18. Sue Grunewold, *Beautiful Merchandise: Prostitution in China, 1860–1936* (New York: Harrington Park Press, 1985), 37–45. See also Maria Jaschok *Concubines and Bondservants: The Serial History of a Chinese Custom* (London: Zed Books, 1988); Julia Kristeva, *About Chinese Women,* trans. Anita Barrows (New York: Marion Boyars, 1986), 66–99.

19. Gloria Anzaldúa, *Borderlands/"La Frontera": The New Mestiza* (San Francisco: Spinsters/Aunt Lute Book Co., 1987), 59; Preface, unpaginated.

20. Patricia Yaeger, *Honey-Mad Women: Emancipatory Strategies in Women's Writing* (New York: Columbia University Press, 1988), 40, 44. For a discussion of a second language as an alternate form of self-inscription, see David Leiwei Li, "The Naming of a Chinese American 'I': Cross-Cultural Sign/ifications in *The Woman Warrior,*" *Criticism* 30 (Fall 1988): 515; Shirley K. Rose, "Metaphors and Myths of Cross-Cultural Literacy: Autobiographical Narratives by Maxine Hong Kingston, Richard Rodriguez, and Malcolm X," *MELUS* 14 (Spring 1987): 3–15. Michael M. J. Fischer has discussed the use of bilingualism and "interlinguistic play" in relation to ethnic autobiography; see "Ethnicity and the Arts of Memory," *Writing Culture: The Politics and Poetics of Ethnography,* ed. James Clifford and George E. Marcus (Berkeley: University of California Press, 1986), 218.

21. Roberta Rubenstein states, "If women are typically muted within their own culture even when they constitute a demographic majority, then women of ethnic minority groups are doubly muted. Both gender and ethnic status render them 'speechless' in patriarchy." See Roberta Rubenstein's *Boundaries of the Self: Gender, Culture, Fiction* (Chicago: University of Illinois Press, 1987), 8. See also Lim, 302; King-Kok Cheung, "'Don't Tell': Imposed Silences in *The Color Purple*

and *The Woman Warrior,*" *PMLA* 103 (March 1988): 162–174; and the selected writings by women of color in *Making Face, Making Soul/"Haciendo Caras": Creative and Critical Perspectives by Women of Color,* ed. Gloria Anzaldúa (San Francisco: Aunt Lute Foundation Books, 1990), 179–220.

22. Lindo's narratives interweave first-person discourse with second-person address throughout. Her first story, "The Red Candle," begins with her addressing Waverly directly, beginning: "I once sacrificed my life to keep my parents' promise. This means nothing to you, because to you promises mean nothing" (p. 49). In her second story, "Double Face," she addresses Waverly by referring to "My mother— your grandmother . . . " (p.256) and asking "Why do you always tell your friends that I arrived in the United States on a slow boat from China? . . . Why do you always tell people that I met your father in the Cathay House . . . This is not true! Your father was not a waiter, I never ate in that restaurant" (p. 259). Ying-Ying begins her story, "The Moon Lady," in the third person; she ends her second story, "Waiting between the Trees," with the declaration that "now I must tell my daughter everything" (p. 252). An-Mei's story, "Magpies," is the most distinctive in its clear shift from first-person narration to second-person address. When the story begins, she describes her daughter Rose's psychiatric treatment: "She lies down on a psychiatrist couch, squeezing tears out about this shame" (p. 215). At the end of the same story, she addresses Rose directly: "You do not need a psychiatrist to do this. A psychiatrist does not want you to wake up" (p. 241).

23. Kim Chernin, *The Hungry Self: Women, Eating, and Identity* (New York: Harper & Row, 1985), 82, 51, 86.

24. Rich, 250.

25. The process by which a mother's death inspires women writers to begin to explore the meaning of the maternal has been written about by a number of scholars. In discussing women's writings in the 1920s, Hirsch has noted (p. 97) a pattern by which works by women artists "are not composed by the daughters until the mothers are dead. Only then can memory and desire play their roles as instruments of connection, reconstruction, and reparation." Similarly, Bell Gale Chevigny has examined how Margaret Fuller imagined her mother's death in her fiction in order to be able to "contemplate her mother's life much more freely than before." See her "Daughters Writing: Toward a Theory of Women's Biography," *Feminist Studies* 9 (Spring 1983): 86. See also Judith Kegan Gardiner, "A Wake for Mother: The Maternal Deathbed in Women's Fiction," *Feminist Studies* 4 (June 1978): 146–165.

26. Valerie Miner, "The Daughters' Journeys," *The Nation,* 24 Apr. 1989, 66.

27. See Joseph Frank, "Spatial Form in Modern Literature," in *Criticism: The Foundations of Modern Literary Judgment,* ed. Mark Schorer, Josephine Miles, and Gordon McKenzie (New York: Harcourt, Brace, World, 1958), 379–392; and Jeffrey R. Smitten and Ann Daghistory, eds. *Spatial Form in Narrative* (Ithaca: Cornell University Press, 1981).

28. Jean Wyatt, *Reconstructing Desire: The Role of the Unconscious in Women's Reading and Writing* (Chapel Hill: University of North Carolina Press, 1990), 3, 201 (I am indebted to an anonymous reader of the manuscript of this essay for referring me to this book).

29. Eric S. Rabkin, "Spatial Form and Plot," in *Spatial Form in Narrative,* 96–97.

30. Wyatt, 201.

31. As Eric S. Rabkin notes (p. 99), the "notion of spatial form directs our attention most specifically to works . . . in which the ultimate point of view must be foisted on the reader by the parataxis of the text."

32. This strategy has emerged as a signature of some recent fiction by women of color. See Deborah E. McDowell's discussion of Alice Walker's construction of a sisterhood of readers in *The Color Purple* in "'The Changing Same': Generational Connections and Black Women Novelists," *New Literary History* 18 (Winter 1987): 297; Gayle Greene's analysis of the participatory reading elicited by Toni Morrison's *Beloved* in "Feminist Fiction and the Uses of Memory," *Signs* 16 (1991): 318; and Wendy Ho's characterization of *The Woman Warrior* as a "self-talking story" that insists on writing as "something to be decoded and reconstructed through the reader's or listener's collaborative efforts" in her essay, "Mother/Daughter Writing and the Politics of Race and Sex in Maxine Hong Kingston's *The Woman Warrior*," in *Asian Americans: Comparative and Global Perspectives*, ed. Shirley Hune, Hyung-chan Kim, Stephen S. Fugita, and Amy Ling (Pullman: Washington State University Press, 1991), 236. See also Fischer, "Ethnicity and the Arts of Memory," 232.

JUDITH CAESAR

Patriarchy, Imperialism, and Knowledge in
The Kitchen God's Wife

If, as Jean-Francois Lyotard says, a "master narrative" is required to legitimate artistic expression, for the past thirty years the legitimizing narrative
of mainstream American literary realism has been the quest for personal
fulfillment. The increasingly stagnant, if not outright polluted, mainstream
has produced novel after novel concerning the mid-life crises (and sometimes accompanying marital infidelities) of self-centered American men,
with even the once rich Jewish and Southern literary traditions now given
over to novels like Bernard Malamud's *Dubin's Lives,* Walker Percy's *The
Second Coming,* and Reynolds Price's *Blue Calhoun,* all concerning a middle-
aged (and in the first two instances, wealthy) white man's discontent. All
are a far cry from the writers' earlier ethical and philosophical concerns. The
consideration of the reflective person's stance toward questions of political
and social justice, central to the 19th- and early 20th-century novel from
Charles Dickens' *Bleak House* to Ernest Hemingway's *For Whom the Bell
Tolls,* seems to have become limited to experimental postmodern novels
(E. L. Doctorow's *Ragtime,* Thomas Pynchon's *Vineland*) and to the kinds
of essays on domestic politics, international affairs, and human rights that
appear in *The New Yorker, Harpers',* and *The Nation.* Worse, American literary realism's concentration on the purely personal has led to a delegitimation
of other experience, namely, the experience of introspective and articulate

North Dakota Quarterly, Volume 64, Number 2 (1994–1995): pp. 164–174. Copyright © 1994
North Dakota Quarterly.

people who have lived lives devastated by social and political forces out-side their control. These people are relegated to inarticulate images on the television screen—in Sarajevo, in Somalia, in the Middle East, in Thai-land, and in China. These people, then, whose real stories and histories remain untold to the American public, become less "real" than many of the characters who populate American literary fiction.

In this context, it is very significant that the supposedly "popular" novels of minority American women—Alice Walker, Toni Morrison, Maxine Hong Kingston, Louise Erdrich, and now Amy Tan—seem to be reaching a larger audience than much mainstream literary realism. In part, this is because all five can create such an engaging and often witty surface and because all seem to deal with the popular topics of TV talk shows: spouse abuse, recovering from divorce, finding one's roots, etc. And of course all are hyphenated Americans of some sort, a fact which engages the curiosity of readers who do not share the writers' backgrounds. (Chicana and Native American writers like Sandra Cis-neros and Leslie Silko, who use more experimental techniques and deal with a wider range of subject matter, have yet to reach the Waldenbooks reader.)

Yet Tan, for one, does much more than articulate popular media issues. She causes us to question the very basis of how we know what we know. She creates her own narrative by seeming to affirm popular American assump-tions in the formula of the popular novel and then undermining that very narrative in a complex political allegory that questions the basic American (indeed Western) concepts of truth and rationality.

In keeping with this subtly deceptive plan, *The Kitchen God's Wife* seems at first like a lively but somewhat clichéd popular novel, a modern pseudo-feminist retelling of the folklore story of the abused wife (patient Griselda in the West, the kitchen god's wife in the East) who wins her husband's love by passing all his tests or his remorse by her generosity of spirit. What makes it modern is that the abused wife is angry at her ill treatment and seemingly "finds herself" in that anger. The women, moreover, are the "good guys" while the men seem quite unrelievedly evil, with the exception of the male rescuer. It seems, in short, to be a type of formula novel which provides women read-ers with clear heroines, heroes, and villains, all without disrupting the Gothic romance's illusion of rescue by "the right man." Jiang Weili, the narrator of the central three-fourths of the novel, endures the most horrifying abuse from her brutal husband, Wen Fu, while traditional Chinese society not only fails to intervene but colludes in her victimization. The only twist seems to be that instead of winning her husband's love, Weili is rescued by a handsome prince, in this case, Jimmy Louie, a Chinese-American soldier who marries her and takes her back to the United States. In fact, one can see the novel as a rather smug indictment of the misery of women in traditional Chinese society in contrast to American society's enlightened feminism. Moreover, the story that frames the story, that of Jiang Weili's daughter Pearl and her relationship with her mother, seems like yet another story about returning to one's roots to discover some less complicated identity. In short, there seems little here to challenge conventional American thinking.

Yet nothing in the novel is as it seems. Certainly, in the beginning, nothing is as it seems to Weili's American-born daughter Pearl, who narrates the opening chapters of the novel and embodies the American sensibility in all its directness and in all its limitations. Like well-meaning Americans in China, Pearl makes cultural gaffes in dealing with the older Chinese-American community and even with her mother because she doesn't seem to understand the differences between outer display and actual feeling or the realm of implied meanings that are so much a part of Chinese tradition. Thus, at the funeral of elderly Grand Auntie Du which opens the novel, Pearl sees a group of sobbing women in threadbare padded jackets and takes them for recent immigrants from China, Grand Auntie Du's "real friends," when in fact they are Vietnamese professional mourners. Worse, with all the confidence of American pop psychology, Pearl advises her mother to speak frankly to her contemporary, Auntie Helen, about her feelings that Auntie Helen should be sharing more in Grand Auntie Du's care. Pearl says,

> "Why don't you just tell Auntie Helen how you feel and stop complaining?" This is what Phil [Pearl's Anglo husband] had suggested I say, a perfectly reasonable way to get my mother to realize what was making her miserable so she could finally take positive action. (13)

Of course, Pearl doesn't realize that her mother is quietly boasting to Pearl about her own dutifulness and implying that more could be expected of Pearl as well. Thus, Pearl is shocked when her mother is so profoundly offended that she will barely speak to her for a month.

She knows her mother as Winnie Louie, her American name, her kindly but often inexplicably crotchety mother to whom she is bound by sometimes tiresome traditions that don't seem to apply to other Americans. She doesn't realize until the end of the novel that her mother is also Jiang Weili, a woman brought up in China who has survived both a disastrous marriage and the invasion and occupation of her country by a brutal enemy army. And because she doesn't know who her mother is, Pearl also doesn't know that she herself is not the daughter of the kindly Jimmy Louie but of Wen Fu, the brutal first husband. This is but one of the novel's pattern of multiple and mistaken identities that suggests the ambiguity of all knowledge and the incompleteness of the official (legitimate) narrative.

In particular, the novel explores the incompleteness of the American narrative, an incompleteness that comes from a refusal to see the validity of the knowledge of other cultures or of the experiences of people who are not Americans. Pearl, with her confident American knowledge of the way things are, her faulty Mandarin, and her imperviousness to implied meanings, misses much of what is going on beneath the surface, although she is sensitive enough sometimes to realize that there are some things she doesn't understand: " . . . apparently, there's a lot I don't know about my mother and Auntie Helen" (49), she thinks at one point. Since the bulk of the novel is Weili's story, it would seem that one of the purposes of having Pearl as the initial narrator is not only to contrast the American sensibility with the Chinese, but to alert the American reader to the subtext beneath Jiang Weili's story as well. Although the reader would first identify with the American, Pearl, it is very clear that Pearl doesn't know all that needs to be known.

Weili's story is also much more than it would first seem to an American reader. Most obviously, Jiang Weili's is the story of a progressively more violent and degrading marriage set against the backdrop of the Japanese invasion of China. Weili is married off to a man of a socially "suitable" family, although both her father and her aunts and uncles clearly have a sense of the man's flawed character. Because they know something of his deceptiveness, if not his outright cruelty, they marry Weili to him and not her favored cousin, nicknamed Peanut, who had wanted to marry her. Wen Fu proves to be a sexual sadist who delights in humiliation games, a liar who uses his dead brother's diplomas to become an officer in the Nationalist air force (another confused identity), and a coward who manages to save his own life throughout the war by deserting his fellow pilots whenever they encounter Japanese aircraft. Because of Wen Fu's social position, however, no one acknowledges any of these failings.

As the war continues and the Nationalist army flees from Shanghai to Nanjing and finally to Kunming, so Wen Fu degenerates. He refuses to leave a card game to get a doctor for his sick daughter, and then he publicly blames Weili when the child dies. He brings a concubine into the house and then discards her when she becomes pregnant. He forces Weili to "admit" publicly to being a prostitute, despite her very obvious fidelity. He is the enemy of whatever is life-affirming and generous (Weili's maternal responses to save her child, her sisterly desire to help the ignorant concubine) disguised as patriarchal morality. Throughout all of this abuse, no one interferes; in fact, when Weili tries to run away from Wen Fu, her friends Hulan (later Helen) and Auntie Du tell him her hiding place. The increasing viciousness of Wen Fu parallels the increasing closeness of the Japanese army, so that by the time Weili has run away and been brought back to a still more degraded life, the Japanese are bombing Kunming.

The parallel between the victimization of Weili and the Japanese conquest of China is further emphasized by the fact that old Jiang, Weili's father, has collaborated with the Japanese, betraying his country in the same way he betrayed his daughter. His pattern of ineffectual resistance and subsequent capitulation, moreover, continues throughout the novel. He throws a teacup against a priceless painting to show that he would rather destroy China's heritage than betray it—and then accedes to Japanese demands; in Shanghai, when both he and Weili are Wen Fu's victims, he gives Weili the money with which to leave Wen Fu—and then is too ill to help her when Wen Fu accuses her of theft and has her imprisoned.

Even at this level of the political allegory, however, there is little in equating Chinese patriarchy with Japanese expansionism and imperialism that would discomfort or challenge an American reader. It is still "those people" who have done these terrible things, not "us." Yet it is not so comforting if one carries the political allegory to its logical conclusions. Weili's victimization couldn't have taken place if Chinese society had not condoned it to such an extent that even her best friends didn't want to blemish their reputations by helping her escape—at least until the very end of the novel, when they try to get her out of jail (ineffectually, it turns out) by saying that they had witnessed her divorce. These friends, who later join her in the United States, are not all that different from the United States itself, which, as Tan points out, helped to keep the Japanese war machine running by supplying the Japanese with oil and scrap metal all through the 1930s and later helped China only after the United States itself was under attack. Hulan thinks that she freed Weili through her second husband's influence with the Nationalist government; in fact, it is Weili's cousin Peanut, now a communist cadre who runs a shelter for abused wives, who gets Weili out of prison because Nationalist officials in charge of Weili's case fear reprisals from the communists. If Weili is China, then it is a communist who helps to liberate her, although the liberation is far from complete.

Moreover, if we interpret the novel as a fairly literal political allegory, there is yet another disturbing implication. Wen Fu is never punished. When Weili finally gets word of his death, she learns that he has died an old man, surrounded by his family and respected by his community—the very definition of a righteous man's proper death in Chinese tradition. In contrast, Weili's good husband Jimmy Louie dies relatively young and in great pain, seemingly denied by Pearl, the daughter whom he raised. The pain and prematurity of Jimmy's death is one reason it so haunts Weili. Weili, furthermore, is eking out a living in a foreign country (America), widowed and at least, as the book opens, culturally estranged from her children. One could see this as paralleling the fact that all the former imperial powers—Japan among them—are both more prosperous and more respected than their former victims. To cite the most literal sort of example, the Western media tends to blame the human rights abuses and the political unrest in China and the rest of the former colonial world on the ideological systems that ejected the colonial powers, not on the after-effects of imperialism itself. And the crimes of imperialism did go unpunished. The war crimes trials after World War II focused on the Japanese abuse of western POWs, not on the Japanese imprisonment and massacre of millions of Chinese civilians.

One reason for Tan's equation of imperialism and patriarchy is essentially rhetorical. It is easier for an American audience to sympathize with the victims of patriarchy than with the victims of imperialism. Many American women have been the victims of patriarchy, after all, while very few have been the victims of imperialism. We have not had our country invaded and occupied by a foreign army or had laws imposed on us by people who didn't know our language or culture—except, of course, for Native Americans. The type of suffering Weili endures, moreover, is primarily emotional and psychological rather than physical. She is humiliated and exploited; she cannot even complain about her plight. But she is not being starved, beaten, or tortured at a time when millions of her countrymen (and women) were, as Weili herself points out. Weili's suffering is that of a middle-class woman married to a bully. An American reader can identify with this, at least to some degree; and once one has done this, one can begin to get a sense of the type of suffering that Tan suggests only metaphorically or seemingly incidentally—the Nanjing massacre, for instance. Then other events fit into place. Weili and Wen Fu's children die, one the direct victim of Wen Fu's neglect, two the indirect victims of the Japanese. Tan's presentation helps to legitimize a narrative of suffering otherwise so far outside the American experience that it could seem beyond our capacity for empathy.

But there are more complex philosophical reasons for linking imperialism and patriarchy. For one thing, they both shape the "legitimate" printed narratives of Weili's story. To the Shanghai press covering Weili's case, Wen Fu is a war hero whose wife has been seduced and corrupted by a lecherous American. In this patriarchal narrative, Weili wants to escape Wen Fu not because she has been abused, but because she is "crazy for American sex." This is as true as the printed leaflets the Japanese drop on Nanjing, explaining that civilians will not be harmed.

Behind these official narratives is the assumption that some people's suffering is more significant than other peoples' sufferings. The Chinese historian Szuma Chien once ironically remarked that some deaths are as heavy as Mount Tai, while others are lighter than a feather—that is, in official versions of events.[1] Thus, the honor of men is more important than the dignity of women, and the deaths of ordinary Chinese simply aren't important at all. This assumption isn't merely Oriental, moreover, since it underlies the current

American narrative that the personal emotional crisis of an American is the only suffering interesting enough to write about. The official narratives are used to ignore or justify the sufferings of the powerless.

Consequently, all the official facts in Tan's novel are questionable. Weili's divorce is officially valid when Wen Fu holds a gun to her head and makes her sign the paper, but it can be made invalid by her ex-husband's tearing up the paper. What is a divorce and what does it mean under those circumstances? Weili can be "officially" a thief for taking the gold her father gave her, and then later be "officially" innocent when her imprisonment is termed an "error of the court." Even Pearl's official American knowledge that World War II began with the bombing of Pearl Harbor is questionable, since, as Weili points out, it began for China with the Japanese invasion of Manchuria. (Or did it begin even earlier, with the German concession of the Shantung peninsula to the Japanese?) The Western narrative is at best an incomplete truth. When does a divorce or a war begin or end?

The narrative structure of the novel also suggests the problematic nature of truth. As Edward Said has pointed out in *Culture and Imperialism,* the narrative structure of the classic 19th-century realistic novel, with its omniscient narrator or reliable first-person narrator, helped to underscore the idea of an authoritative and "correct" version of events (77). Despite the polyphonic narrations of the high modernist novel, the 20th-century popular novel has generally preserved the 19th-century technique, as has much of contemporary literary realism. The modernist novel, moreover, focuses on the psychological and philosophical implications of competing narratives (*Mrs. Dalloway, As I Lay Dying,* etc.), not on their political implication. Much contemporary fiction thus tends to confirm the value of Americanness over foreignness, a kind of contemporary imperialism. (Think, for example, of Cormac McCarthy's National Book Award-winning *All the Pretty Horses* in which the good guys are all American men and the bad guys either Mexican or female. Consider how different it would be if any of the Mexican or women characters gave their version of events.) In contrast, Tan has two narrators and three versions of events—Pearl's, Weili's, and Hulan's, all of which seem credible in some respects.

While Tan's use of a polyphonic narrative is significant in itself, perhaps more significant is who speaks. Through much of the novel, after all, it is an elderly Chinese immigrant whose syntax and word choice reflect the patterns of Chinese-accented English, a speech pattern marginalized and mocked by contemporary mainstream American society. Tan helps to give this voice a validity and dignity in the same way that Walker and Morrison have helped to legitimize African American speech. She has made the sufferings of those who speak in this voice "as heavy as Mount Tai."

The details of the novel confirm both the validity of these Chinese women's experience and the subjective nature of truth. What Hulan remembers is different from what Weili remembers, yet Hulan's insights are given sudden credibility when she tells Pearl, "You know how she [Weili] is, very hard to thank . . ."(408), and we realize how very true this is of both Weili and Pearl. Just as Pearl rejects her "cousin" Mary's comforting casseroles when Mary learns of Pearl's illness, Weili would indeed be repelled by the idea of being indebted to Hulan in any way. We also realize the extent to which Hulan's behavior, which Weili had interpreted as simply contrary and obstructive, was well intended. What is interesting here is that in personal relationships, unlike political ones, conflicting versions of the truth are not necessarily divisive, since neither version is used as a means of control or suppression. Thus even the quarrels between Winnie (once Weili) and Helen (once Hulan) are not precisely quarrels at all. Pearl observes,

> I watch them continue to argue, although perhaps it is not arguing.
> They are remembering together, dreaming together. (410)

Tan also contradicts this idea of a rational Western truth through the pattern of double and shifting identities of her characters and by her clear indications that the commonly accepted criteria for determining identity are sometimes irrelevant. Tan shows a world of multiple and contradictory truths, truth as a series of Chinese boxes, not a unitary truth to be "discovered" in the Western sense. Tan's is not even a Western "postmodernist" truth of multiple linear narratives, but of contradictory truths and partial truths intermixed in layers of meaning. Through the contradictions in Winnie's (Weili's) character, we see that a complete person can be both large-spirited and petty, loving and distant. Indeed, self-knowledge consists of acknowledging these seemingly contradictory traits. At one point Weili tells Pearl,

> I have told you about the early days of my marriage so you can understand why I became strong and weak at the same time. Maybe according to your American mind, you cannot be both, that would be a contradiction. But according to my life, I had to be both. (313)

The simultaneous existence of these opposites is indeed very different from what our American minds tell us is rational, and thus it calls into question the validity of that rationality.

Moreover, none of the characters is precisely what they seem, even concerning the most common determiner of identity, family relationships. Consider, for instance, the ways in which the characters seem to be related but aren't. Pearl calls Hulan "auntie" and thinks of Hulan's children Bao-Bao and Mary as her cousins. Indeed, Winnie and Helen, with all their feuding and tenderness, act like sisters. And Pearl is as exasperated and yet connected to the "cousins" as she would be with any blood relative, a relationship Tan underscores by using them as foils to Pearl. Pearl has believed the "official version" that Helen is the widow of Winnie's younger brother, but she learns very early in her mother's story that Helen is "merely" a person she has known ever since her youth.

Thus it is not surprising that Pearl's discovery of her parentage, her "real identity" does not have the significance the episode's placement in the novel would seem to grant it. Finally, the great climactic revelation that Wen Fu is Pearl's "real" father seems to be irrelevant after all. It is the pattern formed by all the revelations leading up to it that is important. That Jimmy Louie is Pearl's "real" father is simply one more item in the list of things that seems true, isn't true, and finally is in a larger sense as true as any of the novel's other ambiguous truths. And on the level of character, it doesn't matter either. Pearl is not at all like Wen Fu, as Winnie points out. Ancestry and blood relationship finally do not matter very much—a very non-Chinese idea in a very non-American narrative.

Meaning and truth exist in layers, and what is true on the surface is contradicted by another truth underneath, which is in turn contradicted by a third layer. And all are "true." We see this kind of paradox even in the names of minor characters. Pearl's cousin Roger is named Bao-Bao, "precious baby," because his parents were so happy to finally have a child, but the nickname sticks as he grows up because it becomes a sarcastic description of his superficial and immature behavior. The only one of the Chinese-American characters to have a Chinese name, he speaks like a cartoon of an American and gets married and divorced as carelessly as a character in a Woody Allen comedy. Is it then because he is so American that he is so superficial? In fact, in his self-centeredness and sexual inconstancy, he seems like a comic and relatively benign version of Wen Fu. He's a beloved precious baby who has become a spoiled precious baby whose faults are equally American and Chinese.

In this context, it is not surprising that nationality doesn't matter very much in determining the identity of both Weili and Pearl either. It merely determines their modes of expression. Pearl is very much an American version of Weili. Like Weili, she is a concerned and loving mother, she faces difficulties (her multiple sclerosis, for example) with such stoicism that she cuts herself off from both her husband and her mother, she is witty and critical, and she is willing to let things be understood without spelling them out. Yet in her manners and beliefs, she is an American. When, at the end, she accepts her mother's herbal cures and the offering to Lady Sorrowfree, she does so as an acceptance of her mother's solicitude, not her beliefs. She hasn't found a "Chinese identity" in the way the characters in *Song of Solomon* and *The Color Purple* find an African identity; instead she has found a closer relationship

with her mother and an insight into the seemingly conflicting layers of reality
in the world around her, beginning with the multiple identities of her mother
and the Chinese "relatives" whom she thought she knew. Personal identity,
like both personal and political truth, is many layered and elusive, something
accepted rather than discovered.

Under the outward layer of a highly readable popular novel, Tan has
written an extremely complex postmodern literary novel that challenges the
dominant narratives of contemporary American society, particularly our ideas
of who matters and who does not, of whose version is "true" and whose is not,
and indeed of how one can find what is true. Through the voices of characters
like Weili and Hulan, Tan presents a world in which complex and intelligent
people must find a way of accommodating hostile political and social forces
against which they are powerless to rebel—a type of suffering from which
most American readers have been sheltered. Thus, Tan verifies the reality of a
world outside the American experience as nevertheless part of the human experience and questions the sense of entitlement and cultural superiority that
allows Americans to dismiss the sufferings of foreigners. This sense of entitlement, the idea that "our" deaths are as heavy as Mount Tai and "their" deaths
are light as feathers underlies the callousness of all imperial narratives—the
novels of contemporary America, as well as narratives of the Imperial China
of which Szuma Chien wrote and of patriarchal China and Imperial Japan,
of which Jiang Weili speaks. By making us question the validity of American
knowledge and the "otherness" of what Americans consider foreign, Amy Tan
has helped to enlarge the American narrative.

NOTE

1. As quoted by Jia-lin Peng in his short story, "The Typewriter," from the
collection *Wild Cat* (26). Peng's narrator comments, "If Szuma Chien . . . were still
alive, would he think the death of people like us was lighter than a feather . . . ? The
people who used his remark, did they know its original meaning? . . . " Years after
he had been castrated by the emperor for speaking out in defense of an acquaintance,
Szuma Chien wrote this comment in bitterness, to an innocent friend who was about
to be executed!

"I wished in the future there would be an historian as great as Szuma Chien
who would unmistakably say something like this: Any innocent and unnecessary
death should be heavier than Mount Tai. No one should have the right to think any
other human being's life, even an enemy's life, is as light as a feather. Otherwise,
those in power will be able to wipe out anyone in their way. . . . "

Szuma Chien was a Han dynasty scholar who was one of the first writers
to comment on the significance of events rather than merely recording dates and
official views. It is a particular ironic example of the official manipulation of
narrative that his statements were used to justify the killing of "class enemies" during
the Cultural Revolution.

Works Cited

Lyotard, Jean-Francois. *The Post-Modern Condition: A Report on Knowledge.* Trs. Geoff Bennington and Brian Massumi. Minneapolis: University of Minnesota Press, 1984.

Peng, Jia-lin. *Wild Cat: Stories from the Cultural Revolution.* Dunvegan, Canada: Cormorant Books, 1990.

Said, Edward. *Culture and Imperialism.* New York: Knopf, 1993.

Tan, Amy. *The Kitchen God's Wife.* New York: Putnam, 1991.

———. *The Joy Luck Club.* 1989. New York: Ivy Books, 1992.

SAU-LING CYNTHIA WONG

"Sugar Sisterhood": Situating the Amy Tan Phenomenon

The sensational success of Amy Tan's first novel, *The Joy Luck Club* (1989), is the stuff of publishing legend. Before the shrewd eye of agent Sandra Dijkstra spotted a potential winner, Tan was entirely unknown to the literary world. But lavish advance praise—the dust jacket of the hardcover edition bears enthusiastic blurbs by Alice Walker, Alice Hoffman, and Louise Erdrich—and postpublication rave reviews instantly propelled *The Joy Luck Club* onto the *New York Times* best-seller list, where it stayed for nine months. The hardcover edition was reprinted twenty-seven times and sold 275,000 copies (J. Simpson, 66); frenzied bidding by corporate publishers pushed the price for paperback rights from a floor of $100,000 to an astonishing $1.2 million (Holt). *The Joy Luck Club* was a finalist for the National Book Award and the National Book Critics Circle Award, and a recipient of the 1990 Bay Area Book Reviewers Award for Fiction.

Tan's second novel, *The Kitchen God's Wife* (1991), has not duplicated *Joy Luck*'s blockbuster success. However, it too is a highly acclaimed best-seller, with most reviewers declaring it as good as, if not better than, its predecessor (e.g., Dew; Gillespie; Howe; Humphreys; Iyer; James; Perrick; Romano; Yglesias).[1] The $4 million advance that Putnam reputedly paid on it (Solovitch, 18) has apparently been money well spent.[2] The Amy Tan phenomenon continues its momentum with a new children's book, *The Moon Lady*, spun off

The Ethnic Canon: Histories, Institutions, and Interventions, edited by David Palumbo-Liu (Minneapolis: University of Minnesota Press, 1995): pp. 174–210. Copyright © 1995 Sau-Ling Cynthia Wong.

from an episode in *The Joy Luck Club;* a third novel in the works (Rothstein); and a film adaptation of *The Joy Luck Club* made by noted Chinese American director Wayne Wang.[3]

Like Maxine Hong Kingston's *Woman Warrior* (1976), *The Joy Luck Club* is a crossover hit by a female ethnic writer; it also straddles the worlds of "mass" literature and "respectable" literature, stocking the shelves of airport newsstands as well as university bookstores, generating coffee table conversations as well as conference papers. Tan's stellar status in the publishing world, further assured by *The Kitchen God's Wife,* causes one to wonder: wherein does the enormous appeal of her fiction lie?

To say that book buyers and readers are simply responding to Tan's good writing—briskly paced, easy to follow, by turns poignant and hilarious—is to give a naive and decontextualized, if partially true, answer. It goes without saying that the history of literary reputations abounds with instances of "good" writing belatedly recognized, or else of "bad" writing amply rewarded in the marketplace. (Without getting into a general disquisition on the social construction of taste, I use the "good"/"bad" distinction here to refer to either a disjuncture between academic/critical opinion and popular success, or else a revision of judgment over time.) To narrow the consideration to contemporaneous Asian American women's writing alone, the year *The Joy Luck Club* appeared also saw the polished novelistic debut of another young writer, Cynthia Kadohata (*The Floating World*), as well as new books by two established figures: Kingston's *Tripmaster Monkey: His Fake Book* and Bharati Mukherjee's *Jasmine.* All three works show remarkable artistry and garnered strong reviews, but none became a commercial triumph. That elusive element, "timing" or "luck," usually summoned to explain cases of overnight celebrity, must be restored to historicity: What is it about the subject matter of *The Joy Luck Club* and its treatment that somehow "clicked" with the times? What prompts Tan's following to come back loyally to *The Kitchen God's Wife?* Where is her fiction positioned in the multiple discourses that make up American writing? What discursive traditions does it participate in, and to what ideological effect, to create Tan's trademark fictional world and a niche market?

Tan has often been presented in the media as a meteoric individual talent, bursting full-blown from obscurity onto the literary scene (e.g., Kepner). She has even been implicitly credited with singlehandedly ushering in an Asian American literary renaissance (J. Simpson), even though Tan herself takes pains to point out that many of the writers of the 1991 "wave" named by the mainstream media (David Wong Louie, David Mura, Gish Jen, Gus Lee, Laurence Yep, Frank Chin) had been writing and publishing before—some, like Chin and Yep, long, long before—she became known, and that they represent very different, unique voices (Fong-Torres, B4). The media account of Tan's singularity, based on tacit meritocratic assumptions and a late twentieth-century variation on the myth of the original romantic artist, obscures the role of politics in the making (and breaking) of Asian American and other ethnic minority writers. Demythologizing this kind of portrayal, this essay situates the appeal of Amy Tan's fiction in its sociohistorical context and analyzes the discursive demands and contradictions experienced by Chinese American (and to some degree other Asian American) writers at this juncture in American history.

Feminist/Matrilineal Discourse and China Mama's Revenge

One of the most obvious reasons for the success of *The Joy Luck Club* and *The Kitchen God's Wife* is the centrality of the mother-daughter relationship in these books. This subject matter places them squarely in a tradition of matrilineal discourse that has, as a part of the feminist movement, been gathering momentum in the United States over the last ten to fifteen years. In 1976, Adrienne Rich wrote that the "cathexis between mother and daughter—essential, distorted, misused—is the great unwritten story" (225; quoted in Hirsch, "Maternal Narratives," 415). In 1984, Tillie Olsen was still able to lament, "Most of what has been, is, between mothers, daughters, and in motherhood, daughterhood, has never been recorded" (275; quoted in Pearlman, 1). But a scant five years later, as Mickey Pearlman notes, the profusion of creative writing as well as social-science scholarship on the "linked lives" of mothers and daughters had become overwhelming.[4]

That the success of Amy Tan's fiction is a product of, and testimony to, the strength of the feminist movement is easy to see. Both her books capture the contradictions that have been identified as characteristic of the "literature of matrilineage" in Nan Bauer Maglin's simple but convenient schema:

1. the recognition by the daughter that her voice is not entirely her own;

2. the importance of trying to really see one's mother in spite of or beyond the blindness and skewed vision that growing up together causes;

3. the amazement and humility about the strength of our mothers;

4. the need to recite one's matrilineage, to find a ritual to both get back there and preserve it;

5. and still, the anger and despair about the pain and the silence borne and handed on from mother to daughter. (258)

Any number of pithy quotations from *The Joy Luck Club* and *The Kitchen God's Wife* can be culled to illustrate these interconnected themes. What is harder to determine than Tan's place in American matrilineal discourse is the reason why her fiction has so conspicuously eclipsed works by Euro-American writers on similar subject matter,[5] as Kingston's *Woman Warrior* did over a decade ago. The white feminist reading public appears to have an unusually keen appetite for mother-daughter stories by and about people of color.[6] In particular, as one British reviewer wryly observes from across the Atlantic, "Whether by a quirk of literary fate or because it is their psychological destiny, Chinese American women seem to have won the world rights to the mother/daughter relationship" (Perrick). Why? Why this privileging of Chinese American mothers and daughters in literature while no equivalent is forthcoming in the realm of, say, employment opportunities or provision of child care?

I suggest it is neither literary fate nor psychological destiny that has conferred favored status on the Chinese American mother-daughter relationship, but rather a convergence of ethnic group-specific literary tradition and ideological needs by the white-dominated readership—including the feminist readership—for the Other's presence as both mirror and differentiator.

Contrary to popular belief, Kingston did not invent Chinese American matrilineal discourse, and Tan, creating something of an accessible "*Woman Warrior* without tears" in *Joy Luck,* is not so much revisiting Kingston territory as sharing a concern long of interest to many other Chinese American women writers. Antecedents for Kingston's strong Chinese women can be found in the female-centered household in Su-ling Wong and Earl Cressy's little-known collaborative autobiography, *Daughter of Confucius* (1952). Even propatriarchal Chinese American autobiographies from the pre-1965 period,[7] such as Helena Kuo's *I've Come a Long Way* (1942) and Jade Snow Wong's *Fifth Chinese Daughter* (1945), like *Daughter of Confucius,* show occasional interruptions of matrilineal consciousness, as in Kuo's anecdote of mother-daughter complicity in novel reading (24), or Jade Snow Wong's descriptions of hours spent with her grandmother and mother learning about Chinese customs—at once mother-daughter bonding and induction into the woman's submissive role in the culture (28–33; 48–60). That is to say, even earlier male-identified Chinese American women writers are, at some level, aware of the precariousness of their place in a patriarchal society—an awareness also reflected in the virtually obligatory opening explanations of how they come to receive a decent education, thanks to generous fathers willing to mitigate prevailing gender norms (e.g., Kuo, 21, 33–44; J. Wong, 14–15).[8] Chinese American interest in matrilineage continues in the post-1965 period; examples range from Chuang Hua's recurrent image of the majestic matriarch in *Crossings* (1968) (again in spite of an overt obsession with the father's approval);[9] to Alice P. Lin's combined ethnic/matrilineal root-seeking journey in *Grandmother Has No Name* (1988); to the fiction of younger writers like Sarah Lau (1990), Wen-Wen C.

Wang (1990), and Fae Myenne Ng (1993), who, like Kingston, explore their
bond with immigrant mothers simultaneously tough and vulnerable.

Chinese American preoccupation with the mother-daughter bond
can be further situated in a broader Asian American discourse of matrilineage, both pre- and post-*Woman Warrior* (Lim). Hisaye Yamamoto's
classics, "Seventeen Syllables" (1949) and "Yoneko's Earthquake" (1951),
predate *The Woman Warrior* by over two decades; apparent inspiration for
"The Handkerchief" (1961) and "Songs My Mother Taught Me" (1976)
by Wakako Yamauchi, Yamamoto's literary disciple, these stories depict the
ambivalent and largely unspoken emotional exchanges between unhappily
married mothers and daughters on the verge of womanhood, in ways again
reminiscent of Maglin's schema. Despite the protagonists' expressed yearn-
ing for the father's love, the presence of abrasive, abusive, but irrepressibly
vigorous grandmothers is indelible in Burmese American Wendy Law-Yone's
Coffin Tree (1983) as well as Japanese American Cynthia Kadohata's *Floating World* (1989); the grandmother/matriarch figure, coupled again with an
absent mother, resurfaces in Singaporean American writer Fiona Cheong's
Scent of the Gods (1991). The resilient spirit of female ancestors embodied in
the Vietnamese legend of the woman warrior, along with the support of living women relatives, is lovingly recalled in Le Ly Hayslip's account of her life
during and after the Vietnam War, *When Heaven and Earth Changed Places*
(1989). Merle Woo's "Letter to Ma" (1981) articulates a radical, lesbian perspective on Asian American mother-daughter relationships. Ronyoung Kim's
Clay Walls (1987) chronicles the strong ties between a Korean immigrant
woman and her daughter. Short fiction such as South Asian Appachana's
(1989) and Dhillon's (1989), and Japanese American Sasaki's (1989), continue the exploration of matrilineage. If we broaden the Asian American canon
to include Asian Canadian works, then Joy Kogawa's *Obasan* (1982) offers
a distinctly matrilineal text, in which themes like the search for the absent
mother, surrogate motherhood (or maternalistic aunthood), silence breaking,
and rituals of reclamation are woven into an account of the uprooting of Japanese Canadians during the Second World War. More recently, South-Indian
Canadian writer Mara Rachna's *Of Customs and Excise* (1991) places the story
of the "immigrant daughter's revolt" in a multigenerational, postcolonial global
context to deepen one's understanding of matrilineage.[10]

This quick survey of the literature of matrilineage in the Chinese American and Asian American traditions is meant to contextualize Tan's work
more precisely: to dispel the notion that her fiction is simply riding on the
coattails of white feminism, tapping directly into "universal" concerns from
the vantage point of individual insight.[11] Even if there had been no white
buyers of *The Joy Luck Club* and *The Kitchen God's Wife*, there would still have
been a readership for these books among Asian American women, many of

whom are hungry for validation of their own experiences as daughters of immigrant mothers (e.g., Fong and Sit; compare Suzi Wong on Kingston's *Woman Warrior*).

Identifying a matrilineal Asian American tradition is important in terms of not only racial politics within feminism, but also gender politics within cultural nationalism. The kind of rehabilitation of Asian American literary patrilineage undertaken by the *Aiiieeeee* group,[12] essential as it is, is attained at the expense of the female perspective (Cheung). In the influential Introduction to *Aiiieeeee!* (Chin et al. 1974), the numerical superiority of Asian American women writers is categorically denounced as a sign of the literature's emasculation by white society, while not one living Chinese American woman writer is included in *The Big Aiiieeeee!* (Chan et al. 1991), the sequel to the first anthology.[13] Frank Chin's *Year of the Dragon* (1981), a play about a disintegrating Chinatown family in the 1960s, is emblematic of this suppression of the woman's voice. In addition to a scatterbrained American-born mother humming inherent snatches of song, the play features China Mama, the patriarch's first wife left in China because of immigration restrictions and suddenly transported to San Francisco to assuage the dying man's cultural and familial guilt. This *gum sahn paw* (Cantonese for "Gold Mountain wife") is portrayed as totally devoid of subjectivity: a recalcitrant, alien presence unceremoniously deposited in the Eng family's living room, mute except for sporadic attempts to communicate with the children in gibberish-like Cantonese. In Chin's play, the old immigrant woman from China is just a convenient symbol, not a human being with decades' worth of experiences and grievances to recount.[14] In this context, *The Joy Luck Club* and *The Kitchen God's Wife* are China Mama's revenge: the Joy Luck aunties get not only their own voices back but equal time with their American offspring. And when Winnie in *The Kitchen God's Wife* holds forth about her past, she is allowed to do so endlessly, for more than 330 pages, until her daughter Pearl nearly falls off the chair from surprise at revealed secrets (397), and we the readers from sheer fatigue.

It is vital to recognize the Asian American discursive context for Amy Tan's fiction, but the Asian American readership for matrilineal discourse is simply not large enough to support the kind of sales that Tan's fiction has enjoyed. Today's book-buying readers of literature are predominantly white and female (Zill and Winglee).[15] The question thus remains: what do these readers—some with conscious feminist leanings, some without—find so engrossing in Tan's stories of the mother-daughter bond?

"Sugar Sisterhood": The Persistent Allure of Orientalism
This brings me to the odd-sounding title of this essay, "Sugar Sisterhood," derived from the phrase "sugar sister" used by Winnie in *The Kitchen God's*

Wife. Winnie is explaining to Pearl, her English-speaking daughter, her closeness to cousin Peanut. Peanut has found a face-saving way to reveal that she has given up Wen Fu, a charming, wealthy, but as it turns out abusive, young man, for Winnie to marry; the emotionally orphaned Winnie is grateful for Peanut's generosity:

> And that's how we came to be as close as sisters once again for the rest of the time I had left with my family. In fact, from that day forward, until I was married, we called each other *tang jie,* "sugar sister," the friendly way to refer to a girl cousin. (154)

Tang jie, again presented with the "sugar sister" translation for Pearl's benefit, is repeated in a later scene, when Winnie and Peanut are temporarily reunited (350). The phrase "sugar sister" is an egregious mistranslation based on Amy Tan's confusing two Chinese homophones, while the accompanying explanation of how the two young women come to address each other by that term betrays a profound ignorance of the Chinese kinship system. What is most remarkable about this passage is its very existence: that Amy Tan has seen fit to include and elaborate on such a "gratuitous" detail—gratuitous in the sense of not functioning to advance the plot or deepen the characterization, of which more later—on something of which she has little knowledge. Furthermore, this putative clarification issues from the mouth of Winnie, a native Chinese-speaker born and raised in China for whom it should be impossible to make such mistakes.

I use the term "sugar sisterhood," then, to designate the kind of readership Amy Tan has acquired, especially among white women, through acts of cultural interpreting and cultural empathy that appear to possess the authority of authenticity but are often products of the American-born writer's own heavily mediated understanding of things Chinese. By examining the "sugar sister" solecism and related uses of Chinese or Chinese-seeming details, by analyzing the stylistic features and narratological design in both of Tan's works, and by uncovering the culturalist reading practices that such novelistic elements encourage, I argue that the "Amy Tan phenomenon" must ultimately be situated in quasi-ethnographic, Orientalist discourse. Occasional anti-Orientalist statements made by the characters, and the opportunities for anticulturalist interpretation provided by Tan's keen observations of Chinese American life, do not negate my assessment. In fact, they are functional in that they enable Orientalism to emerge in a form palatable to middle-class American readers of the 1980s. Specifically, for the feminist audience, the Chinese American mother/daughter dyad in *The Joy Luck Club* and *The Kitchen God's Wife* allegorizes a Third World/ First World encounter that allows mainstream American feminism to construct itself in a flattering, because depoliticized, manner—an outcome unlikely to be delivered by mother-daughter stories penned by writers from Euro-American traditions.

Since the "sugar sister" phrase provides the entering wedge for my thesis, I will dwell a moment longer on its significance. Besides the confusion of two different characters for *tang*, there are several other implausibilities in this passage. The term *tang jie* does exist and can be used in the relationship between Winnie and Peanut. (Peanut is the daughter of the younger brother of Winnie's father.) But *tang jie* is a descriptive label and a term of address defined stringently by one's position in a patrilineal system of blood ties; it is not, as Tan suggests, a friendly term of endearment, to be assumed at will when two girl cousins feel close to each other. Moreover, in the thoroughly hierarchical, age-conscious Chinese kinship system, *jie*, or "older sister," is always complemented by *mei*, or "younger sister": two women cannot simultaneously be the *jie*—not even in "courtesy" situations where blood ties are not involved, such as *xuejie/xuemei* (fellow students) or *qijie/qimei* ("sworn sisters") relationships.

In citing the "sugar sister" passage, I am not practicing an idle and mean-spirited "Gotcha!" school of criticism. Something larger is at issue: what is sought is a more precise determination of Tan's stance toward her audience(s) and the types of discourses her works participate in, leading to a clearer understanding of her popularity. To readers who protest that Tan is just writing fiction, I concede that a phrase like "sugar sister" does little to detract from her overall achievements as a writer—from the page-turning narrative drive of her novels, or the general contours of Winnie's vivid character. Given this, the question arises, then, of what function is served by this kind of detail—a romanized Chinese phrase with an appositive explanation, tossed off as an aside by a Chinese-speaking character to her English-dominant daughter—or other similar details of language and custom, minimally warranted by the immediate narrative context but providing occasions for elucidating an exotic Chinese culture.

A list can easily be compiled of such highly dubious or downright erroneous details: Lindo Jong's first husband in Taiyuan is described as yanking off her red veil at the wedding ceremony (59)—a suspiciously Western practice, since traditionally the bride's red veil is removed only in the privacy of the wedding chamber, before the consummation of the marriage;[16] in Ying-Ying St. Clair's childhood reminiscences, the customs that are allegedly part of Moon Festival celebrations—burning the Five Evils (68) and eating *zong zi* (73)—actually belong to the *Duanwu* or "Dragon-Boat" Festival on the fifth day of the fifth lunar month; the operatic version of the Moon Lady-Hou Yi story witnessed by Ying-Ying includes a detail from another legend about another festival—the annual meeting of two star-crossed lovers on the seventh night of the seventh month (80); the mother-in-law's rebuke to the young bride Lindo, "*Shemma bende ren!*" rendered in English as "What kind of fool are you!" (55), sounds like a concoction by some first-year Chinese student and necessitates a quiet emendation by the Chinese translator of *The Joy Luck Club* (Tan, *Xifuhui*, 46); the warning Rose Hsu Jordan remembers from her mother, shortly before her younger brother's drowning, likewise sounds gratingly unidiomatic in Chinese—"*Dangsying tamende shenti*," translated by Tan as "Watch out for their bodies" (123); except for the first one, the characters used for the Chinese version of McDonald's name, *mai dong lou*, are not what Lindo Jong says they are, "wheat," "east," and "building" (259); in *The Kitchen God's Wife*, the Chinese pilots allegedly give General Chennault a good Chinese name, *shan*, "lightning," and *nao*, "noisy," but his name actually has a well-known standard Chinese translation, *Chen Naide*. The list goes on.

The function of such insertions of "Chinese" cultural presence is worth investigating not only because a history of controversy exists in Asian American cultural politics concerning issues of authenticity, but also because Tan's books have been showered with praise precisely for their *details*.

Detail and Myth

The Joy Luck Club is repeatedly applauded by reviewers for the specificity of its descriptions—entire "richly textured worlds" (Shapiro, 64) evoked by details "each . . . more haunting and unforgettable than the one before" (Bernikow). The book is called "dazzling because of the *worlds* it gives us"; the word "tapestry" is used to describe this effect of intricacy and richness (Sit). This view of Tan's distinctive gift is carried over to reviews of *The Kitchen God's Wife:* "The power of literature over sociology lies in particularization, and it is in details that *The Kitchen God's Wife* excels"; "it is through vivid minutiae that Tan more often exercises her particular charm" (Yglesias, 1, 3); "what fascinates in *The Kitchen God's Wife* is not only the insistent storytelling, but the details of Chinese life and tradition" (Romano); *The Kitchen God's Wife*'s "convincing detail" is said to give her fiction "the ring of truth" (Humphreys, 1), and Dew urges her readers to give themselves over to Tan's "Tolstoyan tide of event and detail."

This emphasis on details as a main source of Tan's appeal is intriguing because it coexists with a seemingly opposite type of commendation: that details do *not* matter that much in *The Joy Luck Club*, and to a lesser extent *The Kitchen God's Wife*, since they are lyrical, mythical, dreamlike: "full of magic" (See), "rich in magic and mystery" (Fong). Of Tan's second book, Perrick writes, "There is something dizzyingly elemental about Tan's storytelling; it melds the rich simplicities of fairytales with a delicate lyrical style." Fairy tales, we may note, are "generic" stories stripped of historical particulars, and lyricism is generally associated with moments of inwardness set apart from the realm of quotidian social facts.

The Joy Luck Club draws comparisons with myth even more readily. One reviewer calls it "almost mythic in structure, like the hypnotic tales of the legendary Scheherazade" (Bernikow). In the eyes of some readers, the lack of differentiation between the rapidly alternating narrative voices in *Joy Luck*, far from betraying a limited artistic repertoire, is in fact an asset: the mark of universal appeal to women (Sit) or a more capacious sensibility (E. Kim, "'Such Opposite Creatures,'" 82). Orville Schell, who wrote a widely quoted glowing review of *The Joy Luck Club*, acknowledges that the book's segmented structure, with its abrupt transitions in time and space, may be confusing, but argues that "these *recherches* to old China are so beautifully written that one should just allow oneself to be borne along as if in a dream." Juxtaposed with the daughters' "upwardly mobile, design-conscious, divorce-prone and Americanized world," the mothers' vanished world in China seems "more fantastic and dreamlike than real," a product of "memory" and "revery" (28)— and herein, Schell seems to suggest, lies its peculiar charm.

Is there any necessary incompatibility between these two views of Tan's fiction, one lauding her mastery of details, the other deeming them relatively inconsequential in its overall effect? Not at all, if one takes into account another recurrent theme in reviews of the two novels: their value as anthropological documents, giving the non-Chinese reader access to an enigmatic culture.[17] A review of *The Kitchen God's Wife* finds it a convenient lesson in Chinese history and sociology:

> As a backdrop . . . we learn more about the nature of arranged marriages in Chinese societies and also about the kind of inter-wifely accommodation arranged by second or third wives and their offspring. It is like being invited into a dusty room full of castoffs, and being given a chance to reapprehend them in their former richness. We get to understand how, why, and from where Chinese-American society evolved. . . . Tan is handing us a key with no price tag and letting us open the brass-bolted door. (Gillespie, 34)

In view of the inaccurate cultural details we have seen, this coupling of Tan's fiction with anthropological discourse, which carries with it implicit claims of credibility and factual verifiability, may be ironic. But the issue is not so much how Tan has failed as a cultural guide; it is, rather, the text- and reception-oriented question of how and why the American reading public has responded so eagerly to her writings as faithful chronicles of things Chinese. Tan's fiction has apparently been able to hold in colloidal suspension two essential ingredients of quasi-ethnographic Orientalist discourse on China and the Chinese, which both have a long genealogy in this country (E. Kim, *Asian American Literature*, 23–32). These ingredients are "temporal distancing" and "authenticity marking." Tan's ability to somehow keep both details and "nondetails," as it were, in busy circulation allows readers with culturalist propensities—that is to say, a large proportion of the American reading public—to recognize the genre and respond accordingly, with enthusiastic purchases as well as a pleasurable mixture of respect and voyeurism, admiration and condescension, humility and self-congratulation.

Temporal Distancing and Other "Othering" Maneuvers

Johannes Fabian, in his *Time and the Other: How Anthropology Makes Its Object*, suggests that "temporal distancing" is a means of constructing the Other widely employed in ethnographic discourse. He proposes the term "Typological Time" to refer to a use of time "almost totally divested of its vectorial, physical connotations": "instead of being a measure of movement, it may appear as a quality of states" presumably "unequally distributed among human populations of this world." The concept of Typological Time produces familiar distinctions attributed to human societies such as preliterate versus literate, traditional versus modern, peasant versus industrial (23), the term with which the anthropologist identifies himself/herself invariably being the privileged one. The contrast between some such binary states—traditional versus modern, superstitious versus secular, elemental versus materialistic, communal enmeshment versus anomie—is, we may note, precisely what *The Joy Luck Club* and *The Kitchen God's Wife* are engaged in exploring.

Whereas the ethnographer relies on the temporalized protocols of the "field method" to achieve Othering—field notes in the past tense, subsequent generalizations about the culture in the "ethnographic present" tense—Tan's two novels effect it through a number of narratological and stylistic means. (Whether Tan consciously employed them is another matter: *means* here refers not to goal-oriented artistic choices but an after-the-fact reconstruction of how the reader is affected.) Chief among these is the way the stories about old China are "framed" by reference to the present time of America. In *The Joy Luck Club*, except for the short chapter entitled "Scars," all the mothers' narratives open with some kind of time signature in the United States of the 1980s, in the form of a silent addressing of the daughter as "you" or some mention of "my daughter" in her present predicament. In *The Kitchen God's Wife*, of course, Winnie's entire tale is framed by the "now" of Pearl's dealings with her mother in connection with cousin Bao Bao's wedding and Grand Aunt Du's funeral; periodically, too, within what amounts to a lengthy monologue, Winnie supplies answers to queries (unrecorded), rhetorical questions, proleptic allusions, and philosophical musings for the benefit of her daughter.

The temporal distancing that makes possible the Othering of the Chinese mothers does not consist in locating their stories in elapsed time—after all, the daughters too tell about their childhood. Instead, it works through a subtle but insistent positioning of everything in the mothers' lives to a watershed event: arrival in the United States. Like using the arrival of the white man to demarcate two modes of being, the later one redeeming the earlier from cyclical repetition as a matter of inevitable "progress," this practice bears the unmistakable traces of a hegemonic cultural vantage point vis-à-vis a "backward" Third World. The Typological Time in both novels revolves around an unstated aporetic split between the static, ritual-permeated, mythical Time of a China past, where individuals' lives are deprived of choice, shaped by tradition and buffeted by inexorable "natural" circumstances (in terms of which even wars are described), and the unfolding, enlightened, rational, secular Time of contemporary America, where one can exercise decision making and control over one's life and where learning from the past is possible (Dew). The mothers, who are portrayed as fixated on old hurts and secrets and obsessed with cultural transmission in the form of aphorisms, and whose transformation in America from young refugees to stolid matrons is never delineated, belong to the mythical time so beloved of many a non-Chinese reader.

The Othering accomplished by temporal distancing is augmented by the stylistic uniformity of the Joy Luck mothers' voices when recounting their lives in China, which has the effect of constructing the Third World women's experiences as interchangeable and predictably constrained, because so overwhelmingly determined by culture (Ong, 85). As Renato Rosaldo observes, "social analysts commonly speak . . . as if 'we' have psychology and 'they' have culture" (202). The *content* of one set of stories is no doubt distinguishable from the next, but the *manner* of presentation is not. In *The Kitchen God's Wife*, despite Tan's claim of a new departure (Gillespie, 33), her stylistic range can hardly be said to be noticeably extended, and Winnie's voice inevitably recalls Lindo Jong's or An-mei Hsu's.

Both *The Joy Luck Club* and *The Kitchen God's Wife* contrast a "low-resolution" picture of the mothers' lives in China with descriptions of high material specificity or informational density in the daughters' sections. The American-born and -bred daughters—whose world Tan shares—are able to *name* things in their world to a high degree of topical and local precision: a scroll-length calendar from the Bank of Canton hangs on Auntie Hsu's wall; candy is not just candy but See's Nuts and Chews or M&M's (35); Shoshana's outing is to not just any science museum but to the Exploratorium; the trendy restaurants Rose dreams of asking Ted to go to are Cafe Majestic and Rosalie's. In contrast, the items in the mothers' stories are much more "generic": the fish in the Fen River are not identified; the variety of lanterns at the Moon Festival is not differentiated; the bicycle on which An-mei Hsu's little brother rides has no brand name.

This lack of elaboration cannot be explained away as merely a realistic mirroring of the mothers' memory lapses. In the minds of many older people, recollections of remote childhood events often surpass, in clarity and specific-ity, those of more proximate occurrences. And young children are not nearly as oblivious to culturally meaningful distinctions as retrospective idealization makes them out to be. Finally, while the consumer orientation of present-day American society may partly account for the profusion of named objects in the daughters' narratives, it would be ignorant and condescending to attribute a preindustrial simplicity to the mothers' China. Whether uneven distribu-tion of authorial knowledge about the two worlds is a factor in the textural fluctuation in the novels, or whether Tan is consciously manipulating the degree of resolution, remains an open, perhaps unanswerable, question. How-ever, from the point of view of reception analysis, the leveling of descriptive details in the "Chinese" segments is an important source of pleasure for white readers, who accept and appreciate it as a "mythic" treatment of a remote but fascinating China.

Markers of Authenticity: "The Oriental Effect"

Are the reviewers simply misguided then when they laud Tan's "convinc-ing details"? Not at all. The details are there, but their nature and function are probably not what a "commonsense" view would make them out to be: evidence of referential accuracy, of the author's familiarity with the "real" China. Rather, they act as gestures to the "mainstream" readers that the author is familiar with the kind of culturally mediated discourse they have enjoyed, as well as qualified to give them what they expect. I call these details "markers of authenticity," whose function is to create an "Orien-tal effect" by signaling a reassuring affinity between the given work and American preconceptions of what the Orient is/should be.

The term "Oriental effect" borrows from "the reality effect" posited by Roland Barthes.[18] In an essay of that name, Barthes investigates the function of apparently "useless" descriptive details in realist fiction—details that are "scandalous (from the point of view of structure)" or "allied with a kind of nar-rative *luxury*" (11), lacking "predictive" power for plot advancement (12), and salvageable only as a cumulative indicator of "characterization or atmosphere" (11). Citing epideictic discourse in classical rhetoric, in which "plausibility [is] not referential, but overtly discursive"—"it [is] the rules of the discourse genre which laid down the law" (13)—Barthes goes on to argue that in the modern aesthetic of *vraisemblance,* the function of apparently superfluous details is to announce "*we are the real*" and produce a "reality effect." "It is the category of the 'real,' and not its various contents, which is being signi-fied" (16).[19] Extending Barthes's analysis, I argue that, in both *The Joy Luck Club* and *The Kitchen God's Wife,* there are many details whose existence can-not be justified on structural or informational grounds, but whose function seems to be to announce "We are Oriental" to the "mainstream" reader. These are the details for which reviewers have praised Tan. Marking the discourse as "authentic," but in a discursive rather than referential dimension, they are in a sense immune to revelations that "real" Chinese cultural practices are otherwise.

An important class of such details is made up of romanized words of limited, at times nonexistent, utility in structural or informational terms. Their usage ranges from "redundant" romanization (such as the appearance of *pai* in the same sentence where the standard English name for mahjong pieces, *tiles,* also appears (24); or adding "bad *pichi*" to "bad temper" (50), when the latter is a perfectly serviceable equivalent of the Chinese term); to correct renditions of Chinese based on a sophisticated knowledge of the language and culture (such as the clever pun on Suyuan's name); to plausible and justifiable uses of Chinese for concepts without full English equivalents (such as *shou* for filial piety), or for representing the Americanized daughters' cultural gropings (as when Rose remembers the term *huli-hudu* during her postdivorce disorientation). Errors of the "sugar sister" type, like the ones listed earlier in this essay, actually constitute only a small percentage of Tan's handling of Chinese matters. But whether "gratuitously" deployed or not, whether informed or not, the very insertion of italicized words in a page of roman type, or of explanatory asides about what the Chinese do and think in a story, is a signal that the author has adopted a certain stance toward the audience. She is in effect inviting trust in her as a knowledgeable cultural insider and a competent guide familiar with the rules of the genre in question: quasi ethnography about the Orient.

We can extend the concept of authenticity marking to a peculiar variety of prose Amy Tan has developed, which has the effect of announcing "Chineseness" in the speakers. The preponderance of short, choppy sentences and the frequent omission of sentence subjects are oft-used conventions whereby the Chinese can be recognized as Other. In addition to these, Tan employs subtle, minute dislocations of English syntax and vocabulary—jolting the language out of whack just enough—to create an impression of translation from the Chinese even where no translation has taken place. For example, in Ying-Ying's recollections of her childhood trauma at the Moon Festival, an old woman's complaint about her swollen foot takes this form: "Both inside and outside have a sour painful feeling" (71). This is neither an idiomatic English sentence nor a direct English equivalent of an idiomatic Chinese sentence; it cannot be attributed to Ying-Ying's poor command of English, for the mothers' laborious, grammatically mangled, often malapropic English appears only in "real life," that is, when they are in the United States, speaking with their daughters. Elsewhere, when telling their own stories, they are given a different kind of English, fluent if simple, by Tan's own avowal designed to better articulate their subjectivities, do full justice to their native intelligence, and restore them to the dignity they deserve (Tan, "Mother Tongue"). This cause is decidedly not well served by such slight linguistic skewings, which in the American popular imagination have been associated with the "comic" pidginized "Asian English" found in Anglo-American writing on Asians (E. Kim, *Asian American Literature*, 12–14). However, reading exactly like the kind of quaint, circumlocutious literal translations, or purported literal translations, in the tradition of self-Orientalizing texts (e.g., by Lin Yutang and Pardee Lowe), they indicate the comforting presence of cultural mediation to the "mainstream" reader. Thus it is not surprising to find white reviewers like Miner (567) and Schell (28) praising the *authenticity* of the immigrant women's diction. This valorized "Oriental effect" exists independent of Tan's sincerity in wanting to give voice to first-generation Chinese women, which we have no cause to doubt.[20]

If, as Todorov maintains in *The Poetics of Prose*, verisimilitude in literature is less a relation with "reality" than "what most people believe to be reality—in other words, with public opinion," and with "the particular rules of [a] genre" (82), then the reviewers' satisfaction with Tan's details is entirely consistent with their assessment of *The Joy Luck Club* and *The Kitchen God's Wife* as "mythic" or "lyrical." Tan's details may lack referential precision, but what shapes the reviewers' expectations is verisimilitude in Todorov's second and third senses. The reviewers' dual emphases—on a timeless mythic realm and on presumably authentic details—are ultimately Orientalist in spirit. It is it certain image of what China must be like ("public opinion"—here defined, of course, as the opinion of the "mainstream") and familiarity with a certain type of writing about China ("rules of the genre") that have influenced their estimation of Tan's fiction. Paradoxical as it may seem, an author with more direct historical knowledge about China than Amy Tan may well be *less* successful in convincing the American reading public of the "truthfulness" of her picture, since, in such a case, the element of cultural mediation would be correspondingly weaker."

Counter-Orientalist Gestures

It is fair to say that gestures of cultural mediation are an important component in Amy Tan's novels and are responsible, in no small part, for their popularity. But it is also fair to say that the variety of Orientalism informing *The Joy Luck Club* and *The Kitchen God's Wife* is far from simple-minded or unproblematized. It is not the knowingly exploitative misrepresentation described by Peanut in *The Kitchen God's Wife:*

> They sell *Chinese* garbage to the foreigners, especially people from America and England. . . . They sell anything that is broken, or strange, or forbidden. . . . The broken things they call Ming Dynasty. The strange things they say are Ching Dynasty. And the forbidden things—they say they are forbidden, no need to hide that. (156; italics in original)

After all, Tan, born in racially heterogeneous Oakland, California, in 1952 (albeit in a predominantly white neighborhood), grew up in the 1960s; however peripherally or obliquely, her works cannot but bear traces of the ethnic consciousness movement of that era. These traces range from relatively inconsequential information about the characters [22] or satirical observations on ethnic chic (and its cousin, prole chic),[23] to the pervasive, if often implicit, presence of the vocabulary and concepts of identity politics in *The Joy Luck Club*—what does it mean to be Chinese? to be an ethnic minority? to be American? The white middle-class book-reading and book-buying public of the post-civil rights era, likewise touched, has learned to enjoy its exotica flavored by the rhetoric of pluralism and an awareness of domestic and global interethnic connectedness. An unself-consciously ingratiating invitation to the cultural sightseer, such as the tourist brochure-style, zoom-in description of San Francisco Chinatown in the opening paragraph of Jade Snow Wong's *Fifth Chinese Daughter* (1), has a decidedly old-fashioned ring to it and no longer carries the persuasiveness it once possessed.[24] Indeed, this type of writing is no longer produced by any Asian American writers of note. A credible cultural middleman for the contemporary "mainstream" reader needs to demonstrate, in addition to access to an authentic originary culture (or the appearance thereof), some sophistication regarding the limitations of monologism.

On this score Amy Tan fits the bill well. Again, whether by design or not, she manages to balance on a knife edge of ambiguity, producing texts in which Orientalist and counter-Orientalist interpretive possibilities jostle each other, sometimes within the same speech or scene. The complex, unstable interplay of these possibilities makes for a larger readership than that enjoyed by a text with a consistently articulated, readily identifiable ideological perspective. The nonintellectual consumer of Orientalism can find much in *The Joy Luck Club* and *The Kitchen God's Wife* to satisfy her curiosity about China and Chinatown; at the same time, subversions of naive voyeurism can be detected by the reader attuned to questions of cultural production.

Contending Interpretive Possibilities

That Tan's works have a little bit of something for everyone can be illustrated by a few examples from *The Joy Luck Club*. (*The Kitchen God's Wife*, which is fashioned from the same range of elements as its predecessor but contours them differently, will be discussed at greater length in a later section.) Waverly Jong's first chapter, "Rules of the Game," contains a portrayal of the young Chinatown girl as hit-and-run cultural guerrilla: to get back at a Caucasian tourist who poses her with roast ducks, Waverly tries to gross him out with the disinformation that a recommended restaurant serves "guts and duck's feet and octopus gizzards" (91). An anti-Orientalist impulse animates this incident; in Tan's account of daily routines among bakeries, sandlots, and alleyways, one recognizes a desire to demystify the tourist mecca and evoke a sense of Chinatown as home, not spectacle. However, this effect is undermined by what appears to be a retroactive exoticizing reading of an everyday detail: Waverly, now seeming to have adopted the tourist's mentality, recalls that her meals used to begin "with a soup full of mysterious things I didn't want to know the names of" (89). Furthermore, the chapter opens with language highly reminiscent of fortune cookie wisdom, Charlie Chan aphorisms, and the kind of Taoist precepts scattered throughout Lin Yutang's *Chinatown Family* (1948):[25]

> I was six when my mother taught me the art of invisible strength.
> . . . [S]he said, "Wise guy, he not go against wind. In Chinese we
> say, Come back from South, blow with wind—poom!—North will
> follow. Strongest wind cannot be seen.". . . My mother imparted
> her daily truths so she could help my older brothers and me rise
> above our circumstances. (89)

At times, the characters in *The Joy Luck Club* articulate a historicized understanding of their situation and an awareness of the perils of essentializing ethnicity. For example, as her marriage deteriorates, Lena St. Clair begins to appreciate the advice of her friend Rose, herself a disappointed divorcée:

> "At first I thought it was because I was raised with all this Chinese
> humility," Rose said. "Or that maybe it was because when you're
> Chinese you're supposed to accept everything, flow with the Tao
> and not make waves. But my therapist said, Why do you blame
> your culture, your ethnicity? And I remembered reading an article
> about baby boomers, how we expect the best and when we get it
> we worry that maybe we should have expected more, because it's
> all diminishing returns after a certain age." (156)

Coexisting with such insights into Chinese American exigencies, and indeed outnumbering them, are statements encouraging a culturalist view of Chinese American life. Much is made of the so-called Chinese horoscope with the twelve animal signs: Ying-Ying St. Clair emphasizes the mystical, quasi-genetic cultural transmission from her "tiger lady" self (248) to her "tiger girl" daughter (251), while Waverly Jong attributes her conflicts with her mother to incompatible horoscope signs, horse and rabbit (167).[26]

Given the mutually subverting and qualifying copresence of contradictory tendencies in *The Joy Luck Club*—Orientalist, culturalist, essentialist, and ahistorical on the one hand, and counter-Orientalist, anticulturalist, constructionist, and historicist on the other—the same narrative detail may yield widely divergent readings. Lindo Jong's mother, in response to her daughter's mock-innocent question about "Chinese torture," answers, "Chinese people do many things. . . . Chinese people do business, do medicine, do painting. Not lazy like American people. We do torture. Best torture" (91). How is this statement, delivered "simply" (91), to be read? Is it a straightforward expression of the mother's ethnocultural pride? Or is it an ironic gesture of exasperation at, and resistance against, the daughter's early induction into hegemonic discourse? Has she already seen through the daughter's "wickedness" in transforming a personal irritation and minor filial rebellion into an ideological struggle? (If so, then even the mother's air of matter-of-factness is suspect; Waverly could have been simply insensible of her parodic inflection.)

The reader's quandary parallels Jing-mei Woo's puzzlement in the face of her mother's explanation about Jewish versus Chinese mahjong: "Jewish mah jong, they watch only for their own tile, play only with their eyes. . . . Chinese mah jong, you must play using your head, very tricky" (33). For all intents and purposes, Mrs. Woo could be just describing the difference between novice and expert playing—in which case the scene affords an intriguing glimpse of culturalism in action: the mother mobilizing ethnicity xenophobically to reinforce the exclusivity of her cultural authority. But if, like Jing-mei, one is brought up on reified ethnic categories and has an emotional investment in believing the speaker's cultural knowledge-ability, the purported insider's explication might leave one in a curious state of suspended judgment (which could be mistaken for cultural sensitivity and respect for the mysteries of the Other's life).

The temptation to galvanize this uncertainty into a definite interpretation is strong, and, given the current voguishness of multiculturalist rhetoric, the safest course for the befuddled non-Chinese reader might be to take the fictional "insider" speaker at face value. This spells the ultimate, if circuitously achieved, victory of Orientalist readings at the expense of other approaches. A handful of scholars of Asian American literature have argued emphatically against a one-dimensional view of *The Joy Luck Club* as a tale of intergenerational cultural confrontation and resolution. Melani McAlister, for example, has provided compelling evidence that socioeconomic class is as much a factor as culture in the mother-daughter conflicts in *The Joy Luck Club*—that, in fact, "cultural difference" can function as a less volatile or more admissible surrogate term for class anxieties. When the yuppie daughters are embarrassed by their mother's color-mismatched outfits or "un-American" restaurant manners, McAlister observes, they are consumed by the fear of being déclassé, even though they may, in all sincerity, be experiencing their distancing from the mothers *in terms of cultural conflict*. Like McAlister, Lisa Lowe, as part of a larger theoretical project on the "heterogeneity, hybridity, and multiplicity" of Asian American identity, has warned against reductionist readings of *The Joy Luck Club* that leave out class concerns ("Heterogeneity," 35–37; "Rethinking Essentialisms"). Nevertheless, voices such as McAlister's or Lowe's, already a minority in the academy, are unlikely to reach the "airport newsstand" readership of Tan's works.

Furthermore, McAlister's thesis that culturalist readings of *The Joy Luck Club* are *mis*readings—implying that a class-informed reading is somehow closer to Tan's intentions—may itself be a simplification. It is true that, as McAlister points out, when reviewer Orville Schell poses the American-ized daughters against the Joy Luck mothers wearing "funny Chinese dresses with stiff stand-up collars and blooming branches of embroidered silk sewn over their breasts" (28), he is betraying a binarist mind-set. (The Joy Luck mothers have been wearing slacks, print blouses, and sturdy walking shoes for years. "Tonight, there is no mystery" [ibid.].) Schell's telescoping of historical moments—the late 1940s and the late 1980s—freezes the mothers at their moment of immigration, absolutizes the foreign-American distinction, and reproduces the American myth that intergenerational strife is the inevitable price of assimilation. To that extent, one is justified in speaking of a *mis*read-ing. However, in another sense, Schell is not "wrong," for *The Joy Luck Club*, as we have seen, is filled with features that would amply support the spirit if not the letter of his reading. The ending of the novel itself offers a powerful essentialist proposition: despite much wavering throughout the crisscrossing narratives, "family" and "blood" (288) eventually triumph over history. When Jing-mei travels to China to meet her long-lost half sisters, she discovers "what part of [her] is Chinese" and is able to "let [it] go" (288). This ostensible reconciliation presupposes the reality of a self-alienating ethnic malaise (without considering how it could be an ideological construction in the service of monoculturalism), then locates redemption in origin, thus in effect nullifying or at least discounting the "American" temporality of the Chinese American experience.

Joy Luck Club is not a misunderstood, co-opted ethnic text that has been unfortunately obscured by a culturalist haze and awaits recuperation through class- or gender-based readings. To suggest so risks explaining away the persistence of Orientalism as a matter of the individual reader's ignorance, inattention, or misguidedness. It is more defensible to characterize *The Joy Luck Club* as a multidimensional cultural product, one whose many ideological layerings, reflections, and refractions are aligned, for a broad cross section of the American reading public, with the contending needs and projections of the times. The book's popular success—and the "Amy Tan phenomenon" in general—cannot be fully understood apart from its *equivocation* vis-à-vis issues of culture and identity, allowing a profusion of interpretive claims to be made with seemingly equal cogency.

The "Declarative Modality" and Its Implications

Many of the issues raised in the foregoing discussion of how to "read" Amy
Tan recall the controversy surrounding Maxine Hong Kingston's *Woman
Warrior*. Some Chinese American critics have accused Kingston of distort-
ing traditional myths and cultural practices to capitalize on the Orientalist inclinations of the white reader (Sau-ling C. Wong, "Autobiography as
Guided Chinatown Tour?"). Indeed, *The Woman Warrior*, like its successor
The Joy Luck Club, has excited many reviewers who single out its picturesque
details about old China for praise. The tacit assumption, as Kingston notes
in an exasperated complaint about many of her so-called admirers ("Cultural
Mis-readings"), is that the author's Chinese blood is a natural and sufficient
guarantor of reliable knowledge; thus the questions Kingston raises in the
book about the very cultural ignorance and confusion of the American-born
Chinese are casually brushed aside. The question of Kingston's possible
complicity in her own misreading is too vast to examine here; her relationship to Orientalism cannot be summed up in few sentences. And in a way,
any ethnic writer who takes on the issue of stereotyping is caught in a bind:
like the man in the Zen parable who holds on to a tree branch with his teeth
and is asked the way by a straying passer-by, he is lost whatever he does. If
he opens his mouth to give the "right" answer, he falls and gets hurt; but if
he keeps silent he only deepens the surrounding confusion. How does one
protest a problem without mentioning it? But in mentioning it, does one
not risk multiplying its visibility and potency, through reiteration if nothing
else? Generalization aside, confining ourselves to *The Woman Warrior* and
The Joy Luck Club, we may note a crucial difference between the two works:
in modality of presentation.

According to Elliott Butler-Evans, *The Woman Warrior* is distinguished
by an "interrogative modality"—it ceaselessly deconstructs its own narrative authority and overtly thematizes the epistemological difficulties of the
American-born Chinese. Its governing rhetorical trope is the palinode, or
the taking back of what is said (Sau-ling C. Wong, "Ethnic Dimensions").
In other words, despite the first-person form, the narrator/protagonist lays
no claim to referential advantage: the negotiations of her consciousness are
foregrounded. In Naomi Schor's terms, she is an *interpretant* (interpreting
character; as opposed to the interpreter, or interpreting critic/reader of the
book) (122), constantly aware of the hazards of under- or overreading, yet
unable to refrain from trying to wrest cultural meanings from bewildering
details. Through the interpretant, the author Kingston "is trying to tell the
interpreter something *about* interpretation" (Schor, 122). In contrast, *The Joy
Luck Club* is epistemologically unproblematized—in Butler-Evans's view, its
narrative modality is "declarative." The mothers' narratives about their Chinese life are displayed as im-mediate, coming directly from the source, and,

for that reason, are valorized as correctives to the daughters' unenlightened or biased outlook. The intervention of a narrating consciousness is thus erased. This is what creates the space for equivocation about culture and identity: one is never entirely sure when a reinsertion of this mediation is necessary, and whether attribution of a Chinese American cast to such mediation is justified. Whereas the conflation of Chinese and Chinese American is explored in *The Woman Warrior* as a perilous legacy of Orientalism—the need to sort out the conflation defines the narrator/protagonist's lifelong act of self-creation—it is never actively interrogated in *The Joy Luck Club*.

The "declarative modality" of *The Joy Luck Club* is arguably appropriate for the project of giving voice to the immigrant mothers. Of course, this project is not the only one inferable from Tan's first novel. The "four-by-four" structure of the work—four sections each with four chapters, so that, except for the deceased Mrs. Woo (whose story is told through Jing-mei), each mother-daughter set gets to speak twice—allows the alternating accounts to resonate with, balance out, and qualify each other. The daughters' worlds, if depicted as flawed by greed and small-mindedness, are at least fleshed out enough to be counterpoised against the mothers'. Despite the compromised nature of the voice Tan assigns to the mothers, with its many Orientalist stylistic maneuvers, the narrative design does not draw overwhelming attention to the issue of the voice's truthfulness.

The Valorization of Origin

Yet a question remains, one whose ramifications do not become fully evident until *The Kitchen God's Wife*. Unlike *The Woman Warrior*, whose narrator/protagonist has to outgrow the illusion that talking to mother will resolve cultural disorientation and crystallize truth, *The Joy Luck Club*, while posing subjectivities "declaratively" against each other, does not push the relativistic implications of this move to their limit. The ending of *The Joy Luck Club*, as well as the tentative dramas of mother-daughter reconciliation within the body chapters, suggest there is indeed a locus of truth, and that locus is origin. The daughter's task is to break through the obfuscation caused by her American nativity and upbringing. Certainly there is poignancy in the picture of the mother whose voice is not heard by her daughter:

> Because I remained quiet for so long now my daughter does not hear me. She sits by her fancy swimming pool and hears only her Sony Walkman, her cordless phone, her big, important husband asking her why they have charcoal and no lighter fluid. (67)

But there is also an asymmetry in the poignancy of this isolation *à deux:* the burden is on the daughter to educate herself into truth, to put aside her fears and needs, so that she can see her mother for what she is (183–184). The China trip—planned by Waverly, actually undertaken by Jing-mei—is in some ways an extended trope for this embrace of origin. Origin stays put, long-suffering but autotelic, awaiting rediscovery and homage.

But if there is a privileging of origin—which, in the context of Tan's books, means privileging China and the Chinese (whether "native" or dia-sporic)—does it not run counter to the colonialist tenor of Orientalism?

This question becomes even more pertinent when we examine *The Kitchen God's Wife*, in which both the "declarative modality" of narration and the valorization of the mother's life in China are far more pronounced than in *The Joy Luck Club*. The broad shape of characters and story types from the first novel is preserved—the assimilated, upwardly mobile daughter married to a white husband and living in the suburbs; the immigrant mother in China-town with a thing or two to teach her daughter about life; sufferings in China recounted; secrets revealed, old grievances banished, blood ties reaffirmed. But much more explicitly than in *The Joy Luck Club*, the daughter's role is ancillary. The staggered framework has given way to a sandwiching of the mother's tale, which forms the bulk of the novel, between two thin slices of the daughter's life. The daughter's presence, its countervailing function almost reduced to irrelevance, is now little more than a conduit for the True Word from mother, a pretext for Winnie's outpouring.

What is accomplished by this accordion-like redistribution of narrative and thematic priorities? Judging from the way they concentrate on Win-nie, most reviewers of *The Kitchen God's Wife* would probably answer "Not much." Humphreys considers Pearl's opening segment merely a "long pro-logue" making for a "late start" of the "central story," which gathers "energy and momentum" only when Winnie begins speaking (1). Dew bemoans the novel's "slow start" (9), and Howe feels that whenever Pearl and her husband appear the novel "bogs down" (15). To these critics, Pearl's presence might be the result of an artistic miscalculation, a nuisance one has to get past to reach the good stuff, or else a residue from the successful formula of *The Joy Luck Club*. Yet in the context of repackaging Orientalism—considered again as de facto impact on the reader—this apparently awkward or primitive narrative convention in fact serves useful functions for *The Joy Luck Club* and especially for *The Kitchen God's Wife*.

The Americanized Daughter's Functions

The Americanized daughter, who needs to be enlightened on things Chinese, serves as a convenient, unobtrusive stand-in for the mainstream reading public. White readers, their voyeurism concealed and their curi-osity indulged by "naturalized" explanations, are thus relieved of possible historical guilt, free to enjoy Chinese life as a depoliticized spectacle. In such a spectacle, the interesting localness of nomenclature and custom over-shadows larger historical issues. The "sugar sister" statement, besides being a "marker of authenticity" establishing the author's credentials, is thus also a cultural demonstration addressed simultaneously to the Americanized daughter and the mainstream American reader, overtly in one case, covertly in the other. Working in much the same way are Winnie's asides about linguistic trivia, such as her remarks on the formulaic expression *yi wan* (ten thousand) ("That is what Chinese people always say . . . always an exaggeration" [89]), or the distinction between *syin ke* (literally, "heart liver"), a Chinese term of endearment, and English *gizzard* (93). The phrase *taonan* elicits the following from Winnie:

> This word, *taonan*? Oh, there is no American word I can think of that means the same thing. But in Chinese, we have lots of words to describe all kinds of trouble. (207)

The English language can hardly be guilty of lacking words for "all kinds of trouble"—a quick flip through Roget's Thesaurus would show that readily. What Winnie gives Pearl is not empirically grounded contrast but the kind of cultural tidbits Orientalist readers enjoy—decontextualized, overgeneralized, speculative, and confirmative of essential difference.

In the larger scheme of China on display, the propositional content of any specific comparison is relatively immaterial. At times the United States seems to come out ahead, portrayed as institutionally more advanced, such as when Lindo Jong of *The Joy Luck Club* speaks of flood damage: "You couldn't go to an insurance company back then and say, Somebody did this damage, pay me a million dollars" (53). At other times commonality seems to be stressed, such as when Lindo compares herself to an American wife on a TV detergent commercial in terms of eagerness to please the husband (56). What matters more is that, by setting up the Americanized daughter as the one to whom Chinese life has to be explained, while at the same time endowing the mother with ancestral wisdom born of the sheer vastness of her life experiences, the edge is taken off the suffering of the Chinese people (in particular, Chinese women). The enormity of Chinese suffering is now made safe for literary consumption. As Rey Chow remarks of what she calls the "King Kong syndrome," the "Third World," as the "site of the 'raw' material that is 'monstrosity,' is produced for the surplus-value of spectacle, entertainment, and spiritual enrichment for the 'First World'" (84).[27]

This is the process that enables *Newsweek* reviewer Pico Iyer to apply an adjective like *glamorous* to Winnie in *The Kitchen God's Wife*: "the dowdy, pinchpenny old woman has a past more glamorous than any fairy-tale, and more sad." The American-born daughters and the readers they stand in for, from the secure distance of their material privilege, can glamorize suffering as ennobling. They can have their cake and eat it too, constructing the Chinese woman—as a type of Third World woman—in such a way that their own fundamental superiority vis-à-vis the foreigner, the immigrant, is not threatened. The Third World woman is simultaneously simpleminded and crafty, transparent and unfathomable, capable of surviving unspeakable victimization but vulnerable in the modern world. She may be strong and resourceful in privation—a suitable inspiration for those grown soft from the good life—but ultimately she still needs the validation and protection of the West (in the form of immigration, a white husband, or, in the case of Winnie, Jimmy Louie—an American-born Chinese who speaks perfect English, dances, wears an American uniform, and has God on his side).[28] Superficially, to concede that women such as Winnie, Lindo Jong, even Ying-Ying St. Clair could hold the key to truth and be teachers to the Westernized or Western woman may seem a sign of humility before the Third World. But such a concession does not really threaten the Western(ized) woman's image of herself as "secular, liberated, and having control of their own lives" (Mohanty, 81). Rather, the mothers' repeated message to the daughters is that the latter have frittered away their chance to enjoy what women in the West take for granted—freedom, choice, material plenty. The harrowing accounts of arranged marriages, sadistic mothers-in-law, sexual humiliation, floods and famines, bombings and dead babies, government corruption, technological backwardness, and other assorted bane for the Third World woman are meant to bolster, not undermine, the incontrovertible desirability attributed to the Western(ized) woman's station. (The exaltation of origin is not incompatible with this message, for it removes the Chinese American's proper arena of struggle from material and political concerns in the United States, relocating in privatized psychology and dehistoricized geography.) In fact, to those readers with feminist sympathies, the books' emphasis on sexist oppression as the basis for cross-cultural, cross-generational female bonding invites a facile sense of solidarity (e.g., Miner). A reassuring projection of universal Woman obscures the role of the West in causing the very historical catastrophes from which Tan's mothers so gladly escape.

In setting tales of personal tribulation against a Chinese historical backdrop, the mothers' chapters in *The Joy Luck Club* and Winnie's recitation in *The Kitchen God's Wife* overlap the discursive space occupied by a proliferating number of English-language works in which the upheavals of "recent"—meaning post-Western contact (Fabian's Typological Time is again at work here)—Chinese history are used as a foil for personal dramas, often those of women from prominent, Westernized families, or women marrying prominent white Americans. Constituting a subgenre that might be called "the Chinese *Gone with the Wind*,"[29] these works are billed sometimes as memoirs (of varying degrees of fictionalization), sometimes as historical fiction. Virtually all involve a multigenerational family saga interwoven with violent historical events (the "Boxer Rebellion," the Republican Revolution, the Nationalist-Communist Civil War, the Cultural Revolution, the Tiananmen Square massacre), as well as a culminating personal odyssey across the ocean to the West, signaling final "arrival" in both a physical and an ideological sense.[30] From these works of epic sweep about China in turmoil, American readers can derive the concomitant satisfaction of self-congratulation and limited self-flagellation: "Thank heavens we natives of the democratic First World don't have to go through that kind of suffering; but then again, we miss out on the opportunity to build character and we lose touch with the really important things in life—Roots, Culture, Tradition, History, War, Human Evil." So the equation is balanced after all.

The "Psychospiritual Plantation System" in the Reagan Era

Thus the daughters' presence in the narratological apparatus of *The Joy Luck Club* and *The Kitchen God's Wife* serves another vital purpose: it tempers the novels' critique of Reagan-era rapacity and hedonism, rendering it temporarily chastening but ultimately undemanding. After listening with appropriate awe, empathy, and "culture envy" to her mother, the daughter returns to yuppiedom (to which Chinese Americans have been allowed qualified access) and continues to enjoy the fruits of assimilation. In the same manner, the "sugar sisterhood" among Tan's readership returns edified from the cathartic literary excursion, but its core of historical innocence remains undisturbed.

A kind of "psychospiritual plantation system"—a stratified world of privileged whites and colored servers/caregivers—is at work in Amy Tan's novels as well as films from roughly the same period such as Bruce Beresford's *Driving Miss Daisy* (1989), Woody Allen's *Alice* (1990), and Jerry Zucker's *Ghost* (1990).[31] All these products of popular culture make indictments against the shallow, acquisitive, image-conscious (read "middle- and upper-middle-class white") world of wealth and institutional power by putting selected members of this world in physical and/or emotional crisis, and by engineering their education/rescue by a person of color. Tan's mothers, the African American chauffeur in *Driving Miss Daisy*, the Chinese herbalist in *Alice*, and the African American medium in *Ghost* all surpass their uptight, disaffected protégés in vitality, vividness of personality, instinctual wisdom, integration of self, cultural richness, interpersonal connection, and directness of contact with elemental presences (love, death, spirituality). At the same time, these Third World healers, like loyal Black slaves of the past, are remarkably devoid of individual ambition and content with a modest piece of the American pie. If, like the frugal Joy Luck mothers or the flamboyant small-time crook in

Ghost, they value money, that interest has an almost childlike forthrightness to it, dissociated front the "rational" pursuit of status that is the forte of their overcerebral, impeccably schooled charges. In short, the world is neatly stratified into those who have wealth and power but no soul, and those who have soul but neither wealth nor power. The latter group nurtures the former but is not interested in displacing or replacing it.

What Renato Rosaldo says of the discipline of anthropology is a good gloss on "psychospiritual plantation" discourse:

> Social analysts . . . often assert that subordinate groups have an authentic culture at the same time that they mock their own upper-middle-class professional culture. In this view, subordinate groups speak in vibrant, fluent ways, but upper-middle-class people talk like anemic academics. Yet analysts rarely allow the ratio of class and culture to include power. Thus they conceal the ratio's darker side: the more power one has, the less culture one enjoys, and the more culture one has, the less power one wields. (202)

Both *The Joy Luck Club* and *The Kitchen God's Wife* tacitly subscribe to a worldview in which the inverse relationship between political power and cultural visibility is deemed natural. Despite its chatty, upbeat tone and inspirational effectiveness, Tan's fiction, too, has a darker side.

Conclusion

Judging from the frequency with which *The Joy Luck Club* has been anthologized and adopted for courses during the brief period since its publication, and the way Amy Tan has been chosen to perform the Asian American spokeswoman/figurehead function once assigned to Maxine Hong Kingston, Tan currently occupies a place of substantial honor in the "mainstream" literary canon. The movement for curricular diversification in the academy has created a demand for fairly accessible ethnic works of a multiculturalist, preferably also feminist, bent, and *The Joy Luck Club*, whatever its other complexities, fits the bill well. Tan's place in the Asian American canon is less clear: there has been some academic interest in *The Joy Luck Club* (less so for *The Kitchen God's Wife*), but hardly comparable in amount and intensity to what *The Woman Warrior* generated. Only time will tell what the staying power of the "Amy Tan phenomenon" is.

The fortunes of once-popular, now overlooked cultural interpreters in Chinese American literary history, such as Lin Yutang and Jade Snow Wong, suggest that cultural mediation of the Orient for the "mainstream" readership requires continual repackaging to remain in sync with changing times and resultant shifts in ideological needs. It will be interesting to see whether

Tan will be superseded by another "flavor of the month" (Streitfield, F8), and if so, when, how, and to what degree. Unlike Lin Yutang's and Jade Snow Wong's, Amy Tan's books appeared *after* the Asian American consciousness movement, at a time when Asian American cultural production is burgeoning, Asian American literary studies has been instituted as a force (albeit still a weak one) in cultural politics, and Asian American critics are busily engaged in defining a canon dissociated as much as possible from Orientalist concerns, through teaching, practical criticism, and other professional activities if not conscious, explicit theorizing. Although there is obviously no end point in the canon-formation process, there are already signs that the "Asian American" canon, the one arising from contestations within the community, differs considerably from the one shaped by the publishing industry and the critical establishment. It would be intriguing to study how these two canons are related and how they act upon each other.

Whatever the future holds, the extent of Amy Tan's sensational success becomes somewhat more comprehensible when we see her works as standing at the confluence of a large number of discursive traditions, each carrying its own history as well as ideological and formal demands: "mainstream" feminist writing; Asian American matrilineal literature; quasi ethnography about the Orient; Chinese American "tour-guiding" works; post-civil rights ethnic soul-searching; the "Chinese *Gone with the Wind*" genre; multiculturalist rhetoric; and Reagan-era critiques of materialism—to name only those touched on in this essay. (The literature of immigration and Americanization is an obvious tradition that has been omitted in this discussion; the literature of New Age self-healing might be another [Palumbo-Liu].) This heteroglossic situation, where discourses press against each other, generating now synergy, now conflict, is what makes possible the intriguing equivocation in *The Joy Luck Club* and *The Kitchen God's Wife* and allows readers of differing persuasions to see what they expect (or desire) in the texts.

Notes

1. Shapiro is among the few dissenting voices, noting that in *The Kitchen God's Wife* "all the excitement is on the surface" (64).
2. The most recent sales estimate for Tan's novels that I could find, said to be based on publishers' figures, gives 253,000 hardcover (note the difference from J. Simpson's figures) and over two million paperback for *The Joy Luck Club* and nearly 392,000 for *The Kitchen God's Wife* (Sun).
3. The film was released, to generally enthusiastic reviews, just as the final revision of this essay was completed in the fall of 1993. Some of the issues raised about the book are addressed in the film version, some not, but a comparison cannot be undertaken here because of space limitations.
4. The extent of the growth in mother-daughter discourse can be gauged by comparing the bibliographies in Broner and Davidson's review essay (1978),

Davidson and Broner's anthology (1980), Hirsch's review essay (1981), and Hirsch's book-length study (1989). This phenomenon can be placed in a larger context of changing motherhood discourse in American popular culture (Kaplan).

5. For example, Brown (1976); Oates (1986); M. Simpson (1987). Most of the works surveyed in Pearlman ("Introduction") fall into this category.

6. For example, Toni Morrison's *Sula* (1987) and *Beloved* (1987), Terry Mcmillan's *Mama* (1987), and others. See Hirsch ("Maternal Narratives") on the matrilineal tradition in African American literature.

7. 1965 was the year immigration legislation was reformed to end decades of exclusion and restriction and allow Chinese to enter on an equal footing with immigrants from other countries.

8. This immediately recalls the pivotal role of literacy acquisition in African American slave narratives. Autobiographies by Chinese American men from the same period, such as Huie Kin's (1932; alphabetized under Huie) or Pardee Lowe's (1943), do not show this feature.

9. Chuang Hua is a pseudonym; alphabetization is under Chuang.

10. This list does not even include works like Ruthanne Lum McCann's *Thousand Pieces of Gold* (1981) and Yoshiko Uchida's *Picture Bride* (1987), which, though not depicting mother-daughter relationships, may be construed as part of matrilineal literature in that they reconstruct the lives of heroic female ancestors who crossed the ocean to come to America. In addition, there is a large body of Asian American poetry dealing with matrilineage, such as Jessica Hagedorn (1975: "Cristina," pages unnumbered), Nellie Wong (1977: 7, 12, 14, 18, 40–41), Janice Mirikitani (1978: "Desert Flowers" and "Lullabye," pages unnumbered), Fay Chiang (1979: 26), Kitty Tsui (1983: 4–8), Cathy Song (1983: 2–6, 43–48).

11. In a *Washington Post* story on the success of *The Joy Luck Club*, David Streitfield notes: "According to one theory, Tan inadvertently tapped into the mentality of the baby boomer female—who also, coincidentally, forms a huge chunk of the book-buying public. Heading toward and through that crucial dividing line of age 40, these women are realizing, as Tan did, that their mothers won't be with them forever" (F9). The context suggests that the reference here is to "mainstream" female readers.

12. "The *Aiiieeeee* group" refers to writers Frank Chin, Jeffery Paul Chan, Lawson Fusao Inada, and Shawn Wong, who edited *Aiiieeeee!* (1974) and later *The Big Aiiieeeee!* (1991). Though not the first anthology of Asian American literature, *Aiiieeeee!* has been the most influential in that its Introduction sets forth a sort of declaration of independence for Asian American writers. Frank Chin, the informal leader of the group, has been the most vocal spokesman for the cultural nationalist and masculinist position articulated in the 1974 anthology. The 1991 sequel contains both a general Introduction, signed by all four editors, and a lengthy prefatory essay, "Come All Ye Asian American Writers of the Real and the Fake," signed by Frank Chin alone, in which the effeminization of Chinese American literature continues to be bemoaned and Maxine Hong Kingston, Amy Tan, and David Henry Hwang are attacked for producing "fake" Chinese American literature.

13. Works by Japanese American women writers are included. No explicit explanation for this discrepancy is provided.

14. Yung (80–83, esp. 80) provides a woman-centered account of Chinese women married to "Gold Mountain men" who were affected by decades of family separation.

15. I am indebted to Catharine R. Stimpson for this reference.

16. Given China's sheer size and regional variations in cultural practices, it is of course impossible to rule this out entirely, especially since the novel is set in a period of increasing Western influence. However, the inland location of the episode and the lack of corroboration in the ethnographic literature (e.g., Shizhen Wang) make the kind of veil lifting and bride kissing described by Tan an extremely unlikely occurrence. In the film version, the red veil is removed in the wedding chamber.

17. One of the first academic papers I heard on *The Joy Luck Club* borrows anthropologist Clifford Geertz's term, "thick description," to refer to Tan's renditions of Chinese places and mores (Butler-Evans).

18. I am indebted to David Palumbo-Liu for referring me to this highly useful theoretical piece, as well as to Schor.

19. This view is disputed by Schor (141–147), but for our purposes Barthes's framework is quite sufficient.

20. Dasenbrock and Ashcroft, Griffiths, and Tiffin (64–66) offer alternative views of how untranslated words function in "minority" writing. I have no quarrel with their theoretical positions but find Tan's case to constitute a significant complication of them.

21. A good example of this phenomenon is Eileen Chang's (Chang Ai-ling's) masterful "Golden Canque," which deals with the kind of milieu depicted in parts of *The Joy Luck Club* and *The Kitchen God's Wife:* the protagonist is a concubine trapped in a decaying Chinese family in a Westernizing city, much like An-mei Hsu's mother. Filled with precise details of dress and decor, highly respected by Chinese readers as a classic of short fiction, and available in English translation, "The Golden Canque" is yet little known to the American reading public.

22. For example, Lena St. Clair majors in Asian American studies, a field that did not exist prior to the 1969 Third World student strikes in San Francisco and Berkeley.

23. See, for example, in *The Joy Luck Club*, Lindo Jong's complaint, "Now she wants to be Chinese, it is so fashionable" (253), and Jing-mei's attitude toward her jade pendant (197); in *The Kitchen God's Wife*, Pearl's changing attitude toward the once detested "art deco" dressing table in her mother's house (17).

24. *Fifth Chinese Daughter* enjoyed immense popularity in the 1940s and 1950s; in 1952 Jade Snow Wong was sent on a State Department-sponsored tour of Asia to speak on behalf of American democracy (E. Kim, *Asian American Literature*, 60).

25. See, for example, the Confucian and Taoist dicta in chap. 7, sec. 3; chap. 12, sec. 1; chap. 18, sec. 2 and sec. 3. Lin Yutang is alphabetized under Lin.

26. It might be noted that the Chinese horoscope, in China proper, was used more for reckoning than for fortune-telling, which more often called for information not only about the year of birth but also the date and hour (*shichen bazi*). The fascination with the twelve animals of the horoscope appears to be the combined effect of American cultural appropriation and Chinese American cultural evolution/accommodation. Although it is plausible for the American-born Waverly to have internalized this fascination, China-born Ying-Ying St. Clair is less likely to be as preoccupied with "tiger attributes" as Tan makes her out to be.

27. Interestingly, Amy Tan links the writing of *The Kitchen God's Wife* to the bloody events in Tiananmen Square; of both the abused Chinese wife (her mother) and the repressed Chinese students, she wanted to know why rising-up did not take place sooner (Fong-Torres, B4).

28. It might be instructive to relate this process to what Chandra Mohanty calls the production of "third-world difference" in Western feminist discourse: "Third-world women as a group or category are automatically and necessarily defined as: religious (read 'not progressive'), family oriented (read 'traditional'), legal minors (read 'they-are-still-not-conscious-of-their-rights'), illiterate (read 'ignorant'), domestic (read 'backward') and sometimes revolutionary (read 'their-country-is-in-a-state-of-war; they-must-fight!')" (80).

29. This is a promotional phrase used on the dust jacket of Linda Ching Sledge's *Empire of Heaven*.

30. In this category can be included Anna Chennault's *Education of Anna* (1980); Bette Bao Lord's *Spring Moon* (1981); Katherine Wei and Terry Quinn's *Second Daughter* (1984); Nien Cheng's *Life and Death in Shanghai* (1986); C. Y. Lee's *China Saga* (1987); Tsai Chin's *Daughter of Shanghai* (1988); Linda Ching Sledge's *Empire of Heaven* (1990); Bette Bao Lord's *Legacies* (1990); Jung Chang's *Wild Swans* (1991); Lillian Lee's translated *The Last Princess of Manchuria: A Novel* (1992); C. Y. Lee's *Gate of Rage* (1992); and Ching Yun Bezine's trilogy, *Children of the Pearl* (1991), *Empire of the Moon* (1992), and *On Wings of Destiny* (1992). C. Y. Lee is the author of *The Flower Drum Song* (1957), source of the notoriously Orientalist musical of the same name.

31. These and other films portraying physical and psychospiritual caregiving by people of color are analyzed in my "Diverted Mothering."

WORKS CITED

Appachana, Anjana. "My Only Gods." In *The Forbidden Stitch: An Asian American Women's Anthology,* ed. Shirley Geok-lin Lim and Mayumi Tsutakawa. Corvallis, Ore.: Calyx, 1989. 228–234.

Ashcroft, Bill, Gareth Griffiths, and Helen Tiffin. *The Empire Writes Back: Theory and Practice in Post-colonial Literatures.* London: Routledge, 1989.

Asian Women United of California. *Making Waves: An Anthology of Writings by and about Asian American Women.* Boston: Beacon, 1989.

Barthes, Roland. "The Reality Effect." In *French Literary Theory To/day: A Reader,* ed. Tzvetan Todorov. New York: Cambridge University Press, 1982. 11–17.

Bernikow, Louis:, Review of Amy Tan's *The Joy Luck Club, Cosmopolitan,* October 1989: 42.

Bezine, Ching Yun. *Children of the Pearl.* New York: Signet, 1991.

———. *Empire of the Moon.* New York: Signet, 1992.

———. *On Wings of Destiny.* New York: Signet, 1992.

Broner, E. M., and Cathy N. Davidson. *Mothers and Daughters in Literature.* Special issue. *Women's Studies* 6.1 (1978).

Brown, Rosellen. *The Autobiography of My Mother.* New York: Doubleday, 1976.

Butler-Evans, Elliot. "Strategies of Self-Fashioning in Amy Tan's *The Joy Luck Club.*" Paper presented at "Reading Each Other: Cross-Cultural Perspectives on Literatures Other Than One's Own." Modern Language Association Convention, Washington, D.C., December 27–30, 1989.

Chan, Jeffery Paul, Frank Chin, Lawson Fusao Inada, and Shawn Wong, eds. *The Big Aiiieeeee! An Anthology of Chinese American and Japanese American Literature.* New York: Meridian, 1991.

Chang, Eileen (Chang Ai-ling). "The Golden Canque." Trans. author. In *Twentieth Century Chinese Stories*, ed. C. T. Hsia, with Joseph S. M. Lau. New York: Columbia University Press, 1971. 138–191.

Chang, Jung. *Wild Swans.* New York: Simon & Schuster, 1991.

Cheng, Nien. *Life and Death in Shanghai.* 1986. New York: Penguin, 1988.

Chennault, Anna. *The Education of Anna.* New York: Times Books, 1980.

Cheong, Fiona. *The Scent of the Gods.* New York: Norton, 1991.

Cheung, King-Kok. "The Woman Warrior versus the Chinaman Pacific: Must a Chinese American Critic Choose between Feminism and Heroism?" In *Conflicts in Feminism*, ed. Marianne Hirsch and Evelyn Fox-Keller. New York: Routledge, 1990. 234–251.

Chiang, Fay. *In the City of Contradictions.* New York: Sunbury Press, 1979.

Chin, Frank. *The Chickencoop Chinaman* and *The Year of the Dragon.* Seattle: University of Washington Press, 1981.

———. "Introduction'" In *Aiiieeeee!* ed. Frank Chin et al. xxi–xlviii.

Chin, Frank, Jeffery Paul Chan, Lawson Fusao Inada, and Shawn Wong, eds. *Aiiieeeee! An Anthology of Asian-American Writers.* 1974. Washington, D.C.: Howard University Press, 1983.

Chin, Tsai. *Daughter of Shanghai.* New York: St. Martin's Press, 1988.

Chow, Rey. "Violence in the Other Country: China as Crisis, Spectacle, and Woman." In *Third World Women and the Politics of Feminism*, ed. Mohanty, Russo, and Torres, 81–100. Chuang, Hua [pseud.]. *Crossings.* 1968. Boston: Northeastern University Press, 1986.

Dasenbrock, Reed Way. "Intelligibility and Meaningfulness in Multicultural Literature in English." *PMLA* 102.1 (1987): 10–19.

Davidson, Cathy N., and E. M. Broner, eds. *The Lost Tradition: Mothers and Daughters in Literature.* New York: Ungar, 1980.

Dew, Robb Forman. "Pangs of an Abandoned Child." Review of Amy Tan's *The Kitchen God's Wife. New York Times Book Review,* June 16, 1991, sec. 7: 9.

Dhillon, Kartar. "The Parrot's Beak." In Asian Women United, 214–222.

Fabian, Johannes. *Time and the Other: How Anthropology Makes Its Object.* New York: Columbia University Press, 1983.

Fong, Yem Siu. Review of Amy Tan's *The Joy Luck Club. Frontiers* 11.2–3 (1990): 122–123.

Fong-Torres, Ben. "Can Amy Tan Do It Again?" *San Francisco Chronicle,* June 12, 1991: B3, B4.

Gillespie, Elgy. "Amy, Angst, and the Second Novel." Review of Amy Tan's *The Kitchen God's Wife. San Francisco Review of Books,* Summer 1991: 33–34.

Hagedorn, Jessica. *Dangerous Music.* San Francisco: Momo's Press, 1975.

Hayslip, Le Ly. With Jay Wurts. *When Heaven and Earth Changed Places: A Vietnamese Woman's Journey from War to Peace.* New York: Doubleday, 1989.

Hirsch, Marianne. "Maternal Narratives: 'Cruel Enough to Stop the Blood.'" In *Reading Black, Reading Feminist: A Critical Anthology,* ed. Henry Louis Gates Jr. New York: Meridian, 1990.

———. *The Mother/Daughter Plot: Narrative, Psychoanalysis, Feminism.* Bloomington: Indiana University Press, 1989.

———. "Mothers and Daughters." Review essay. *Signs* 7.1 (1981): 200–222.

Holt, Patricia. "The Shuffle over 'Joy Luck.'" *San Francisco Chronicle Review,* July 16, 1989: 2.

Howe, Joyce. "Chinese in America: Telling the Immigrant Story." Review of Gish Jen's *Typical American,* Gus Lee's *China Boy,* Amy Tan's *The Kitchen God's Wife,* David Wong

Louie's *Pangs of Love,* and Frank Chin's *Donald Duk. Express Books,* a supplement to the East Bay *Express,* October 1991, 1: 14–15.

Huie, Kin. *Reminiscences.* Peiping [Beijing]: San Yu Press, 1932.

Humphreys, Josephine. "Secret Truths: Amy Tan Writes of Fate and Luck." Review of Amy Tan's *The Kitchen God's Wife. Chicago Tribune,* June 9, 1991, sec. 14: 1, 5.

Iyer, Pico. "The Second Triumph of Amy Tan." *Newsweek,* June 3, 1991: 67.

James, Caryn. "Relax, But Don't Leave Your Mind Behind." Review of Amy Tan's *The Kitchen God's Wife* and other works. *New York Times,* late ed., May 31, 1991: C1, C25.

Kadohata, Cynthia. *The Floating World.* New York: Viking, 1989.

Kaplan, E. Ann. *Motherhood and Representation: The Mother in Popular Culture and Melodrama.* London: Routledge, 1992.

Kepner, Susan. "Imagine This: The Amazing Adventure of Amy Tan." *San Francisco Focus,* May 1989: 58–60, 160–162.

Kim, Elaine H. *Asian American Literature: An Introduction to the Writings and Their Social Context.* Philadelphia: Temple University Press, 1982.

———. "'Such Opposite Creatures': Men and Women in Asian American Literature." *Michigan Review,* Winter 1990: 68–93.

Kim, Ronyoung. *Clay Walls.* 1987. Seattle: University of Washington Press, 1990.

Kingston, Maxine Hong. "Cultural Mis-readings by American Reviewers." In *Asian and Western Writers in Dialog: New Cultural Identities,* ed. Guy Amirthanayagam. Hong Kong: Macmillan, 1982. 55–65.

———. *Tripmaster Monkey: His Fake Book.* New York: Knopf, 1989.

———. *The Woman Warrior: Memoirs of a Girlhood among Ghosts.* New York: Knopf, 1976.

Kogawa, Joy. *Obasan.* 1981. Boston: Godine, 1982.

Kuo, Helena. *I've Come a Long Way.* New York: Appleton, 1942.

Lau, Sarah. "Long Way Home." In Watanabe and Bruchac, 87–95.

Law-Yone, Wendy. *The Coffin Tree.* New York: Knopf, 1983.

Lee, C. Y. *China Saga.* New York: Weidenfeld, 1987.

———. *The Flower Drum Song.* New York: Farrar, Straus & Cudahy, 1957.

———. *Gate of Rage.* New York: William Morrow, 1991.

Lee, Lillian (Lee Pik-Wah). *The Last Princess of Manchuria: A Novel.* Trans. Andrea Kelly. New York: William Morrow, 1992.

Li, Leslie. *Bittersweet.* Boston: Tuttle, 1992.

Lim, Shirley Geok-lin. "Asian American Daughters Rewriting Asian Maternal Texts." In *Asian Americans: Comparative and Global Perspectives,* ed. Shirley Hune, Hyung-chan Kim, Stephen S. Fugita, and Amy Ling. Pullman: Washington State University Press, 1991. 239–248.

Lin, Alice P. *Grandmother Has No Name.* San Francisco: China Books and Periodicals, 1988.

Lin, Yutang. *Chinatown Family.* New York: John Day, 1948.

Lord, Bette Bao. *Legacies: A Chinese Mosaic.* New York: Fawcett Columbine, 1990.

———. *Spring Moon: A Novel of China.* New York; Harper, 1981.

Lowe, Lisa. "Heterogeneity, Hybridity, Multiplicity: Making Asian American Differences." *Diaspora* 1.1 (Spring 1991): 24–44.

———. "Rethinking Essentialisms: Gender and Ethnicity in Amy Tan's *The Joy Luck Club.*" Paper presented at the American Literature Association Conference, San Diego, June 2, 1990.

Lowe, Pardee. *Father and Glorious Descendant.* Boston: Little, Brown, 1943.

Maglin, Nan Bauer. "'Don't Never Forget the Bridge That You Crossed Over On': The Literature of Matrilineage." In Davidson and Broner, 257–267.

Mara, Rachna. *Of Customs and Excise.* Toronto: Second Story Press, 1991.

McAlister, Melani. "(Mis)reading *The Joy Luck Club.*" *Asian America: Journal of Culture and the Arts* 1 (winter 1992): 102–118.

McCunn, Ruthanne Lum. *Thousand Pieces of Gold.* San Francisco: Design Enterprises, 1981

Mcmillan, Terry. *Mama.* New York: Washington Square Press, 1987.

Miner, Valerie. "The Daughters' Journeys." Review of Amy Tan's *The Joy Luck Club* and Hisaye Yamamoto's *Seventeen Syllables and Other Stories. The Nation,* April 24, 1989: 566–569.

Mirikitani, Janice. *Awake in the River.* N.p.: Isthmus Press, 1978.

Mohanty, Chandra Talpade. "Under Western Eyes: Feminist Scholarship and Colonial Discourses." In *Third World Women and the Politics of Feminism,* ed. Mohanty, Russo, and Torres, 51–80.

Mohanty, Chandra Talpade, Ann Russo, and Lourdes Torres, eds. *Third World Women and the Politics of Feminism.* Bloomington: Indiana University Press, 1991.

Morrison, Toni. *Beloved.* New York: Knopf, 1987.

———. *Sula.* New York: Bantam, 1973.

Mukherjee, Bharati. *Jasmine.* New York: Weidenfeld, 1989.

Ng, Fae Myenne. *Bone.* New York: Hyperion, 1993.

Oates, Joyce Carol. *Marya: A Life.* New York: Dutton, 1986.

Olsen, Tillie. *Mother to Daughter, Daughter to Mother.* Ed. Tillie Olsen. New York: Feminist Press, 1984. 275. Cited in Pearlman, 1.

Ong, Aihwa. "Colonialism and Modernity: Feminist Re-presentations of Women in Non-Western Societies." *Inscriptions* 3.4 (1988): 79–93.

Palumbo-Liu, David. "Model Minority Discourse and the Course of Healing." Forthcoming in *Minority Discourse: Ideological Containment and Utopian/Heterotopion Potential,* ed. Abdul JanMohamed.

Pearlman, Mickey. "Introduction." In *Mother Puzzles: Daughters and Mothers in Contemporary American Literature,* ed. Mickey Pearlman. New York: Greenwood, 1989. 1–9.

Perrick, Penny. "Daughters of America." Review of Amy Tan's *The Kitchen God's Wife. Sunday Times Book Review,* July 14, 1991: 6.

Rich, Adrienne. *Of Woman Born: Motherhood as Experience and Institution.* New York: Norton, 1976. 225.

Romano, Nancy Forbes. "The Disorientation of Pearl and Kai." Review of Amy Tan's *The Kitchen God's Wife. Los Angeles Times Book Review,* June 16, 1991, home ed.: 2.

Rosaldo, Renato. *Culture and Truth: The Remaking of Social Analysis.* Boston: Beacon, 1989.

Rothstein, Mervyn. "A New Novel by Amy Tan." *New York Times,* June 11, 1991, late ed.: C13–C14.

Sasaki, Ruth. "The Loom." In *Asian Women United,* 199–214.

Schell, Orville. "Your Mother Is in Your Bones." Review of Amy Tan's *The Joy Luck Club. New York Times Book Review,* March 19, 1989: 3, 28.

Schor, Naomi. *Reading in Detail: Aesthetics and the Feminine.* New York: Methuen, 1987.

See, Carolyn. "'Joy Luck' Readers: Extraordinary Good Fortune." Review of Amy Tan's *The Joy Luck Club. Oakland Tribune,* March 15, 1989: D8.

Shapiro, Laura. "From China, with Love." Review of Amy Tan's *The Kitchen God's Wife. Newsweek* 117.25, June 24, 1991: 63–64.

Simpson, Janice C. "Fresh Voices above the Noisy Din." *Time,* June 3, 1991: 66–67.

Simpson, Mona. *Anywhere but Here.* New York: Knopf, 1986.

Sit, Elaine. "Taking 'My Mother's Place . . . On the East, Where Things Begin.'" Review of
    Amy Tan's *The Joy Luck Club*. *East/West News*, April 13, 1989: 6.

Sledge, Linda Ching. With Gary Allen Sledge. *Empire of Heaven*. New York: Bantam,
    1990.

Solovitch, Sara. "Finding a Voice." *West*, June 30, 1991: 18–22.

Song, Cathy. *Picture Bride*. New Haven: Yale University Press, 1983.

Streitfield, David. "The 'Luck' of Amy Tan: Bestselling Writer Puts Newfound Fame in
    Perspective." *Washington Post*, October 8, 1989: F1, F8, F9.

Sun, Qingfeng. (In Chinese) *"Tan Enmei de ertongshu Yueniang"* [Amy Tan's children's book
    The Moon Lady]. *World Journal*, November 29, 1992: C8.

Tan, Amy. *The Joy Luck Club*. New York: Putnam, 1989.

———. *The Kitchen God's Wife*. New York: Putnam, 1991.

———. *The Moon Lady*. Illustrated by Gretchen Shields. New York: Macmillan, 1992.

———. "Mother Tongue," 1990. Repr. in *The Best American Essays 1991*. New York: Ticknoer
    & Fields, 1991. 196–202.

———. *Xifuhui* [*The Joy Luck Club*]. Trans. Yu Renrui. Tabei: Lianhe wenxue chubanshe,
    1990.

Todorov, Tzvetan. *The Poetics of Prose*. Trans. Richard Howard. New Foreword by Jonathan
    Culler. Ithaca, N.Y.: Cornell University Press, 1977.

Tsui, Kitty. *The Words of a Woman Who Breathes Fire*. San Francisco: Spinsters, 1983.

Uchida, Yoshiko. *Picture Bride*. Flagstaff, Ariz.: Northland Press, 1987.

Wang, Shizhen. (In Chinese) *Zhongguo gesheng hunsu* [Wedding customs in various provinces
    of China]. Taibei: Xingguang chubanshe, 1981.

Wang, Wen-Wen C. "Bacon and Coffee." In Watanabe and Bruchac, 97–105.

Watanabe, Sylvia, and Carol Bruchac, eds. *Home to Stay*. Greenfield Center, N.Y.: Greenfield
    Review Press, 1990.

Wei, Katherine, and Terry Quinn. *Second Daughter: Growing up in China, 1930–1949*. 1984.
    New York: Holt, Rinehart and Winston, 1985.

Wong, Jade Snow. *Fifth Chinese Daughter*. 1945• Seattle: University of Washington Press,
    1989. With a new Introduction by the author.

Wong, Nellie. *Dreams in Harrison Railroad Park*. N.p.: Kellsey Street Press, 1977.

Wong, Sau-ling C. "Autobiography as Guided Chinatown Tour? Maxine Hong Kingston and
    the Chinese-American Autobiographical Controversy." In *Multicultural Autobiography:
    American Lives*, ed. James Robert Payne. Knoxville: University of Tennessee Press,
    1992. 248–279.

———. "Diverted Mothering: Representations of Caregivers of Color in the Age of
    'Multiculturalism.'" In *Mothering: Ideology, Experience, and Agency*, ed. Evelyn Nakano
    Glenn, Grace Chang, and Linda Rennie Forcie. New York: Routledge, 1993. 67–91.

———. "Ethnic Dimensions of Postmodern Indeterminacy: Maxine Hong Kingston's *The
    Woman* Warrior as Avant-garde Autobiography." In *Autobiographie & Avant-garde*,
    ed. Alfred Hornung and Ernstpeter Ruhe. Tübingen: Gunter Narr Verlag, 1991.
    273–284.

Wong, Su-ling [pseud.], and Earl Herbert Cressy. *Daughter of Confucius: A Personal History*.
    New York: Farrar, Straus & Giroux, 1952.

Wong, Suzi. Review of Maxine Hong Kingston's *The Woman Warrior*. *Amerasia Journal* 4.1
    (1977): 165–167.

Woo, Merle. "Letter to Ma." In *This Bridge Called My Back: Writings by Radical Women of
    Color*, ed. Cherríe Moraga and Gloria Anzaldúa. Watertown, Mass.: Persephone Press,
    1981: 140–147.

Yamamoto, Hisaye. "Seventeen Syllables." 1949. Repr. in *Seventeen Syllables,* 8–19.

———. *Seventeen Syllables and Other Stories.* Latham, N.Y.: Kitchen Table: Women of Color Press, 1988.

———. "Yoneko's Earthquake." 1951. Repr. in *Seventeen Syllables,* 46–56.

Yamauchi, Wakako. "The Handkerchief." 1961. Repr. in *Amerasia Journal* 4.1 (1977): 143–150.

———. "Songs My Mother Taught Me." *Amerasia Journal* 3.2 (1976): 63–73.

Yglesias, Helen. Review of Amy Tan's *The Kitchen God's Wife. Women's Review of Books* 8.12 (1991): 1, 3, 4.

Yung, Judy. *Chinese Women in America: A Pictorial History.* Published for the Chinese Culture Foundation of San Francisco. Seattle: University of Washington Press, 1986.

Zill, Nicholas, and Marianne Winglee. *Who Reads Literature? The Future of the United States as a Nation of Readers.* Foreword by Jonathan Yardley. Commissioned by the Research Division of the National Endowment for the Arts. Cabin John, Md./Washington, D.C.: 1990.

WENYING XU

A Womanist Production of Truths:
The Use of Myths in Amy Tan

Women as sexed subjects[1] are produced by centuries of ideological indoctrination inscribing social and sexual mores in girls and women. Mythologies are one of the most appetizing, saturating, and thus most vicious components of gender ideologies, for mythologies are capable of shaping female subjects who take as their own vital survival the perpetuation of existent social and sexual order. As we have often seen and read, sometimes women have a more desperate sense of peril than men when there is any transgression of sexual morals, particularly if the transgression is done by another woman. Humanist and individualist traditions have further captivated women under their oppression with the philosophy of the Intended Subject. If one fails to recognize the subject as ideologically molded and thus fractured and incoherent, one cannot understand women as gendered subjects who are not identical to their intentions. If there were a self before language and culture that was identical to its intentions, it has been irretrievably lost.

It is not my desire, however, to speculate on the nature of the primordial; rather I would like to discuss through the reading of Amy Tan's novels how women can take possession of myths and make them produce truths that enable women to revise their self-understanding and thus gain a renewed sense of self. Their production of truths is an act of transgression

Paintbrush, Volume 22 (Autumn 1995): pp. 56–66. Copyright © 1995 Wenying Xu.

against established norms and ideals, facilitating the loosening of the foundations of female subject constitution.

How Asian American writers use myths and legends has been at the center of a debate concerning the truthfulness of the representation of Chinese culture. In *The Big Aiiieeee!* Frank Chin tries to distinguish the real Chinese myths and legends from the fake ones as he finds them in Maxine Hong Kingston, Amy Tan., and David Henry Hwang.[2] Chin accuses these Asian American writers of having "faked" Chinese legends and myths to confirm "the white racist" belief that Chinese are cruel and misogynous. These writers' revision of Chinese myths and legends is condemned as "a device for destroying history and literature" (Chan 2–3).

It seems that what Frank Chin demands of Chinese American writers is their loyalty to their ancestral culture and history to such an extent that it precludes any concern about gender issues which challenge the patriarchal order, for his charge against Kingston, Tan, and Hwang is that these writers have rewritten Chinese myths and legends in order to highlight either the victimization of women or women's self-empowerment. As a man well versed in Chinese culture and history, Chin has to work very hard to forget the misogynous portrayals of women in Chinese literature and the gendered Chinese language. In his "This Is Not An Autobiography," Chin's repeated use of "Chinaman" functions to demarcate "the yellow agents of yellow extinction" or "ornamental orientals" (among whom he locates Maxine Hong Kingston, Betty Bao Lord, and David Henry Hwang) from the "real Chinaman" (Chin 110). This male universal as the incorruptible genuine embodiment of Chinese culture and history further blinds Chin to the blatant male domination inherent in the Chinese language. He writes: "Whatever language a Chinaman speaks, it is always Chinaman, and the first person pronoun I, in any language, means "I am the law'" (Chin 111). In order to make this Kwan Kung bold statement (Chin 121–122), Chin must forget the humble Chinese female pronoun "I" (nu) which is synonymous with slave.

Chin's desire to separate the real from the fake is thus gender driven. In opposing the feminization of Chinese myths or legends, he is not simply (and naively) guarding the purity of his ancestral culture; he is glorifying and continuing the male militant heroism in that culture.[3] What Frank Chin does not seem to understand is the fact that myths and legends are neither unmutable nor unmediated in the sense of being sacred and gender free. The story of Fa Mu Lan, for example, has several versions in the Tang, Ming, and Qing dynasties as well as in the modern period.[4] Myths and legends also are the very stuff that renders ideologies invisible.[5]

For me it was a rare pleasure to find in Amy Tan's novels revisions of mythologies that subvert gender ideologies and gain women a measure of freedom from patriarchal domination. The two main myths Amy Tan uses are the myth of the Moon Lady in *The Joy Luck Club* (1989) and that of the Kitchen God in *The Kitchen God's Wife* (1991).[6] For my purpose I will give a fuller account of both myths than that given by Amy Tan.

The Moon Lady myth tells the story of the master archer, Yi, and his wife, Chang Eh, who became the Moon Lady.[7] Both were originally lesser gods but as a punishment they had been turned into mere mortals by the supreme father god and his wife, the sun goddess. Normally only one solar son at a time was permitted to appear in the sky and meet the needs of the mortals on earth. Once, however, choosing to be playful rather than dutiful, all ten sons appeared at the same time, scorching the earth. Yi, the master archer, had been sent to earth merely to discipline the sons of the sun goddess so as to restore the order normal to the relation between the heaven and the earth. Yi, in overzealous compassion for mortals, angrily shot down nine of the sons and thus, with his wife, was forced to become mere mortals. Yi and Chang Eh never gave up hope of recapturing immortality. Yi eventually found a creature who possessed a tree on which grew a ten-thousand-year rare fruit which either could provide human immortality for two people or could send one to heaven as a god. Because of Yi's earlier compassion for mortals, the creature gave him the fruit, and in similar compassion he chose to share it with his wife so both could become immortal. His wife, Chang Eh, however, who had killed no one but still had been punished along with her husband, was not content to share the fate of being merely an immortal human with her husband; she ate the fruit by herself in order to again become a goddess. Instantly, she felt as light as a feather and floated out of an open window up to the moon. In one ending of the myth, as soon as she got to the moon she became a toad in punishment for her disloyalty. In the other ending, she was compelled to live for eternity on the moon as a beautiful but utterly lonely young woman. In *The Joy Luck Club* Ying-Ying recalls a celebration of the Moon Festival in her childhood. The opera of the Moon Lady is customarily staged on the night of August 15 when the moon is the fullest. After the Moon Lady takes the "peach" of immortality, the drama turns didactic.

> As soon as she tasted it, she began to rise, then fly—not like the Queen Mother—but like a dragonfly with broken wings. "Flung from this earth by my own wantonness!" she cried just as her husband dashed back home, shouting, "Thief! Life-stealing wife!". . . . there stood the poor lady against a moon as bright as the sun. Her hair was now so long it swept the floor, wiping up her tears. An eternity had passed since she last saw her husband, for this was her fate: to stay lost on the moon, forever seeking her own selfish wishes.

"For woman is yin," she cried sadly, "the darkness within, where untempered passions lie. And man is yang, bright truth lighting our minds." (*Club* 81)

The moral lesson of the Moon Lady aims at curbing women's desire for agency by describing it as "wanton" and "selfish." Myths mapping such explicit limitations on women's desires and actions are analogous to what Spivak calls "symbolic clitoridectomies" (10). They mark, expose, and slice off the place of women's desire. The agents of perpetrating such removal of desire are often women themselves. Myths and traditional wisdom engender and legitimate the removal of agency in women. As a child Waverly Jong learns from her mother "Bite back your tongue. . . . Strongest wind cannot be seen" (*Club* 89). Only silent wishes get fulfilled. Ying-Ying as a child cannot understand why a secret wish is "what you want but cannot ask." She demands an answer from Amah, "Why can't I ask?" "It's because . . . if you ask it . . . it is no longer a wish but a selfish desire," says Amah. "Haven't I taught you that it is wrong to think of your own needs? A girl can never ask, only listen" (*Club* 70).

The real beginning of the narrative of *The Joy Luck Club* is the mother's killing secret. When Jing-mei is summoned by her father to take her mother's "corner" at the mah jong table, he tells her his suspicions: "My Father thinks she was killed by her own thoughts." "'She had a new idea inside her head,' said my father. 'But before it could come out of her mouth, the thought grew too big and burst. It must have been a very bad idea'" (*Club* 19). It is a desire too great to be good for a woman. A mortal woman dies because of a great desire and an immortal woman becomes exiled for it. Tales or myths of this sort are gendering and regulating biographies for the constitution of the sexed subject. Through them Chinese women learn not to desire, not to demand, not to act out of their wishes. Winnie remembers that all the stories she knows

> had to do with lessons learned too late—not to eat too much, not to talk too loudly, not to wander out at night by yourself—in any case, always about people who fell off the earth and into the sky because of their willful ways. (*Wife* 230)

Amy Tan gives the Moon Lady an alternative ending that counteracts the gendering "truth" of the myth. After the opera is over, Ying-Ying follows the Moon Lady hoping to get her wish granted.

> "I have a wish," I said in a whisper, and still she did not hear me. So I walked closer yet, until I could see the face of the Moon Lady: shrunken cheeks, a broad oily nose, large glaring teeth, and

red-stained eyes. . . . And as the secret wish fell from my lips, the
Moon Lady looked at me and became a man. (*Club* 82)

This ending removes the glamour of the Moon Lady as a beautiful yet piti-
ful sinner, thus disclosing the ugliness of women's victimization and crys-
tallizing the insidious "secret" behind the making of the myth. Now if we
recall the truth uttered by the Moon Lady at the end of the opera, "Women
are yin, the darkness within. . . . And man is yang, bright truth lighting our
minds," we see the comical twist in Tan's telling of the Moon Lady. The
"truth," declared by a declining man disguised as a beautiful young woman,
now appears to be a bad joke that strips the grandeur of the universal claim
about the sexes. With this comical twist of the story of the Moon Lady,
Amy Tan reminds her reader that mythologies are not authorless and therefore free from intentions to manipulate. Rather myths have been authored
by the intentions of gender ideologies to subjugate women and turn them
into sexed subjects.

In *The Kitchen God's Wife* Winnie Louie chooses to tell the unknown
story of a god's wife who was the hand behind his glory and wealth.

Fish jumped in his river, pigs grazed his hand, ducks flew around
his yard as thick as clouds. And that was because he was blessed
with a hardworking wife named Guo. She caught his fish and
herded his pigs. She fattened his ducks, doubled all his riches, year
after year . . . (*Wife* 54)

But the husband "was not satisfied" and began philandering around (54).
His wife, refusing to wait on his lovers, left him for good. Years later, having
squandered all his wealth, Zhang as a beggar met his wife again, who now
was a lady of a rich house. Out of shame he jumped into the fireplace and his
ashes flew up to heaven. "For having the courage to admit you were wrong,"
the Jade Emperor (ruler of heaven) declared to Zhang, "I make you Kitchen
God, watching over everyone's behavior. Every year you let me know who
deserves good luck, who deserves bad" (*Wife* 55).

In one of the common versions of the Kitchen God myth, the god began as a good, hard working, and honest man, fated, however, to be poor all
his life.[8] The extreme poverty forced him to sell his wife to a wealthy man as
a concubine. She never forgot him and once when he came to work for her
new husband, even though he never even recognized her, she gave him some
cakes into which she had hidden money. Not knowing they contained money,
this man on his way home shared one of them with a hungry stranger at a
tea house. Discovering the money in the cake, the stranger swindled him into
selling them for almost nothing. Later, learning that his ever loving former

wife had filled the cakes with money, he decided that his fate was too heavy and ended his own life. With his efforts in this life receiving no reward, he nevertheless was rewarded by being appointed the God of the Kitchen.

Winnie's rendition of the myth focuses on the injustice that the wife suffered. Winnie also denaturalizes the husband's poverty, explaining it as the result of his bad character rather than his fate. In her story the husband and his lover "slaughtered ducks just to eat a plate of their tongues. And in two years' time, all of Zhang's land was empty, and so was his heart" (*Wife* 54). Such revision enables Winnie to indignantly disavow this myth. "Why should I want that kind of person to judge me, a man who cheated his wife? His wife was the good one, not him" (*Wife* 55).

For someone from the old China, Winnie is not only courageous but also enlightened to denounce the god and demand justice for the forgotten wife. After all, as she very well knows,

> "All year long you have to show him [the kitchen god] respect—give him tea and oranges. When Chinese New Year's time comes, you must give him even better things—maybe whiskey to drink, cigarettes to smoke, candy to eat, that kind of thing. You are hoping all the time his tongue will be sweet, his head a little drunk, so when he has his meeting with the big boss, maybe he reports good things about you. This family has been good, you hope he says. Please give them good luck next year." (*Wife* 55)

Following further Winnie's account of her life in China, one finds out that the story of the Kitchen God is also her own story. She is the kind-hearted hard-working wife, who is constantly humiliated and abused by her ruthless and black hearted husband, Wen Fu. It seems that her life in China is an unbreakable chain of bad luck—female child of a concubine, abandoned by both parents, married to a murderous man, two dead children, several abortions, China's war with Japan, and her one and one half years in jail. . . . Perhaps it is her incessant bad luck that has made her defiant of the Kitchen God, for she certainly deserves good luck because of her unbending observation of the traditional codes for women. But in contradiction with the tradition she also learns that being born a female (in the old China) certifies all kinds of rotten luck to appear on her path of life.[9]

In her narrative of her past life, Winnie casts herself in the role of the Kitchen God's wife whose good behavior secured her nothing. She has followed closely the prescription of a virtuous woman and a good wife, but she has always been made to feel inadequate by her husband's dissatisfaction expressed in torrents of abuse. Winnie becomes furious but helpless as she watches her husband being rewarded with good luck for simply being his horrible self. Winnie's revision of the myth of the Kitchen God produces the truth of the masculine use of women as instruments of self-assertion. She makes it clear that it is through the use of women that Zhang became a kitchen god, and it is by abusing women that Wen Fu perceives himself as a "real man."

When Winnie finally understands that if she does not fight back, she will be like many other women who become sacrifices on the altar of the patriarchal tradition, she casts off the respectable robe of tragedy and compares herself to "a chicken in a cage, mindless, never dreaming of freedom, but never worrying when your neck might be chopped off" (*Wife* 313). It is this recognition of the inhumanity of her life that finally motivates her to seek a change in life. In retrospect she tells her daughter, "If I had had to change the whole world to change my own life, I would have done that" (*Wife* 355–356).

To save herself Winnie chooses to do what only "bad" women do—running away from her husband and moving in with the man she loves. Only when she refuses to be a virtuous woman and good wife does good luck begin to flow into her life. Even the good luck, however, does not come without the company of patriarchal bullying. When Winnie is sued by her husband, Wen Fu, the court sentences her to two years in prison for "deserting her husband" (*Wife* 373). Already disentangled from the grip of her traditional female consciousness, Winnie feels no shame but anger over the injustice of China's legal system. After one and one half years in prison, after being raped by Wen Fu once again, and after she has pointed his gun at his head, Winnie finally gains her freedom from Wen Fu and begins her new life with Jimmie Louie in America. In the new country she refuses to continue the tradition that demands in women silent desires and self-effacement. She teaches her daughter with her own life stories the courage to be "selfish."[10]

At the end of *The Kitchen God's Wife*, Winnie shops for a goddess for the red altar which her daughter Pearl has inherited from Auntie Du. Dissatisfied with all the existent goddesses, who are helplessly entrenched in the tradition of female servility, she tells the shop owner: "I am looking for a goddess that nobody knows. Maybe she does not yet exist" (*Wife* 413). The shop owner is delighted to part with the statue of a goddess on which the factory forgot to inscribe her name.

> So I bought that mistake. I fixed it. I used my gold paint and wrote her name on the bottom. . . . I could see this lady statue in her new house, the red temple altar with two candlesticks lighting up her face from both sides. She would live there, but no one would call her Mrs. Kitchen God. Why would she want to be called that, now that she and her husband are divorced. (*Wife* 414)

This "mistake," the object that has made the husband of the shop owner "so mad," takes on the life that has been traditionally impossible for women—she is named "Lady Sorrowfree" (*Wife* 414–415). Now divorced and deified, she finally becomes a goddess by her own merit. "She will listen. She will wash away everything sad with her tears. She will use her stick to chase away everything bad" (*Wife* 414–415).

This gesture of celebration and self-affirmation is also present in Tan's use of the myth of the Moon Lady. At the end of her children's book, *The Moon Lady* (1992),[11] Nai-nai (Grandma Ying-Ying) tells her three granddaughters that her secret wish to the Moon Lady has already been answered—"I had found myself. I found out what kind of tiger I really was. . . . And I knew what the best wishes were: those I could make come true by myself" (*Lady* 27). The story ends with Nai-nai and her granddaughters dancing "by the light of the full moon," casting Nai-nai as the *new* Moon Lady who has outlived the punishment, the misery, and the loneliness (*Lady* 27).

NOTES

1. See Gayatri Spivak, *The Post-Colonial Critic; Interviews, Strategies, Dialogues* (New York: Routledge, 1990) Chapter I.

2. See Frank Chin's "Come All Ye Asian American Writers of the Real and the Fake," *The Big Aiiieeee!*, 1–92.

3. For an excellent study of Frank Chin's charge against Kingston's feminist revision of Chinese myths, see King-Kok Cheung, "The Woman Warrior versus The Chinaman Pacific: Must a Chinese American Critic Choose between Feminism and Heroism?" *Conflicts in Feminism*, eds. Marianne Hirsch et al.

4. See Sau-ling Cynthia Wong, "Kingston's Handling of Traditional Chinese Sources," *Approaches to Teaching Kingston's Woman Warrior*, 26–36.

5. My critique focusing on the issue of gender should not be interpreted as a total rejection of Chin's criticism of Asian Americans for buying into the hegemonic Christian culture.

6. Amy Tan, *The Joy Luck Club* (New York: G. P. Putnam's Sons, 1989). *The Kitchen God's Wife* (New York: G. P. Putnam's Sons, 1991). All further references to these editions will be cited parenthetically in the text, as *Club* and *Wife*.

7. My narration of the myth is based on the untranslated *Chinese Mythology* by Yuan Ke.

8. This version of the Kitchen God is based on "The Kitchen Deity" in *Folk Tales of China*, ed. Wolfram Eberhard.

9. Marina Heung succinctly describes the life of women in the old China. She writes: "Because of their historical devaluation, women in the Chinese family are regarded as disposable property or detachable appendages despite their crucial role in maintaining the family line through childbearing. Regarded as expendable 'objects to be invested in or bartered,' the marginal status of Chinese women shows itself in their forced transfer from natal families to other families through the practice of arranged marriage, concubinage, adoption, and pawning. The position of women—as daughters, wives, and mothers—in Chinese society is therefore

markedly provisional, with their status and expendability fluctuating according to their families' economic circumstances, their ability to bear male heirs, and the proclivities of authority figures in their lives" (601).

10. This, of course, does not guarantee that the daughter would be less vulnerable than her mother to gender ideologies. In Amy Tan America does not dissolve women's oppression. She has An-mei, Rose's mother, complain: "I was raised the Chinese way; I was taught to desire nothing, to swallow other people's misery, to eat my own bitterness. And even though I taught my daughter the opposite, still she came out the same way . . . she was born a girl" (*Club* 215). Through the stories of the daughters in *The Joy Luck Club,* Tan successfully portrays the asymmetrical power relations between men and women in this country. However, Tan is also naive in seeing sexism in the U.S. mainly as unmediated male domination in families and heterosexual relationships. This critique will be the subject of another essay.

11. Amy Tan, *The Moon Lady* (New York: Macmillan, 1992). All further references will be to this edition and will be cited parenthetically in the text, abbreviated *Lady*.

WORKS CITED

Chan, Jeffery Paul et al. eds. *The Big Aiiieeee!* New York: A Meridian Book, 1991.

Cheung, King-Kok, "The Woman Warrior versus The Chinaman Pacific: Must a Chinese American Critic Choose between Feminism and Heroism?" *Conflicts in Feminism,* eds. Marianne Hirsch et al. New York: Routledge, 1990. 234–251.

Chin, Frank, "This Is Not An Autobiography," *Genre* 18 (Summer 1985): 109–130.

Eberhard, Wolfram. ed. *Folk Tales of China.* Chicago: The University of Chicago Press, 1965.

Heung, Marina. "Daughter-Text/Mother-Text: Matrilineage in Amy Tan's *Joy Luck Club*" *Feminist Studies* Fall 1993: 597–616.

Lim, Shirley Geok-lin. *Approaches to Teaching Kingston's The Woman Warrior.* New York: The Modern Language Association of America, 1991.

Spivak, Gayatri. *The Post-Colonial Critic: Interviews, Strategies, Dialogues.* New York: Routledge, 1990.

Tan, Amy. *The Joy Luck Club.* New York: G. P. Putnam's Sons, 1989.

———. *The Kitchen God's Wife.* New York: G. P. Putnam's Sons, 1991.

———. *The Moon Lady.* New York: Macmillan, 1992.

Yuan, Ke. *Chinese Mythology.* Beijing: Chinese Book Bureau Press, 1960.

M. MARIE BOOTH FOSTER

Voice, Mind, Self: Mother-Daughter Relationships in Amy Tan's The Joy Luck Club and The Kitchen God's Wife

In *The Joy Luck Club* and *The Kitchen God's Wife*, Amy Tan uses stories from her own history and myth to explore the voices of mothers and daughters of Chinese ancestry. Each woman tells a story indicative of the uniqueness of her voice. Mary Field Belensky, in *Women's Ways of Knowing*, argues that voice is "more than an academic shorthand for a person's point of view. . . . it is a metaphor that can apply to many aspects of women's experience and development. . . . Women repeatedly used the metaphor of voice to depict their intellectual and ethical development; . . . the development of a sense of voice, mind, and self were intricately intertwined" (18). In Tan's fiction, the daughters' sense of self is intricately linked to an ability to speak and be heard by their mothers. Similarly, the mothers experience growth as they broaden communication lines with their daughters. Tan's women are very much like the women Belensky portrays in *Women's Ways of Knowing*: "In describing their lives, women commonly talked about voice and silence: 'speaking up,' 'speaking out,' 'being silenced,' 'not being heard,' 'really listening,' 'really talking,' 'words as weapons,' 'feeling deaf and dumb,' 'having no words,' 'saying what you mean,' 'listening to be heard'" (18). Until Tan's women connect as mothers and daughters, they experience strong feelings of isolation, a sense of disenfranchisement and fragmentation. These feelings

Women of Color: Mother-Daughter Relationships in 20ᵗʰ Century Literature, edited by Elizabeth Guillory-Brown (Austin: University of Texas Press, 1996): pp. 207–227. Copyright © 1996 University of Texas Press.

often are a result of male domination, as Margery Wolf and Roxanne Witke describe in *Women in Chinese Society* (1–11).

A photo that is in part a pictorial history of Tan's foremothers is the inspiration for many of her portrayals of women. Tan writes in "Lost Lives of Women" of a picture of her mother, grandmother, aunts, cousins:

> When I first saw this photo as a child, I thought it was exotic and remote, of a faraway time and place, with people who had no connection to my American life. Look at their bound feet! Look at that funny lady with the plucked forehead. The solemn little girl was in fact, my mother. And leaning against the rock is my grandmother, Jing mei. . . . This is also a picture of secrets and tragedies. . . . This is the picture I see when I write. These are the secrets I was supposed to keep. These are the women who never let me forget why stories need to be told. (90)

In her remembrances, Tan presents Chinese American women who are forging identities beyond the pictures of concubinage and bound feet, women encountering new dragons, many of which are derived from being "hyphenated" American females. She views mother-daughter relationships in the same vein as Kathie Carlson, who argues, "This relationship is the birthplace of a woman's ego identity, her sense of security in the world, her feelings about herself, her body and other women. From her mother, a woman receives her first impression of how to be a woman" (xi).

The Joy Luck Club and *The Kitchen God's Wife* are studies in balance—balancing hyphenation and the roles of daughter, wife, mother, sister, career woman. In achieving balance, voice is important: in order to achieve voice, hyphenated women must engage in self-exploration, recognition and appreciation of their culture(s), and they must know their histories. The quest for voice becomes an archetypal journey for all of the women. The mothers come to the United States and have to adapt to a new culture, to redefine voice and self. The daughters' journeys become rites of passage; before they can find voice or define self they must acknowledge the history and myth of their mothers—"her-stories" of life in China, passage to the United States, and assimilation. And each must come to grips with being her mother's daughter.

The Joy Luck Club is a series of stories by and about narrators whose lives are interconnected as a result of friendship and membership in the Joy Luck Club: Suyuan and Jing-mei Woo, An-mei Hsu and Rose Hsu Jordan, Lindo and Waverly Jong, and Ying-ying and Lena St. Clair. The stories illuminate the multiplicity of experiences of Chinese women who are struggling to fashion a voice for themselves in a culture where women are conditioned to be silent. The stories are narrated by seven of the eight women in the group—four daughters and three mothers; one mother has recently died of a cerebral aneurysm. Jing-mei, nicknamed June, must be her mother's voice. The book is divided into four sections: Feathers from a Thousand Li Away, The Twenty-six Malignant Gates, American Translation, and Queen Mother of the Western Skies. Each chapter is prefaced with an introductory thematic tale or myth, all of which tend to stress the advice given by mothers.

Tan tells her mother's stories, the secret ones she began to tell after the death of Tan's father and brother in *The Kitchen God's Wife*. Patti Doten notes that Tan's mother told stories of her marriage to another man in China and of three daughters left behind when she came to the United States in 1949 (14), a story that is in part remembered in *The Joy Luck Club* with An-mei's saga. In *The Kitchen God's Wife*, a mother and daughter, Winnie Louie and Pearl Louie Brandt, share their stories, revealing the secrets that hide mind and self—and history—and veil and mask their voices. Winnie Louie's tale is of the loss of her mother as a young girl, marriage to a sadistic man who sexually abused her, children stillborn or dying young, a patriarchal society that allowed little room for escape from domestic violence (especially against the backdrop of war), and her flight to America and the love of a "good man." Daughter Pearl Louie Brandt's secrets include her pain upon the loss of her father and the unpredictable disease, multiple sclerosis, that inhibits her body and her life.

Tan's characters are of necessity storytellers and even historians, empowered by relating what they know about their beginnings and the insufficiencies of their present lives. Storytelling—relating memories—allows for review, analysis, and sometimes understanding of ancestry and thus themselves. The storytelling, however, is inundated with ambivalences and contradictions which, as Suzanna Danuta Walters argues, often take the form of blame in mother-daughter relationships (1).

Voice balances—or imbalances—voice as Chinese American mothers and daughters narrate their sagas. Because both mothers and daughters share the telling, the biases of a singular point of view are alleviated. Marianne Hirsch writes, "The story of female development, both in fiction and theory, needs to be written in the voice of mothers as well as in that of daughters. . . . Only in combining both voices, in finding a double voice that would yield a multiple female consciousness, can we begin to envision ways to live 'life afresh'" (161). Tan's fiction presents ambivalences and contradictions in the complicated interactions of mothers' and daughters' voices.

Regardless of how much the daughters try to deny it, it is through their mothers that they find their voice, their mind, their selfhood. Voice finds its form in the process of interaction, even if that interaction is conflict. "Recognition by the daughter that her voice is not entirely her own" comes in time and with experiences (one of the five interconnecting themes referred to by

Nan Bauer Maglin in *The Literature of Matrilineage* as a recurring theme in such literature [258]). The experiences in review perhaps allow the daughters to know just how much they are dependent upon their mothers in their journey to voice. The mothers do not let them forget their own importance as the daughters attempt to achieve self-importance.

As Jing-mei "June" Woo tells her story and that of her deceased mother, the importance of the mother and daughter voices resonating, growing out of and being strengthened by each other, is apparent in her state of confusion and lack of direction and success. Perhaps her name is symbolic of her confusion: she is the only daughter with both a Chinese and an American name. As she recalls life with her mother, Jing-mei/June relates that she is constantly told by her mother, Suyuan Woo, that she does not try and therefore cannot achieve success. June's journey to voice and balance requires self-discovery—which must begin with knowing her mother. June has to use memories as a guide instead of her mother, whose tale she tells and whose saga she must complete. She must meet the ending to the tale of life in China and daughters left behind that her mother has told her over and over again, a story that she thought was a dark fairy tale.

The dark tale is of a previous life that includes a husband and daughters. Suyuan's first husband, an officer with the Kuomintang, takes her to Kweilin, a place she has dreamed of visiting. It has become a war refuge, no longer idyllic. Suyuan Woo and three other officers' wives start the Joy Luck Club to take their minds off the terrible smells of too many people in the city and the screams of humans and animals in pain. They attempt to raise their spirits with mah jong, jokes, and food.

Warned of impending danger, June's mother leaves the city with her two babies and her most valuable possessions. On the road to Chungking, she abandons first the wheelbarrow in which she has been carrying her babies and her goods, then more goods. Finally, her body weakened by fatigue and dysentery, she leaves the babies with jewelry to provide for them until they can be brought to her family. America does not make Suyuan forget the daughters she left as she fled. June Woo secretly views her mother's story as a fairy tale because the ending always changed. Perhaps herein lies the cause of their conflict: neither mother nor daughter listens to be heard, so each complains of not being heard. June Woo's disinterest and lack of knowledge of her mother's history exacerbate her own voicelessness, her lack of wholeness.

At a mah jong table where, appropriately, June takes her mother's place, she is requested by her mother's friends to go to China and meet the daughters of her mother. Thus her journey to voice continues and begins: it is a journey started at birth, but it is only now that she starts to recognize that she needs to know about her mother in order to achieve self-knowledge. She is to tell her sisters about their mother. The mothers' worst fears are realized when

June asks what she can possibly tell her mother's daughters. The mothers see their daughters in June's response, daughters who get irritated when their mothers speak in Chinese or explain things in broken English.

Although it startles her mother's friends, June's question is a valid one for a daughter whose relationship with her mother was defined by distance that developed slowly and grew. According to June, she and her mother never understood each other. She says they translated each other's meanings: she seemed to hear less than what was said, and her mother heard more. It is a complaint leveled by mothers and daughters throughout *The Joy Luck Club* and later in *The Kitchen God's Wife*. Both women want to be heard, but do not listen to be heard. They must come to understand that a voice is not a voice unless there is someone there to hear it.

Jing-mei is no longer sitting at the mah jong table but is en route to China when she summons up memories of her mother that will empower her to tell the daughters her mother's story. In the title story and in the short story "A Pair of Tickets," she occupies her mother's place in the storytelling, much as she occupies it at the mah jong table, and she is concerned with the responsibilities left by her mother. In her own stories, "Two Kinds" and "Best Quality," she is concerned with her selves: Jing-mei and June—the Chinese and the American, her mother's expectations and her belief in herself. Her stories are quest stories, described by Susan Koppelman in *Between Mothers and Daughters* as "a daughter's search for understanding" of her mother and herself (xxii). As June makes soup for her father, she sees the stray cat that she thought her mother had killed, since she had not seen it for some time. She makes motions to scare the cat and then recognizes the motions as her mother's; the cat reacts to her just as he had to her mother. She is reminded that she is her mother's daughter.

According to Judith Arcana in *Our Mothers' Daughters*, "we hold the belief that mothers love their daughters by definition and we fear any signal from our own mother that this love, which includes acceptance, affection, admiration and approval does not exist or is incomplete" (5). It does not matter to Jing-mei that she is not her mother's only disappointment (she says her mother always seemed displeased with everyone). Jing-mei recalls that something was not in balance and that something always needed improving for her mother. The friends do not seem to care; with all of her faults, she is their friend. Perhaps it is a "daughter's" expectations that June uses to judge her mother. Suyuan tells the rebellious June that she can be the best at anything as she attempts to mold her child into a piano-playing prodigy. She tells June she's not the best because she's not trying. After the request by the Joy Luck Club mothers June, in really listening to the voice of her mother as reserved in her memory, discovers that she might have been able to demonstrate ability had she tried: "for unlike my mother I did not believe I could be anything

I wanted to be. I could only be me" (154). But she does not recognize that the "me" is the one who has made every attempt to escape development. The pendant her late mother gave her is symbolic. It was given to her as her life's importance. The latter part of the message is in Chinese, the voice of wisdom versus the provider of American circumstances.

In archetypal journeys, there is always a god or goddess who supports the "traveler" along his or her way. In *The Kitchen God's Wife*, Lady Sorrowfree is created by Winnie Louie, mother of Pearl, when the Kitchen God is determined by her to be an unfit god for her daughter's altar, inherited from an adopted aunt. The Kitchen God is unfit primarily because he became a god despite his mistreatment of his good wife. A porcelain figurine is taken from a storeroom where she has been placed as a "mistake" and is made into a goddess for Pearl, Lady Sorrowfree. Note Winnie's celebration of Lady Sorrowfree:

> I heard she once had many hardships in her life. . . . But her smile is genuine, wise, and innocent at the same time. And her hand, see how she just raised it. That means she is about to speak, or maybe she is telling you to speak. She is ready to listen. She understands English. You should tell her everything. . . . But sometimes, when you are afraid, you can talk to her. She will listen. She will wash away everything sad with her tears. She will use her stick to chase away everything bad. See her name: Lady Sorrowfree, happiness winning over bitterness, no regrets in this world. (414–415)

Perhaps Tan's mothers want to be like Lady Sorrowfree; they are in a sense goddesses whose altars their daughters are invited to come to for nurturance, compassion, empathy, inspiration, and direction. They are driven by the feeling of need to support those daughters, to give to them "the swan" brought from China—symbolic of their her-stories and wisdom, and the advantages of America, like the mother in the preface to the first round of stories. In the tale, all that is left of the mother's swan that she has brought from China after it is taken by customs officials is one feather; the mother wants to tell her daughter that the feather may look worthless, but it comes from her homeland and carries with it all good intentions. But she waits to tell her in perfect English, in essence keeping secrets. The mothers think that everything is possible for the daughters if the mothers will it. The daughters may come willingly to the altar or may rebelliously deny the sagacity of their mothers.

The mothers struggle to tell their daughters the consequences of not listening to them. The mother in the tale prefacing the section "Twenty-six Malignant Gates" tells her daughter not to ride her bike around the corner where she cannot see her because she will fall down and cry. The daughter questions how her mother knows, and she tells her that it is written in the book *Twenty-six Malignant Gates* that evil things can happen when a child goes outside the protection of the house. The daughter wants evidence, but her mother tells her that it is written in Chinese. When her mother does not tell her all twenty-six of the Malignant Gates, the girl runs out of the house and around the corner and falls, the consequence of not listening to her mother. Rebellion causes conflict—a conflict Lady Sorrowfree would not have to endure. June Woo and Waverly Jong seem to be daughters who thrive on the conflict that results from rebellion and sometimes even the need to win their mother's approval. June trudges off every day to piano lessons taught by an old man who is hard of hearing. Defying her mother, she learns very little, as she reveals at a piano recital to which her mother has invited all of her friends. June notes the blank look on her mother's face that says she has lost everything. Waverly wins at chess, which pleases her mother, but out of defiance she stops playing until she discovers that she really enjoyed her mother's approval. As an adult she wants her mother to approve of the man who will be her second husband; mother and daughter assume the positions of chess players.

Tan's mothers frequently preach that children are to make their mothers proud so that they can brag about them to other mothers. The mothers engage in fierce competition with each other. Suyuan Woo brags about her daughter even after June's poorly performed piano recital. All of the mothers find fault with their daughters, but this is something revealed to the daughters, not to the community.

Much as Lindo Jong credits herself with daughter Waverly's ability to play chess, she blames herself for Waverly's faults as a person and assumes failures in raising her daughter: "It is my fault she is this way—selfish. I wanted my children to have the best combination: American circumstances and Chinese character. How could I know these things do not mix?" (289). Waverly knows how American circumstances work, but Lindo can't teach her about Chinese character: "How to obey parents and listen to your mother's mind. How not to show your own thoughts, to put your feelings behind your face so you can take advantage of hidden opportunities. . . . Why Chinese thinking is best" (289). What she gets is a daughter who wants to be Chinese because it is fashionable, a daughter who likes to speak back and question what she says, and a daughter to whom promises mean nothing. Nonetheless, she is a daughter of whom Lindo is proud.

Lindo Jong is cunning, shrewd, resourceful; Waverly Jong is her mother's daughter. Waverly manages to irritate her mother when she resists parental guidance. Judith Arcana posits that "some daughters spend all or most of their energy trying futilely to be as different from their mothers as possible in behavior, appearance, relations with friends, lovers, children, husbands" (9).

Waverly is a strategist in getting her brother to teach her to play chess, in winning at chess, in gaining her mother's forgiveness when she is rude and getting her mother's acceptance of the man she plans to marry. Lindo proudly reminds Waverly that she has inherited her ability to win from her.

In literature that focuses on mother/daughter relationships, feminists see "context—historical time and social and cultural group" as important (Rosinsky, 285), Lindo relates in "The Red Candle" that she once sacrificed her life to keep her parents' promise; she married as arranged. Chinese tradition permits Lindo's parents to give her to Huang Tai for her son—to determine her fate—but Lindo takes control of her destiny. On the day of her wedding, as she prepares for the ceremony, she schemes her way out of the planned marriage and into America, where "nobody says you have to keep the circumstances somebody else gives to you" (289).

It takes determination to achieve voice and selfhood, to take control of one's mind and one's life from another, making one's self heard, overcoming silence. Lindo does not resign herself to her circumstances in China. Waverly reveals that she learns some of her strategies from her mother: "I was six when my mother taught me the art of invisible strength. It was a strategy for winning arguments, respect from others, and eventually, though neither of us knew it at the time, chess games" (89). Therein lies Lindo's contribution to her daughter's voice.

Lindo uses the same brand of ingenuity to play a life chess game with and to teach her daughter. Adrienne Rich writes in *Of Woman Born:* "Probably there is nothing in human nature more resonant with charges than the flow of energy between two biologically alike bodies, one which has lain in amniotic bliss inside the other, one which has labored to give birth to the other. The materials are there for the deepest mutuality and the most painful estrangement" (226). Lindo has to contend with a headstrong daughter: "'Finish your coffee,' I told her yesterday. 'Don't throw your blessings away.' 'Don't be old-fashioned, Ma,' she told me, finishing her coffee down the sink. 'I'm my own person.' And I think, how can she be her own person? When did I give her up?" (290).

Waverly is champion of the chess game, but she is no match for her mother in a life chess game. She knows her chances of winning in a contest against her mother, who taught her to be strong like the wind. Waverly learns during the "chess years" that her mother was a champion strategist. Though she is a tax attorney able to bully even the Internal Revenue Service, she fears the wrath of her mother if she is told to mind her business: "Well, I don't know if it's explicitly stated in the law, but you can't ever tell a Chinese mother to shut up. You could be charged as an accessory to your own murder" (191). What Waverly perceives as an impending battle for her mother's approval of her fiancé is nothing more than the opportunity for her mother and her to communicate with each other. She strategically plans to win her mother's approval of her fiancé, Rick, just as if she is playing a game of chess. She is afraid to tell her mother that they are going to be married because she is afraid that her mother will not approve. The conversation ends with her recognition that her mother also needs to be heard and with her mother's unstated approval of her fiancé. Waverly Jong recognizes her mother's strategies in their verbal jousts, but she also recognizes that, just like her, her mother is in search of something. What she sees is an old woman waiting to be invited into her daughter's life. Like the other mothers, Lindo views herself as standing outside her daughter's life—a most undesirable place.

Sometimes Tan's mothers find it necessary to intrude in order to teach the daughters to save themselves; they criticize, manage, and manipulate with an iron fist. An-mei Hsu and Ying-ying St. Clair play this role. "My mother once told me why I was so confused all the time," says Rose Hsu during her first story, "Without Wood" (212). "She said that I was without wood. Born without wood so that I listened to too many people. She knew this because she had almost become this way" (212). Suyuan Woo tells June Woo that such weaknesses are present in the mother, An-mei Hsu: "Each person is made of five elements. . . . Too little wood and you bend too quickly to listen to other people's ideas, unable to stand on your own. This was like my Auntie An-mei" (19). Rose's mother tells her that she must stand tall and listen to her mother standing next to her. If she bends to listen to strangers, she'll grow weak and be destroyed. Rose Hsu is in the process of divorce from a husband who has labeled her indecisive and useless as a marriage partner. She is guilty of allowing her husband to mold her. He does not want her to be a partner in family decisions until he makes a mistake in his practice as a plastic surgeon. Then he complains that she is unable to make decisions: he is dissatisfied with his creation. Finding it difficult to accept divorce, she confusedly runs to her friends and a psychiatrist seeking guidance.

Over and over again her mother tells her to count on a mother because a mother is best and knows what is inside of her daughter. "A psyche-atricks will only make you hulihudu, make you heimongmong" (210). The psychiatrist leaves her confused, as her mother predicts. She becomes even more confused as she tells each of her friends and her psychiatrist a different story. Her mother advises her to stand up to her husband, to speak up. She assumes the role of Lady Sorrowfree. When Rose does as her mother advises, she notices that her husband seems scared and confused. She stands up to him and forces him to retreat. She is her mother's daughter. She listens to her mother and finds her voice—her self.

Like the other mothers, An-mei demonstrates some of the qualities of "Lady Sorrowfree." An-mei is concerned that her daughter sees herself as having no options. A psychologist's explanation is "to the extent that women perceive themselves as having no choice, they correspondingly excuse themselves from the responsibility that decision entails" (Gilligan, 67). An-mei was "raised the Chinese way": "I was taught to desire nothing, to swallow other people's misery, to eat my own bitterness" (241). She uses the tale of the magpies to indicate that one can either make the choice to be in charge of one's life or continue to let others be in control. For thousands of years magpies came to the fields of a group of peasants just after they had sown their seeds and watered them with their tears. The magpies ate the seeds and drank the tears. Then one day the peasants decided to end their suffering and silence. They clapped their hands and banged sticks together, making noise that startled and confused the magpies. This continued for days until the magpies died of hunger and exhaustion from waiting for the noise to stop so that they could land and eat. The sounds from the hands and sticks were their voices. Her daughter should face her tormentor.

An-mei tells stories of her pain, a pain she does not wish her daughter to endure. Memory is, in part, voices calling out to her, reminding her of what she has endured and of a relationship wished for: "it was her voice that confused me," "a familiar sound from a forgotten dream," "she cried with a wailing voice," "voices praising," "voices murmuring," "my mother's voice went away" (41–45). The voices of her mothers confused her. She was a young girl in need of a mother's clear voice that would strengthen her circumstances and her context. The voices remind her, in "Scar," of wounds that heal but leave their imprint and of the importance of taking control out of the hands of those who have the ability to devour their victims, as in the story "Magpies." A scar resulting from a severe burn from a pot of boiling soup reminds her of when her mother was considered a ghost: her mother was dead to her family because she became a rich merchant's concubine. With time the scar "became pale and shiny and I had no memory of my mother. That is the way it is with a wound. The wound begins to close in on itself, to protect what is hurting so much. And once it is closed, you no longer see what is underneath, what started the pain" (40). It is also the way of persons attempting to assimilate—the wounds of getting to America, the wounds of hyphenation, close in on themselves and then it is difficult to see where it all began.

An-mei remembers the scar and the pain when her mother returns to her grandmother Poppo's deathbed. Upon the death of Poppo, she leaves with her mother, who shortly afterward commits suicide. Poppo tells An-mei that when a person loses face, it's like dropping a necklace down a well: the only way you can get it back is to jump in after it. From her mother An-mei learns that tears cannot wash away sorrows; they only feed someone else's joy. Her mother tells her to swallow her own tears.

An-mei knows strength and she knows forgetting. Perhaps that is why her daughter tells the story of her loss. It is Rose Hsu who tells the story of her brother's drowning and her mother's faith that he would be found. She refuses to believe that he is dead; without any driving lessons, she steers the car to the ocean side to search once more for him. After her son Bing's death, An-mei places the Bible that she has always carried to the First Chinese Baptist Church under a short table leg as a way of correcting the imbalances of life. She gives her daughter advice on how to correct imbalances in her life. The tale prefacing the section "Queen of the Western Skies" is also a fitting message for Rose Hsu. A woman playing with her granddaughter wonders at the baby's happiness and laughter, remembering that she was once carefree before she shed her innocence and began to look critically and suspiciously at everything. She asks the babbling child if it is Syi Wang, Queen Mother of the Western Skies, come back to provide her with some answers: "Then you must teach my daughter this same lesson. How to lose your innocence but not your hope. How to laugh forever" (159).

Like all the other daughters, Lena must recognize and respect the characteristics of Lady Sorrowfree that are inherent in her mother, Ying-ying. Ying-ying describes her daughter as being devoid of wisdom. Lena laughs at her mother when she says "arty-tecky" (architecture) to her sister-in-law. Ying-ying admits that she should have slapped Lena more as a child for disrespect. Though Ying-ying serves as Lena's goddess, Lena initially does not view her mother as capable of advice on balance. Ying-ying's telling of her story is very important to seeing her in a true mothering role; her daughter's first story makes one think that the mother is mentally unbalanced.

Evelyn Reed in *Woman's Evolution* writes: "A mother's victimization does not merely humiliate her, it mutilates her daughter who watches her for clues as to what it means to be a woman. Like the traditional foot-bound Chinese woman, she passes on her affliction. The mother's self-hatred and low expectations are binding rags for the psyche of the daughter" (293). Ying-ying, whose name means "Clear Reflection," becomes a ghost. As a young girl she liked to unbraid her hair and wear it loose. She recalls a scolding from her mother, who once told her that she was like the lady ghosts at the bottom of the lake. Her daughter is unaware of her mother's previous marriage to a man in China twenty years before Lena's birth. Ying-ying falls in love with him because he strokes her cheek and tells her that she has tiger eyes, that they gather fire in the day and shine golden at night. Her husband opts to run off with another woman during her pregnancy, and she aborts the baby because she has come to hate her husband with a passion. Ying-ying tells Lena that she was born a tiger in a year when babies were dying and because she was strong she survived. After ten years of reclusive living with cousins in the country, she goes to the city to live and work. There she meets Lena's father, an American she marries after being courted for four years, and continues to be a ghost. Ying-ying says that she willingly gave up her spirit.

In Ying-ying's first story, "The Moon Lady," when she sees her daughter lounging by the pool she realizes that they are lost, invisible creatures. Neither, at this point, recognizes the importance of "listening harder to the silence beneath their voices" (Maglin, 260). Their being lost reminds her of the family outing to Tai Lake as a child, when she falls into the lake, is rescued, and is put on shore only to discover that the moon lady she has been anxiously awaiting to tell her secret wish is male. The experience is so traumatic that she forgets her wish. Now that she is old and is watching her daughter, she remembers that she had wished to be found. And now she wishes for her daughter to be found—to find herself.

Lena, as a young girl, sees her mother being devoured by her fears until she becomes a ghost. Ying-ying believes that she is already a ghost. She does not want her daughter to become a ghost like her, "an unseen spirit" (285). Ying-ying begins life carefree. She is loved almost to a fault by her mother and her nursemaid, Amah. She is spoiled by her family's riches and wasteful. When she unties her hair and floats through the house, her mother tells her that she resembles the "lady ghosts . . . ladies who drowned in shame and floated in living people's houses with their hair undone to show everlasting despair" (276). She knows despair when the north wind that she thinks has blown her luck chills her heart by blowing her first husband past her to other women.

Lena, Ying-ying's daughter, is a partner in a marriage where she has a voice in the rules; but when the game is played, she loses her turn many times. Carolyn See argues that "in the name of feminism and right thinking, this husband is taking Lena for every cent she's got, but she's so demoralized, so 'out of balance' in the Chinese sense, that she can't do a thing about it" (11). In the introductory anecdote to the section "American Translation," a mother warns her daughter that she cannot put mirrors at the foot of the bed because all of her marriage happiness will bounce back and tumble the opposite way. Her mother takes from her bag a mirror that she plans to give the daughter as a wedding gift so that it faces the other mirror. The mirrors then reflect the happiness of the daughter. Lena's mother, as does Rose's mother, provides her with the mirror to balance her happiness; the mirror is a mother's advice or wisdom. It is Lena's mother's credo that a woman is out of balance if something goes against her nature. She does not want to be like her mother, but her mother foresees that she too will become a ghost; her husband will transform her according to his desires. Ying-ying recalls that she became "Betty" and was given a new date of birth by a husband who never learned to speak her language. Her review of her own story makes her know that she must influence her daughter's "story" that is in the making. Lena sees herself with her husband in the midst of problems so deep that she can't see where the bottom is. In the guise of a functional relationship is a dysfunctional one. Her mother predicts that the house will break into pieces. When a too-large vase on a too-weak table crashes to the floor, Lena admits that she knew it would happen. Her mother asks her why she did not take steps to keep the house from falling, meaning her marriage as well as the vase.

The goddess role becomes all important to Ying-ying as she becomes more determined to prevent her daughter from becoming a ghost. She fights the daughter that she has raised, "watching from another shore" and "accept[ing] her American ways" (286). After she uses the sharp pain of what she knows to "penetrate [her] daughter's tough skin and cut the tiger spirit loose," she waits for her to come into the room, like a tiger waiting between the trees, and pounces. Ying-ying wins the fight and gives her daughter her spirit, "because this is the way a mother loves her daughter" (286). Lady Sorrowfree helps her "charge" achieve voice.

From the daughter with too much water, to the mother and daughter with too much wood, to the tiger ghosts and just plain ghosts, to the chess queens, Tan's women in *The Joy Luck Club* find themselves capable of forging their own identities, moving beyond passivity to assertiveness—speaking up. They are a piece of the portrait that represents Amy Tan's family history—her own story included; they are, in composite, her family's secrets and tragedies. Tan is unlike some Asian American writers who have had to try to piece together and sort out the meaning of the past from shreds of stories overheard or faded photographs. As in her stories, her mother tells her the stories and explains the photographs. Bell Gale Chevigny writes that "women writing about other women will symbolically reflect their internalized relations with their mothers and in some measure re-create them" (80). From Tan's own accounts, her interaction with her mother is reflected in her fiction.

Tan's women with their American husbands attempt often without knowing it to balance East and West, the past and the future of their lives. A level of transcendence is apparent in the storytelling, as it is in *The Kitchen God's Wife*. Mothers and daughters must gain from the storytelling in order to have healthy relationships with each other.

In *The Kitchen God's Wife*, Winnie Louie and her daughter Pearl Louie Brandt are both keepers of secrets that accent the distance that characterizes their relationship. Pearl thinks after a trip to her mother's home: "Mile after mile, all of it familiar, yet not this distance that separates us, me from my mother" (57). She is unsure of how this distance was created. Winnie says of their relationship: "That is how she is. That is how I am. Always careful to be polite, always trying not to bump into each other, just like strangers" (82). When their secrets begin to weigh down their friends who have known them for years, who threaten to tell each of the other's secrets, Winnie Louie decides that it is time for revelation. The process of the revelation is ritual: "recitation of the relationship between mother and daughter," "assessment of the relationship," and "the projection of the future into the relationship"

(Koppelman, xxvii). At the same time revelation is a journey to voice, the voice that they must have with each other. Again, voice is a metaphor for speaking up, being heard, listening to be heard. No longer will stories begin as Pearl's does: "Whenever my mother talks to me, she begins the conversation as if we were already in the middle of an argument" (11). That they argue or are in conflict is not problematic; it is the "talks to" that should be replaced with "talks with." As much as Pearl needs to know her mother's secrets, Winnie Louie needs to tell them in order to build a relationship that is nurturing for both mother and daughter.

Pearl's secret is multiple sclerosis. At first she does not tell her mother because she fears her mother's theories on her illness. What becomes her secret is the anger she feels toward her father, the inner turmoil that began with his dying and death. Sometimes the mother's voice drowns the voice of the daughter as she attempts to control or explain every aspect of the daughter's existence. "If I had not lost my mother so young, I would not have listened to Old Aunt," says Winnie Louie (65) as she begins her story. These might also be the words of her daughter, though Pearl's loss of mother was not a physical loss. The opportunity for the resonating of mother and daughter voices seems to be the difference between balance and imbalance. American circumstances are to be blamed for the distance; the need to keep secrets grows out of the perceived necessity of assimilation and clean slates. Because her mother was not there, Winnie "listened to Old Aunt" (65). Winnie Louie's dark secret begins with her mother, who disappeared without telling her why; she still awaits some appearance by her mother to explain. Her mother's story is also hers: an arranged marriage—in her mother's case, to curb her rebelliousness; realization that she has a lesser place in marriage than purported; and a daughter as the single lasting joy derived from the marriage. The difference is that Winnie's mother escaped, to be heard from no more.

Winnie's family abides by all of the customs in giving her hand in marriage to Wen Fu: "Getting married in those days was like buying real estate. Here you see a house you want to live in, you find a real estate agent. Back in China, you saw a rich family with a daughter, you found a go-between who knew how to make a good business deal" (134). Winnie tells her daughter, "If asked how I felt when they told me I would marry Wen Fu, I can only say this: It was like being told I had won a big prize. And it was also like being told my head was going to be chopped off. Something between those two feelings" (136). Winnie experiences very little mercy in her marriage to the monstrous Wen Fu.

Wen Fu serves as an officer in the Chinese army, so during World War II they move about China with other air force officers and their wives. Throughout the marriage, Winnie knows abuse and witnesses the death of her babies. She tries to free herself from the tyranny of the marriage, but her husband enjoys abusing her too much to let her go. Her story is a long one, a lifetime of sorrow, death, marriage, imprisonment, lost children, lost friends and family. Jimmie Louie saves her life by helping her to escape Wen Fu and to come to the United States. She loves Jimmie Louie and marries him. The darkest part of her secret she reveals to Pearl almost nonchalantly: Pearl is the daughter of the tyrant Wen Fu.

The daughter asks her mother: "Tell me again . . . why you had to keep it a secret." The mother answers: "Because then you would know. . . . You would know how weak I was. You would think I was a bad mother" (398). Winnie's actions and response are not unexpected. She is every mother who wants her daughter to think of her as having lived a blemish-free existence. She is every mother who forgets that her daughter is living life and knows blemishes. Secrets revealed, the women begin to talk. No longer does Winnie have to think that the year her second husband, Jimmie Louie, died was "when everyone stopped listening to me" (81). Pearl knows her mother's story and can respect her more, not less, for her endurance. She is then able to see a woman molded by her experiences and her secrets—a woman who has lived with two lives. With the tiptoeing around ended, the distance dissipates. By sharing their secrets, they help each other to achieve voice. The gift of Lady Sorrowfree is symbolic of their bonding; this goddess has all of the characteristics of the nurturing, caring, listening mother. Her imperfections lie in her creation; experiences make her. She has none of the characteristics of the Kitchen God.

The story of the Kitchen God and his wife angers Winnie Louie; she looks at the god as a bad man who was rewarded for admitting that he was a bad man. As the story goes, a wealthy farmer, Zhang, who had a good wife who saw to it that his farm flourished, brought home a pretty woman and made his wife cook for her. The pretty woman ran his wife off without any objection from the farmer. She helped him use up all of his riches foolishly and left him a beggar. He was discovered hungry and suffering by a servant who took him home to care for him. When he saw his wife, whose home it was, he attempted to hide in the kitchen fireplace; his wife could not save him. The Jade Emperor, because Zhang admitted he was wrong, made him Kitchen God with the duty to watch over people's behavior. Winnie tells Pearl that people give generously to the Kitchen God to keep him happy in the hopes that he will give a good report to the Jade Emperor. Winnie thinks that he is not the god for her daughter. How can one trust a god who would cheat on his wife? How can he be a good judge of behavior? The wife is the good one. She finds another god for her daughter's altar, Lady Sorrowfree. After all, she has already given her a father.

Even as Winnie tells her story, one senses that the women are unaware of the strength of the bond between them that partly originates in the biological connection and partly in their womanness. Storytelling/revealing secrets gives both of them the opportunity for review; Winnie Louie tells Pearl that she has taught her lessons with love, that she has combined all of the love that she had for the three she lost during the war and all of those that she did not allow to be born and has given it to Pearl. She speaks of her desire "to believe in something good" (152), her lost hope and innocence: "So I let those other babies die. In my heart I was being kind. . . . I was a young woman then. I had no more hope left, no trust, no innocence" (312). In telling her story, she does not ask for sympathy or forgiveness; she simply wants to be free of the pain that "comes from keeping everything inside, waiting until it is too late" (88).

Perhaps this goddess, Lady Sorrowfree, to whom they burn incense will cause them never to forget the importance of voice and listening. On the heels of listening there is balance as both Winnie and Pearl tell their secrets and are brought closer by them. East and West, mother and daughter, are bonded for the better. Arcana notes that "mother/daughter sisterhood is the conscious-ness we must seek to make this basic woman bond loving and fruitful, power-ful and deep . . . " (34). It ensures that women do lot smother each other and squelch the voice of the other or cause each other to retreat into silence.

In exploring the problems of mother-daughter voices in relationships, Tan unveils some of the problems of biculturalism—of Chinese ancestry and American circumstances. She presents daughters who do not know their mothers' "importance" and thus cannot know their own; most seem never to have been told or even cared to hear their mothers' history. Until they do, they can never achieve voice. They assimilate; they marry American men and put on American faces. They adapt. In the meantime, their mothers sit like Lady Sorrowfree on her altar, waiting to listen. The daughters' journeys to voice are completed only after they come to the altars of their Chinese mothers.

Works Cited

Arcana, Judith. *Our Mothers' Daughters*. Berkeley: Shameless Hussy Press, 1979.

Belensky, Mary Field, et al. *Women's Ways of Knowing*. New York: Basic Books, 1986.

Blicksilver, Edith. *The Ethnic American Woman: Problems, Protests, Lifestyle*. Dubuque, Ia.: Kendall / Hunt Publishing, 1978.

Carlson, Kathie. *In Her Image: The Unhealed Daughter's Search for Her Mother*. Boston: Shambhala, 1990.

Chevigny, Bell Gale. "Daughters Writing: Toward a Theory of Women's Biography." *Feminist Studies* 9 (1983): 79–102.

Chodorow, Nancy. *Feminism and Psychoanalytic Theory*. New Haven: Yale University Press, 1989.

Doten, Patti. "Sharing Her Mother's Secrets." *Boston Globe*, June 21, 1991, E9–14.

Friday, Nancy. *My Mother/My Self*. New York: Delacorte Press, 1977.

Gardiner, Judith Kegan. "Mind Mother: Psychoanalysis and Feminism." In *Making a Difference: Feminist Literary Criticism*, ed. Gayle Greene and Coppélia Kahn, 113–145. New York: Methuen, 1985.

Gilligan, Carol. *In a Different Voice.* Cambridge, Mass.: Harvard University Press, 1982.

Hirsch, Marianne. *The Mother-Daughter Plot: Narrative, Psychoanalysis, Feminism.* Bloomington: Indiana University Press, 1989.

Hirsch, Marianne, and Evelyn Fox Feller. *Conflicts in Feminism.* New York: Routledge, 1990.

Kim, Elaine H. *Asian American Literature: An Introduction to the Writings and Their Social Context.* Philadelphia: Temple University Press, 1982.

Koppelman, Susan. *Between Mothers and Daughters, Stories across a Generation.* New York: Feminist Press at the City University of New York, 1985.

Maglin, Nan Bauer. "The Literature of Matrilineage." In *The Lost Tradition: Mothers and Daughters in Literature,* ed. Cathy N. Davidson and E. M. Broner, 257–267. New York: Frederick Ungar, 1980.

Marbella, Jean. "Amy Tan: Luck But Not Joy." *Baltimore Sun,* June 30, 1991, E–11.

"Mother with a Past." *Maclean's* (July 15, 1991): 47.

Reed, Evelyn. *Woman's Evolution.* New York: Pathfinder Press, 1975.

Rich, Adrienne. *Of Woman Born: Motherhood as Experience and Institution.* New York: Norton, 1976, 1986.

Rosinsky, Natalie M. "Mothers and Daughters: Another Minority Group." In *The Lost Tradition: Mothers and Daughters in Literature,* ed. Cathy N. Davidson and E. M. Broner, 281–303. New York: Frederick Ungar, 1980.

See, Carolyn. "Drowning in America, Starving in China." *Los Angeles Times Book Review,* March 12, 1989, 1, 11.

Spence, Jonathan D. *The Search for Modern China.* New York: W. W. Norton, 1990.

Tan, Amy. *The Joy Luck Club.* New York: Ivy Books, 1989.

———. *The Kitchen God's Wife.* New York: G. P. Putnam's Sons, 1991.

———. "Lost Lives of Women." *Life* (April 1991), 90-91.

Walters, Suzanna Danuta. *Lives Together/Worlds Apart: Mothers and Daughters in Popular Culture.* Berkeley: University of California Press, 1992.

Wolf, Margery, and Roxanne Witke. *Women in Chinese Society.* Stanford: Stanford University Press, 1975.

Yamada, Mitsuye. "Invisibility Is an Unnatural Disaster: Reflections of an Asian American Woman." In *This Bridge Called My Back: Writings of Radical Women of Color,* ed. Cherríe Moraga and Gloria Anzaldúa, 35–40. Latham, N.Y.: Kitchen Table/ Women of Color Press, 1982.

LINA UNALI

Americanization and Hybridization in
The Hundred Secret Senses *by Amy Tan*

At the beginning of Amy Tan's *The Hundred Secret Senses,* we observe what I wish to define as a partial or total *discharge of ethnicity* on the part of a Chinese American character. The word "*discharge*" is used in this sense to refer to the idea of the release of a *burden* of a particular kind. In this sense, the burden is connected with the psychological condition of belonging to a minority group, something which appears at times to be felt as an encumbrance, as something undesirable, as a traumatic experience. A major part of the novel is thus devoted to the reflection of the role of ethnicity in the life and choices of the narrator, as she is often forced to face this question and make decisions that have to take the question of her Chinese and American heritages into account. More specifically, the narrative will center on the character of the narrator's half-sister, Kwan, and the drama of ethnicity and identity this person will occasion. As a European professor, I find the presentation of ethnicity in this novel proves an interesting exercise in the understanding of the problems and paradigms of Asian American literature in general. In this paper, I wish to begin a discussion on the manner in which Tan presents the diverse characters in the novel which clearly invites a comparative analysis and a revelation of possible attitudes and modes of defining and living with ethnicity.

Hitting Critical Mass: A Journal of Asian American Cultural Criticisms, Volume 4, Number 1 (1996): pp. 135–144. Copyright © 1996 Lina Unali.

The narrator of *The Hundred Secret Senses* is inclined to consider herself simply *American*. But she goes on to inform readers that, like her brothers, she was born in San Francisco from one Chinese parent. After the death of his Chinese wife in 1948, her father had left for Hong Kong in search of work and, a year later, in 1949, "immigrated here and married (her) mother Louise Kenfield" (3). He died when the narrator was four. With a Chinese father and a mother probably identifiable as *Anglo*, in the writer's own terminology, the narrator feels no particular sense of either dependence or allegiance towards any specific ethnic group. Intermarriage among the descendants of immigrants of different origin has intervened to alter in a permanent way the *monoculturality* of the immigrant's situation, the non-heterogeneous ethnicity of Chinatown. What we are invited to reflect on is the presentation of a contemporary American society characterized by the welding of different cultural and biological traits, the dissipation of the original unmixed cultural features which distinguished the Chinese immigrant, the prevalence of what might be called the American way in all aspects of life—in a word, a thorough Americanization of all ethnic components. The *American way of life* prevails apparently undisturbed with its network of public services, social activities, popular habits, aspirations, brands of modernity, freeways and rush hours. The *American family* and all that implies appears to prevail as the common denominator of all experience.

Further considerations along this vein may be made with regards to Olivia, the narrator of *The Hundred Secret Senses,* and on her family. In the very first page of the novel the narrator's mother is quoted as describing in culinary jargon the mixture of races which occurred within her blood as "mixed grille" (3), and glorifying mixed marriages. A model to which she wishes to conform is Louise Rainer, who played the part of O-lan in *The Good Earth* (3): it may be noted that she prefers the idea of being an American with Asian glamour rather than Chinese with Western charm. The mention of Pearl Buck's once very popular novel, be it said incidentally, seems particularly interesting because it may be seen as the indication of a point of departure in intercontinental cultural and literary interactions. Upon receiving the Nobel Prize in 1938, Buck declared that, in her process of formation as a writer, she owed as much to the Chinese narrative tradition as she did to those of her own country.

We understand that Louise's childhood and upbringing had little to do with either the inhabitants of an American Chinatown or, directly, with China itself. This woman's married life is presented as varied, and as anybody would say, "normally American," with importance attributed to *significant others,* an often light-hearted succession of husbands and love affairs, the cessation of which is never accompanied by excesses of dramatization as occurs in traditional societies, but rather by new energy and hope. Referring to the brief marriage with her first husband, she says, in her enthusiasm, that she intermarried at a time in which it was forbidden by law, a notion that Olivia wryly observes is a lie because in reality, those laws didn't apply in California (3). What counts is Louise's enthusiasm for what she considers emancipated behavior. Both this woman's second husband and succeeding boyfriends belong to ethnic groups different from that of Olivia's father. Some of their names might be identified as originally Indian, such as Bharat Singh (98), or Iranian, as Sharam Shirazi—a man she met "at an advanced salsa dance class" (121). Also the mention of the *salsa dance* class illustrates the fact that ethnic barriers have been crossed in all directions through a kind of international cultural surfing, or better *dancing*, devoid of excessive emotional overtones. Apart from the narrator's father we are not told of any other Chinese husbands or boyfriends that Louise Kenfield might have had. We are only informed of the fact that before Sharam Shirazi, she had gone out with a Samoan (121). So the reader is led to the conclusion that her first marriage with a Chinese might have even been a mere accident. Her shifting from one love affair to the other has nothing particularly remarkable in it.

Among her most permanent partners we count an Italian, Laguni by name, in the function of the most serious of second husbands, who was once mistaken for a Mexican (8) and whose later career as former husband, although sparsely mentioned, we may follow from the first page of the novel to the last. He is sometimes referred to as Daddy Bob, and his influence on the family does leave a mark. The narrator comments that "my brothers look almost as Italian as their last name implies. Their faces are more angular than mine. Their hair has a slight curl and is a lighter shade of brown" (39). We will even find an explanation regarding the origin of the surname Laguni according to which it was "a made-up name that nuns gave to orphans" (141) in Northern Italy. Together with the Jews, the Italians are probably the most frequently mentioned minority with whom most of the characters are vaguely associated. In one passage Bob Laguni is described as having a big nose, something which would appear not particularly relevant if we were not acquainted with the fact that the Chinese have a way—among many—of speaking of foreigners with a certain amount of scorn as of people who have big noses (*ta pi ze*). Maxine Hong Kingston in *The Woman Warrior* is more explicit than Amy Tan when she writes that "an orange creature with a great nose was a barbarian from the West" (8). Furthermore, "barbarian from the West" is a common way of referring to foreigners. Familiarity with colloquial Chinese may help the reader to capture meanings which would otherwise pass unnoticed; further on, I will point out another quite interesting instance of this practice on the part of the narrator.

One of the conclusions which we may reach through a close reading of the first part of the novel, which is set in the United States (the setting of the second half is China), is that the writer refuses all ethnic seclusion and exclusion in favor of intermarriage, cultural hybridization, amalgamation and the routines of the *mainstream American family*. We might coin the neologism *desinization* and apply it to most of the characters. In Tan's narrative we even find, besides the word *hybridization*, the less felicitous *mongrelization*, the result of the crossing of different ethnicities and cultures. It is posed both as a common practice and a goal and even recommended as a "long-term answer to racism" (59).

It is interesting to note that, as with her mother, Olivia's love affairs only occur with non-Chinese Americans. Simon, first her husband and later a former husband, with certain privileges of familiarity and even affection, knows little or nothing about Chinese Americans or China before the couple's adventurous intercontinental expedition to a strangely outlandish and mysterious China. During this visit, both he and his former wife will feel and behave as foreigners, newcomers, American tourists, photographers, reporters of an alien reality—at times, almost, as visitors from another planet. In *The Hundred Secret Senses* Simon is introduced as "a perfectly balanced blend, half Hawaiian-Chinese, half *Anglo*, a fusion of different racial genes and not a dilution" (59), a notation which may even be read as a prescription. We understand that "dilution" is contrasted to "balanced blend," a more praise-worthy process which may leave all component elements recognizable and appreciable both in their singularity and in their fusion. Also, the fact that Simon is Hawaiian-Chinese and not American Chinese makes things more varied, implying all kinds of seclusion of ethnic groups in the urban village, totally disputable and carefully avoided. Simon has not much to do with the concomitants of a mother-in-law's Chinatown family, business and mental-ity. Having no Chinese American mother-in-law, as some of the characters in Amy Tan's other novels, he may, at least before his *grand tour* to China, be free from all problems arising out of complicated family relations, deep-seated secrets, engagements and funeral ceremonies, performed in strident contrast to mainstream American behavior. Moreover, his former girlfriend was the daughter of Polish Jews who changed her name from the "Elsie" given to her by her adoptive parents to the more European "Elza" (64). Later on, we are in-formed that Elza's parents had been at Auschwitz (65). She, too, is connected with Italy. She visits the Etruscan tombs scattered in the Italian territory (39) and sends postcards from the country. Italy and the Jews frequently recur in the narrative in very subtle ways. As in other American novels they may per-haps act as *discharges of ethnic tension* by means of projection and assimilation.

But how, we may ask, does the writer maintain what can be called the *status* of Chinese American character while *discharging* ethnicity? It is im-portant to discover and analyze how such an outstanding piece of fiction as *The Hundred Secret Senses* was created, what kind of intelligent device or set of devices was used in its composition, and how, after what we signaled as one of the main features of the novel—hybridization—can we explain and justify the copious reference to China in the narrative. The answer may probably be that what always appears to be a carefully structured novel, exhibits something which we would like to define as a *presiding fictional arrangement,* a most important literary contrivance; a *Chinese trick,* it might even be called, which helps to make the novel a real masterpiece laden with remarkable cultural and social implications. This *trick* consists in the projection of a "pure" ethnicity, at its utmost level of concentration, on the only character that the narrator seems to want to acknowledge it in, a real foreign national. In this case, the ethnicity is embodied specifically in a Chinese woman endowed with the peculiar traits resonant of the *personage* which, particularly in the Elizabethan drama, was termed as the *fool.* Since the first pages of the novel, the reader has to deal with what appears to be both a true Chinese female character of exceptional power and a *fool.* The character named Kwan stands for both and for many things more.

What in this novel appears as really memorable is the character of an unmixed, non-integrated, American-resistant, Chinese young woman, *imported* into the United States for purely humanitarian reasons, who always performs in ways which show her as absolutely incapable of assimilation, integration, and cultural hybridization. Far from losing her well-marked Chinese identity in favor of more modern attitudes, she is even capable of imposing her "chinoiserie," (in Olivia's eyes) or what might perhaps be termed her "profound ethos," her apparently extravagant and esoteric theories and practices, on everybody around, from her half-sister, to the whole of her father's American family, to all the people with whom she happens to have a contact both in the American environment and in the territory of China. Quoting Ann McClintock, she may be seen as the carrier of "alternative female power" (3). Kwan entertains *alternative* notions of time and knowledge. Her most more profound opinions and convictions seem to regard the underworld of yin and reincarnation which are always intermingled with China's often unfortunate relationship with the West. Her *weltenschauung* derives from a traditional way of looking at humanity, characteristic of ancient societies in general, from which life in the United States totally diverges.

Kwan's logic and understanding have their source in a culture distant in time and space. Hers is the self-reliance of those who have never seriously exposed themselves to any kind of intercultural conflict. She neither loses her individuality nor the perceptions provided by what she calls her *hundred secret senses,* by her special insights into what we are led to see as the inner workings of life, by a familiarity with the world of the dead, and also by her unique sense of humor. Her introduction to the *yin* world is very often amusing, probably another sign of human superiority. She never takes things too seriously. She jokingly says, for instance, that "Also people who miss Chinese food, they go yin world wait there. Later can be born into other person" (89). Reincarnation is dealt with at length in the novel, coming to occupy one of the central themes of Kwan's life and stories.

One certainty the reader acquires about Kwan is that she neither represents the world of acquisition, profit and wealth nor that of the subjection of women in ancient Asiatic societies. Although having nothing to do with powerful ancient matron figures, she moves beyond the dimension of inferiority. Interestingly, Kwan is sacrificed in the end of the novel in order to allow the survival of the other characters. But her presence poses the problem of why, in the economy of the book, is she so necessary?

In the formulation of the character of Kwan, the writer has developed the potentialities of one of Maxine Hong Kingston's female figures in *The Woman Warrior*. In that emblematic novel, we encounter another unforgettable narrator's aunt, Moon Orchid, another *fool* we might say, who starts to behave and speak crazily as soon as she lands at the San Francisco airport. One of her first observations about the Chinese Americans living in Chinatown is that the Americans and Chinese speak the same language. Moon Orchid may also be said to be America-resistant. But differently from her, Chinese Kwan is not a secondary character, the producer and victim of occasional states of craziness and utter maladjustment. Being an exceptional *cultural carrier*, Kwan always overflows with words, memories, considerations, producing discourse throughout the length of the novel. This may be one of the rare cases of the *fool* serving as a main character and absorbing most of the reader's attention. And never had a *fool* had such a chance of expounding fearful truths, of implicitly and explicitly criticizing, of explaining her surprising ways of perceiving reality, of *penetrating* into space and time, of moving with deftness from the present century back to the previous one, from one era to the next. While a resident of the United States, she is the exceptional *misfit*, uncomprehending and incomprehensible, expressing herself in funny broken English. But in China her talk is smooth, even eloquent. At the beginning of her American sojourn she is sent to a mental hospital only because the people around her are not accustomed to hearing the things she says, nor do they share her sensibility. But she does not care. She never feels offended. When in China, in the company of the narrator and her former husband, she turns out to be the most profound interpreter of Chinese life, and even of the historical memory of China. She is transformed into a historian, the only person who is well adjusted to both past and present, to poverty and mystery, to the ways of the living and of the dead. In the second part of the novel Kwan comes to function as a sort of medicine woman with a shaman's powers. As in the case of masters, she explains things which the others are required to understand, she opens up new and old worlds, reveals secrets. What is always clear is that having never become Chinese American while living in the United States, she will reaffirm her full and true Chinese identity when she returns to China.

The narrator, on her part, will remain and reaffirm her being American. In China, Olivia will always be the foreign photographer, the reporter, the tourist, the stranger, the outsider, the alien American woman, an American divorcee still psychologically involved with her former husband, full of resentments, fears and regrets, ever on the point of losing herself in the most exotic of adventures abroad. She turns out to be always fascinated by the exotic natural landscapes, by the acculturation daily provided by her half-sister, and by the exceptional character of the information she receives. But, we as readers, may ask why the narrator decided to embark on that adventure, and what may be the purpose of that attempt towards acculturation to Chinese ways?

Something different may perhaps be observed at this point. The Chinese territory which the narrator presents may be said to be "oriental" in the old, British Empire manner that Edward Said has highly criticized. What for the international reader was always typical of the exotic Indian landscape is here applied to China. This representation of China is that of a strangely *hyperexoticized* country, distant from civilization. In certain passages we may be reminded of Indian exoticism produced by writers such as Kipling or Forster or of ancient Chinese stories such as the *Story of Monkey* or the *Dream of the Red Chamber*, with their abundance of fabulous invention and atmosphere. Far from being depicted as a familiar country, a pacific motherland, a peaceful ancestral cradle, Amy Tan's China in this novel turns out to be, in a possible inversion of all Orientalism, the most conventional of Eastern settings. We are taken to isolated, formerly unvisited places, where are ravines with caves occupied by bats, where the wind howls eerily, where one may lose the sense of gravity, where some people may get temporarily lost while others will be lost forever.

And as all visitors of strange countries try to support their troubled souls with remembrances of what they have left at home, it may be said of them that it is as though they really psychologically never left home (see Unali 1993). The narrator is reminded of a brochure she and her husband wrote on a special effect that the wind performs in the corridors formed by the skyscrapers of Manhattan. She uses the word *Manhattanization*, which sounds similar to Americanization and hybridization. We are taken to caves which remind us of the Marabar caves in Forster's famous novel. We find all the most famous incidents of an oriental journey, including the disappearance of one of the characters as in Samuel Johnson's *Rasselas Prince of Abyssinia*, the Western prototype of all "oriental" literary adventures.

An analysis of the novel brings to light perhaps more questions than answers, and invites to a discussion of the themes we have begun to bring up. Why is that extraordinary experience in China used? Why is Simon's "sterility" healed after a sojourn in a distant country in which only one of his ancestors was born? What is the meaning of this new fertility? Perhaps a new approach is needed. Did it offer only superficial solutions to the abandonment of *overripe* "Oriental" cultures (Wong 6)? Is re-acculturation to Chinese culture felt as necessary at least from the point of view of literary creation? Is a discharge of ethnicity necessary or recommendable? Which are the ways in which it may safely occur?

My answers may differ from those of others. I agree with what may be observed in Tan's novel, which highlights a tendency towards inclusion and limitation of loss, against cultural void, in favor of the characters freely following intellectual and cultural drives, and in the direction of change. What, in my opinion, makes this and many other novels by Chinese American writers really extraordinary is what I wish to define as *progressive memory:* not simply a memory of a dead past and of dead things, not stagnation, but the presentation of the healing of a trauma rather than simply a contemplation of foreign territories. The fictional presence of Kwan aptly represents that trauma and that past, but points hopefully to the future. It is another way of revealing how a process of hybridization and Americanization may have occurred.

WORKS CITED

Buck, Pearl S. *The Chinese Novel.* London: Macmillan, 1939.

Tan, Amy. *The Hundred Secret Senses.* London: HarperCollins Publishers, 1996.

Kingston, Maxine Hong. *The Woman Warrior: Memoir of a Girlhood Among Ghosts.* London: Picador, 1977.

McClintock, Anne. *Imperial Leather: Race, Gender and Sexuality in the Colonial Context.* London: Routledge, 1995.

Unali, Lina. *Stella d'India.* Rome: Edizioni Mediterranee, 1993.

Wong, Sau-ling Cynthia. *Reading Asian American Literature: From Necessity to Extravagance.* Princeton: Princeton University Press, 1993.

PATRICIA L. HAMILTON

Feng Shui, Astrology, and the Five Elements: Traditional Chinese Belief in Amy Tan's The Joy Luck Club

A persistent thematic concern in Amy Tan's *The Joy Luck Club* is the quest for identity. Tan represents the discovery process as arduous and fraught with peril. Each of the eight main characters faces the task of defining herself in the midst of great personal loss or interpersonal conflict. Lindo Jong recalls in "The Red Candle" that her early marriage into a family that did not want her shaped her character and caused her to vow never to forget who she was. Ying-ying St. Clair's story "Waiting Between the Trees" chronicles how betrayal, loss, and displacement caused her to become a "ghost." Rose Hsu Jordan recounts her effort to regain a sense of self and assert it against her philandering husband in "Without Wood." Framing all the other stories are a pair of linked narratives by Jing-mei Woo that describe her trip to China at the behest of her Joy Luck Club "aunties." The journey encompasses Jing-mei's attempts not only to understand her mother's tragic personal history but also to come to terms with her own familial and ethnic identity. In all the stories, whether narrated by the Chinese-born mothers or their American-born daughters, assertions of self are shaped by the cultural context surrounding them. However, there is a fundamental asymmetry in the mothers' and daughters' understanding of each other's native cultures. The mothers draw on a broad experiential base for their knowledge of American patterns of thought and behavior, but the daughters have only fragmentary,

MELUS, Volume 24, Number 2 (Summer 1999): pp. 125–145. Copyright © 1999 MELUS.

second-hand knowledge of China derived from their mothers' oral histories and from proverbs, traditions, and folktales.[1] Incomplete cultural knowledge impedes understanding on both sides, but it particularly inhibits the daughters from appreciating the delicate negotiations their mothers have performed to sustain their identities across two cultures.

Language takes on a metonymic relation to culture in Tan's portrayal of the gap between the mothers and daughters in *The Joy Luck Club*. Jing-mei, recalling that she talked to her mother Suyuan in English and that her mother answered back in Chinese, concludes that they "never really understood one another": "We translated each other's meanings and I seemed to hear less than what was said, while my mother heard more" (37). What is needed for any accurate translation of meanings is not only receptiveness and language proficiency but also the ability to supply implied or missing context. The daughters' inability to understand the cultural referents behind their mothers' words is nowhere more apparent than when the mothers are trying to inculcate traditional Chinese values and beliefs in their children. The mothers inherited from their families a centuries-old spiritual framework, which, combined with rigid social constraints regarding class and gender, made the world into an ordered place for them. Personal misfortune and the effects of war have tested the women's allegiance to traditional ideas, at times challenging them to violate convention in order to survive. But the very fact of their survival is in large measure attributable to their belief that people can affect their own destinies. In the face of crisis the mothers adhere to ancient Chinese practices by which they try to manipulate fate to their advantage. Their beliefs and values are unexpectedly reinforced by the democratic social fabric and capitalist economy they encounter in their adopted country. Having immigrated from a land where women were allowed almost no personal freedom, all the Joy Luck mothers share the belief along with Suyuan Woo that "you could be anything you wanted to be in America" (132)

Ironically, the same spirit of individualism that seems so liberating to the older women makes their daughters resistant to maternal advice and criticism. Born into a culture in which a multiplicity of religious beliefs flourishes and the individual is permitted, even encouraged, to challenge tradition and authority, the younger women are reluctant to accept their mothers' values without question. Jing-mei confesses that she used to dismiss her mother's criticisms as "just more of her Chinese superstitions, beliefs that conveniently fit the circumstances" (31). Furthermore, the daughters experience themselves socially as a recognizable ethnic minority and want to eradicate the sense of "difference" they feel among their peers. They endeavor to dissociate themselves from their mothers' broken English and Chinese mannerisms,[2] and they reject as nonsense the fragments of traditional lore their mothers try to pass along to them. However, cut adrift from any spiritual moorings, the younger women are overwhelmed by the number of choices that their materialistic culture offers and are insecure about their ability to perform satisfactorily in multiple roles ranging from dutiful Chinese daughter to successful American career woman. When it dawns on Jing-mei that the aunties see that "joy and luck do not mean the same to their daughters, that to these closed American-born minds 'joy luck' is not a word, it does not exist," she realizes that there is a profound difference in how the two generations understand fate, hope, and personal responsibility. Devoid of a worldview that endows reality with unified meaning, the daughters "will bear grandchildren born without any connecting hope passed from generation to generation" (41).

Tan uses the contrast between the mothers' and daughters' beliefs and values to show the difficulties first-generation immigrants face in transmitting their native culture to their offspring. Ultimately, Tan endorses the mothers' traditional Chinese worldview because it offers the possibility of choice and action in a world where paralysis is frequently a threat. However, readers who are not specialists in Chinese cosmology share the same problematic relation to the text as the daughters do to their mothers' native culture: they cannot always accurately translate meanings where the context is implied but not stated. Bits of traditional lore crop up in nearly every story, but divorced from a broader cultural context, they are likely to be seen as mere brushstrokes of local color or authentic detail. Readers may be tempted to accept at face value the daughters' pronouncements that their mothers' beliefs are no more than superstitious nonsense. To ensure that readers do not hear less than what Tan is actually saying about the mothers' belief systems and their identities, references to Chinese cosmology in the text require explication and elaboration.

Astrology is probably the element of traditional Chinese belief that is most familiar to Westerners. According to the Chinese astrological system, a person's character is determined by the year of his or her birth. Personality traits are categorized according to a twelve-year calendrical cycle based on the Chinese zodiac. Each year of the cycle is associated with a different animal, as in "the year of the dog." According to one legend, in the sixth century B.C. Buddha invited all the animals in creation to come to him, but only twelve showed up: the Rat, Ox, Tiger, Rabbit, Dragon, Snake, Horse, Ram, Monkey, Cock, Dog, and Pig. Buddha rewarded each animal with a year bearing its personality traits (Scott). In addition to animals, years are associated with one of the Five Elements: Wood, Fire, Earth, Metal, and Water. Metal years end in zero or one on the lunar calendar; Water years end in two or three; Wood years end in four or five; Fire years end in six or seven; and Earth years end in eight or nine. Thus, depending on the year in which one is born, one might be a Fire Dragon, a Water Dragon, and so on. The entire animal-and-element cycle takes sixty years to complete.

Tan draws on astrology in *The Joy Luck Club* in order to shape character and conflict. Lindo Jong, born in 1918, is a Horse, "destined to be obstinate and frank to the point of tactlessness," according to her daughter Waverly (167). Other adjectives that describe the Horse include diligent, poised, quick, eloquent, ambitious, powerful, and ruthless (Rossbach 168). At one point or another in the four Jong narratives, Lindo manifests all of these qualities, confirming her identity as a Horse. In accordance with tradition, Lindo's first husband is selected by his birth year as being a compatible partner for her. The matchmaker in "The Red Candle" tells Lindo's mother and mother-in-law: "An earth horse for an earth sheep. This is the best marriage combination" (50). At Lindo's wedding ceremony the matchmaker reinforces her point by speaking about "birthdates and harmony and fertility" (59). In addition to determining compatibility, birth years can be used to predict personality clashes. Waverly notes of her mother Lindo, "She and I make a bad combination, because I'm a Rabbit, born in 1951, supposedly sensitive, with tendencies toward being thin-skinned and skittery at the first sign of criticism" (167). Lindo's friend Suyuan Woo, born in 1915, is also a Rabbit. No doubt the Joy Luck aunties have this in mind when they note that Suyuan "died just like a rabbit: quickly and with unfinished business left behind" (19). The friction between Horse and Rabbit mentioned by Waverly suggests why Lindo and Suyuan were not only best friends but also "arch enemies who spent a lifetime comparing their children" (37).[3]

Adherents of Chinese astrology contend that auspicious dates for important events can be calculated according to predictable fluctuations of *ch'i*, the positive life force, which is believed to vary according to the time of day, the season, and the lunar calendar. Thus, the matchmaker chooses "a lucky day, the fifteenth day of the eighth moon," for Lindo's wedding (57). Later, Lindo picks "an auspicious day, the third day of the third month," to stage her scheme to free herself from her marriage. Unlucky dates can be calculated as well. Rose Hsu Jordan recalls that her mother An-mei had a "superstition" that "children were predisposed to certain dangers on certain days, all depending on their Chinese birthdate. It was explained in a little Chinese book called *The Twenty-Six Malignant Gates*" (124). The problem for An-mei is how to translate the Chinese dates into American ones. Since the lunar calendar traditionally used in China is based on moon cycles, the number of days in a year varies. Lindo similarly faces the problem of translating dates when she wants to immigrate to San Francisco, but her Peking friend assures her that May 11, 1918 is the equivalent of her birthdate, "three months after the Chinese lunar new year" (258). Accuracy on this point would allow Lindo to calculate auspicious dates according to the Gregorian calendar used in the West. In a broader sense, Lindo's desire for exactness is a strategy for preserving her identity in a new culture.

Tan uses astrology to greatest effect in the life history of Ying-ying St. Clair, who does not fare at all well in the matter of translated dates or preserved identity. Ying-ying is a Tiger, born in 1914, "a very bad year to be born, a very good year to be a Tiger" (248). Tigers are typically passionate, courageous, charismatic, independent, and active, but they can also be undisciplined, vain, rash, and disrespectful (Jackson; Rossbach 167). Tiger traits are central to Ying-ying's character. As a teenager she is wild, stubborn, and vain. As a four-year-old in "The Moon Lady," she loves to run and shout, and she possesses a "restless nature" (72). According to Ruth Youngblood, "As youngsters [Tigers] are difficult to control, and if unchecked, can dominate their parents completely." Ying-ying's Amah tries to tame her into conformity to traditional Chinese gender roles: "Haven't I taught you—that it is wrong to think of your own needs? A girl can never ask, only listen" (70). Ying-ying's mother, too, admonishes her to curb her natural tendencies: "A boy can run and chase dragonflies, because that is his nature. But a girl should stand still" (72). By yielding to the social constraints placed on her gender and "standing perfectly still," Ying-ying discovers her shadow, the dark side of her nature that she learns to wield after her first husband leaves her.

Long before adulthood, however, Ying-ying experiences a trauma regarding her identity. Stripped of her bloodied Tiger outfit at the Moon Festival, she tumbles into Tai Lake and is separated from her family for several hours. Ying-ying's physical experience of being lost parallels her family's suppression of her active nature and curtailment of her freedom. Whenever she wears her hair loose, for example, her mother warns her that she will become like "the lady ghosts at the bottom of the lake" whose undone hair shows "their everlasting despair" (243). After Ying-ying falls into the lake, her braid becomes "unfurled," and as she drifts along in the fishing boat that picks her up, she fears that she is "lost forever" (79). When one of the fishermen surmises that she is a beggar girl, she thinks: "Maybe this was true. I had turned into a beggar girl, lost without my family" (80). Later she watches the Moon Lady telling her tragic story in a shadow play staged for the festival: "I understood her grief. In one small moment, we had both lost the world, and there was no way to get it back" (81). Even though Ying-ying is eventually rescued, she is afraid that her being found by her family is an illusion, "a wish granted that could not be trusted" (82). The temporary loss of her sense of security and belonging is so disturbing that her perception of her identity is forever altered. She is never able to believe her family has found "the same girl" (82).

Ying-ying's traumatic childhood experience prefigures the profound emotional loss and identity confusion she experiences as an adult. Looking back on her experience at the Moon Festival, she reflects that "it has happened many times in my life. The same innocence, trust, and restlessness, the wonder, fear, and loneliness. How I lost myself" (83). As an adult she is stripped of her Tiger nature once again when she immigrates to America. Since there is no immigration category for "the Chinese wife of a Caucasian citizen," Ying-ying is declared a "Displaced Person" (104). Then her husband proudly renames her "Betty St. Clair" without seeming to realize he is effacing her Chinese identity in doing so. The final stroke is his mistakenly writing the wrong year of birth on her immigration papers. As Ying-ying's daughter Lena puts it, "With the sweep of a pen, my mother lost her name and became a Dragon instead of a Tiger" (104). Unwittingly, Clifford St. Clair erases all signs of Ying-ying's former identity and, more importantly, symbolically denies her Tiger nature.

The belief that personality and character are determined by zodiacal influences imposes predictable and regular patterns onto what might otherwise seem random and arbitrary, thereby minimizing uncertainty and anxiety. In this light, the anchor for identity that astrology offers Ying-ying is beneficial. Over the years she comes to understand what her mother once explained about her Tiger nature: "She told me why a tiger is gold and black. It has two ways. The gold side leaps with its fierce heart. The black side stands still with cunning, hiding its gold between trees, seeing and not being seen, waiting patiently for things to come" (248). The certainty that these qualities are her birthright eventually guides Ying-ying into renouncing her habitual passivity. The catalyst for this decision is her perception that her daughter Lena needs to have her own "tiger spirit" cut loose. She wants Lena to develop fierceness and cunning so that she will not become a "ghost" like her mother or remain trapped in a marriage to a selfish man who undermines her worth. Ying-ying expects resistance from Lena, but because of the strength of her belief system, she is confident about the outcome: "She will fight me, because this is the nature of two tigers. But I will win and give her my spirit, because this the way a mother loves her daughter" (252). Tan uses the Chinese zodiacal Tiger as a potent emblem of the way culturally determined beliefs and expectations shape personal identity.

Another element of Chinese cosmology that Tan employs in *The Joy Luck Club* is *wu-hsing*, or the Five Elements, mentioned above in conjunction with astrology.[4] The theory of the Five Elements was developed by Tsou Yen about 325 B.C. As Holmes Welch notes, Tsou Yen "believed that the physical processes of the universe were due to the interaction of the five elements of earth, wood, metal, fire, and water" (96). According to eminent French sinologist Henri Maspero, theories such as the Five Elements, the Three Powers, and *yin* and *yang* all sought to "explain how the world proceeded all by itself through the play of transcendental, impersonal forces alone, without any intervention by one or more conscious wills" (55). Derek Walters specifies how the Five Elements are considered to "stimulate and shape all natural and human activity":

The Wood Element symbolizes all life, femininity, creativity, and organic material; Fire is the Element of energy and intelligence; Earth, the Element of stability, endurance and the earth itself; Metal, in addition to its material sense, also encompasses competitiveness, business acumen, and masculinity; while Water is the Element of all that flows—oil and alcohol as well as water itself, consequently also symbolizing transport and communication. (29)

The Elements correspond to certain organs of the body and physical ailments as well as to particular geometric shapes. An extended array of correspondences includes seasons, directions, numbers, colors, tastes, and smells (Lam 32). In the physical landscape the Elements can be placed in a productive order, in which each Element will generate and stimulate the one succeeding it, or a destructive order, in which Elements in close proximity are considered harmful. To avoid negative effects, a "controlling" Element can mediate between two elements positioned in their destructive order.

Suyuan Woo subscribes to a traditional application of the theory of the Five Elements in what Jing-mei calls her mother's "own version of organic chemistry" (31). As Ben Xu has observed, the Five Elements are "the mystical ingredients that determine every person's character flaw according to one's birth hour." *Wu-hsing* theory posits that "none of us has all the five character elements perfectly balanced, and therefore, every one of us is by nature flawed" (Xu 12). Accordingly, Suyuan believes that too much Fire causes a bad temper while too much Water makes someone flow in too many directions. Too little Wood results in one bending "too quickly to listen to other people's ideas, unable to stand on [one's] own" (31). Jing-mei, who does not understand how Suyuan's pronouncements tie to a larger belief system, associates her mother's theories with displeasure and criticism: "Something was always missing. Something always needed improving. Something was not in balance. This one or that had too much of one element, not enough of another."

According to *wu-hsing* theory, flaws can be amended and balance attained by symbolically adding the element a person lacks. Xu points out that "the 'rose' in Rose Hsu Jordan's name, for example, is supposed to add wood to her character" (12). Conversely, elements can be removed to create an imbalance. When Lindo Jong does not become pregnant in her first marriage, the matchmaker tells her mother-in-law: "A woman can have sons only if she is deficient in one of the elements. Your daughter-in-law was born with enough wood, fire, water, and earth, and she was deficient in metal, which was a good sign. But when she was married, you loaded her down with gold bracelets and decorations and now she has all the elements, including metal. She's too balanced to have babies" (63). Although Lindo knows that the direct cause of her failure to become pregnant is not her having too much metal but rather her husband's refusal to sleep with her, she accepts the matchmaker's reasoning about the Five Elements. Years later Lindo comments: "See the gold metal I can now wear. I gave birth to your brothers and then your father gave me these two bracelets. Then I had you [Waverly]" (66). The implication here is that the gender of Lindo's male children corresponds to her natural deficiency in Metal. Adding Metal back into her composition through the bracelets causes her next child to be female.

More significantly, Lindo, like Suyuan, believes that the Elements affect character traits: "After the gold was removed from my body, I felt lighter, more free. They say this is what happens if you lack metal. You begin to think as an independent person" (63). Tan suggests that Lindo's natural "imbalance" is key to her true identity, the self that she promises never to forget. As a girl she had determined to honor the marriage contract made by her parents, even if it meant sacrificing her sense of identity. But on her wedding day she wonders "why [her] destiny had been decided, why [she] should have an unhappy life so someone else could have a happy one" (58). Once Lindo's gold and jewelry are repossessed by her mother-in-law to help her become fertile, Lindo begins to plot her escape from the marriage. Her feeling lighter and more free without Metal corresponds to her assertion of her true identity. Destiny is not so narrowly determined that she cannot use her natural qualities as a Horse—quickness, eloquence, ruthlessness—to free herself from her false position in the marriage. Because Lindo has secretly blown out the matchmaker's red candle on her wedding night, she has in effect rewritten her fate without breaking her parents' promise. Rather than restricting her identity, her belief in astrology and *wu-hsing* gives her a secure base from which to express it.

As with astrology, Tan uses the theory of the Five Elements not only for characterization but also for the development of conflict in *The Joy Luck Club*. "Without Wood" deals with the disastrous effects of Rose Hsu Jordan's not having enough Wood in her personality, at least according to her mother An-mei's diagnosis. An-mei herself has inspired "a lifelong stream of criticism" from Suyuan Woo, apparently for bending too easily to other's ideas, the flaw of those who lack Wood (30–31). An-mei admits to having listened to too many people when she was young. She almost succumbed to her family's urgings to forget her mother, and later she was nearly seduced by the pearl necklace offered to her by her mother's rival. Experience has shown An-mei that people try to influence others for selfish reasons. To protect her daughter from opportunists, An-mei tells Rose that she must listen to her mother if she wants to grow "strong and straight." If she listens to others she will grow "crooked and weak." But Rose comments, "By the time she told me this, it was too late. I had already begun to bend" (191).

Rose attributes her compliant nature to the strict disciplinary measures of an elementary school teacher and to the influences of American culture:

"Chinese people had Chinese opinions. American people had American opinions. And in almost every case, the American version was much better" (191). Not until much later does she realize that in the "American version" there are "too many choices," so that it is "easy to get confused and pick the wrong thing." Rose, emotionally paralyzed at fourteen by a sense that she is responsible for the death of her four-year-old brother, grows into an adult who not only listens to others but lets them take responsibility for her so that she may avoid committing another fatal error. Her husband, Ted, makes all the decisions in their marriage until a mistake of his own brings on a malpractice suit and shakes his self-confidence. When Ted abruptly demands a divorce, Rose's lack of Wood manifests itself: "I had been talking to too many people, my friends, everybody it seems, except Ted" (188). She tells a "different story" about the situation to Waverly, Lena, and her psychiatrist, each of whom offers a different response. An-mei chides Rose for not wanting to discuss Ted with her, but Rose is reluctant to do so because she fears that An-mei will tell her she must preserve her marriage, even though there is "absolutely nothing left to save" (117).

Contrary to Rose's expectations, her mother is less concerned that she stay married than that she deal with her inability to make decisions. An-mei wants her daughter to address the personality deficiencies that are the cause of her circumstances. Believing that Rose needs to assert her identity by acting on her own behalf, An-mei admonishes: "You must think for yourself, what you must do. If someone tells you, then you are not trying" (130). An-mei's advice is embedded in the broader context of her Chinese world-view. When Rose complains that she has no hope, and thus no reason to keep trying to save her marriage, An-mei responds: "This is not hope. Not reason. This is your fate. This is your life, what you must do" (130). An-mei believes life is determined by fate, by immutable celestial forces. But like Lindo Jong, she sees fate as having a participatory element. Earthly matters admit the influence of human agency. Consequently, her admonition to Rose is focused on what Rose must "do."

As a child Rose observes that both her parents believe in their *nengkan*, the ability to do anything they put their minds to. This belief has not only brought them to America but has "enabled them to have seven children and buy a house in the Sunset district with very little money" (121). Rose notes that by taking into account all the dangers described in *The Twenty-Six Malignant Gates*, An-mei has "absolute faith she could prevent every one of them" (124).

However, An-mei's optimism about her ability to manipulate fate is challenged when her youngest child, Bing, drowns. An-mei does everything she can to recover her son, but she realizes she cannot "use faith to change fate" (130). Tragedy teaches her that forethought is not the same thing as control. Still, she wedges a white Bible—one in which Bing's name is only lightly pencilled in under "Deaths"—beneath a short table leg as a symbolic act, "a way for her to correct the imbalances of life" (116). Although An-mei accepts that her power over fate is limited, she continues to believe that she can positively influence her circumstances. The idea of balance she is enacting is a fundamental element of *yin-yang* philosophy, according to which two complementary forces "govern the universe and make up all aspects of life and matter" (Rossbach 21). As Johndennis Govert notes, "to remove an obstruction to your happiness, regain a state of health, or create a more harmonious household, *yin* and *yang* must be in balance" (7). An-mei may use a Bible to balance the kitchen table, but she rejects the Christian beliefs it represents. Rose notes that her mother loses "her faith in God" after Bing's death (116). The belief system that governs An-mei's actions is Chinese, an amalgam of luck, house gods, ancestors, and all the elements in balance, "the right amount of wind and water" (122).

In contrast to her mother, Rose lacks a means by which she can delineate or systematize her notions of causality and responsibility. Moreover, she eschews any real sense that people can have control over their circumstances. As a teenager Rose is appalled to discover she is powerless to prevent little Bing from falling into the ocean as she watches. Later Rose thinks "that maybe it was fate all along, that faith was just an illusion that somehow you're in control. I found out the most *I* could have was hope, and with that I was not denying any possibility, good or bad" (121). When her husband Ted wants a divorce, Rose compares the shock she receives to having the wind knocked out of her: "And after you pick yourself up, you realize you can't trust anybody to save you—not your husband, not your mother, not God. So what can you do to stop yourself from tilting and falling all over again?" (121). Added to her sense of helplessness is the suspicion that whenever she is forced into making a decision, she is walking through a minefield: "I never believed there was ever any one right answer, yet there were many wrong ones" (120). Rose's lack of any sort of a belief system fosters a crippling passivity characterized by a fear that whatever she chooses will turn out badly. Her inability to make even the smallest decisions becomes the equivalent, in Ted's mind at least, of her having no identity.

Ironically, once Rose realizes that Ted has taken away all her choices, she begins to fight back. She seizes on the metaphor An-mei has used to explain the lack of Wood in her personality: "If you bend to listen to other people, you will grow crooked and weak. You will fall to the ground with the first strong wind. And then you will be like a weed, growing wild in any direction, running along the ground until someone pulls you out and throws you away" (191). Inspired by the weeds in her own neglected garden that cannot be dislodged from the masonry without "pulling the whole building down" (195), Rose demands that Ted let her keep their house. She explains,

"You can't just pull me out of your life and throw me away" (196). For the first time in her life she stands up for what she wants without soliciting the advice of others. After her assertion of selfhood, Rose dreams that her "beaming" mother has planted weeds that are "running wild in every direction" in her planter boxes (196). This image, which suggests that An-mei has finally accepted Rose's nature instead of trying to change her, is consistent with the desires the Joy Luck daughters share regarding their mothers. Each one struggles to feel loved for who she is. In part the younger women's insecurity stems from having a different set of cultural values than their mothers. The older women try to encourage their daughters but do not always know how to cope with the cultural gap that separates them. As Lindo states: "I wanted my children to have the best combination: American circumstances and Chinese character. How could I know these two things do not mix?" (254). But Rose's dream-image submerges the fact that Rose has finally acted on her mother's admonition to speak up for herself. An-mei has guessed that Ted is engaged in "monkey business" with another woman, and it is at the moment when Rose realizes her mother is right that she begins to move intuitively toward standing up for her own needs and desires. As it turns out, An-mei is correct in wanting Rose to listen to her mother rather than to her bored and sleepy-eyed psychiatrist in order to be "strong and straight." Ultimately, An-mei's belief that one's fate involves making choices instead of being paralyzed as a victim is validated by Rose's assertion of her identity.

A third element of traditional belief in *The Joy Luck Club* is *feng shui*, or geomancy. The most opaque yet potentially the most important aspect of Chinese cosmology to Tan's exploration of identity, *feng shui* plays a pivotal role in Lena St. Clair's story "The Voice from the Wall," which chronicles her mother Ying-ying's gradual psychological breakdown and withdrawal from life. Ten-year-old Lena, having no knowledge of her mother's past, becomes convinced that her mother is crazy as she listens to Ying-ying rave after the death of her infant son. Even before Ying-ying loses her baby, however, her behavior appears to be erratic and compulsive. When the family moves to a new apartment, Ying-ying arranges and rearranges the furniture in an effort to put things in balance. Although Lena senses her mother is disturbed, she dismisses Ying-ying's explanations as "Chinese nonsense" (108). What Lena does not understand is that her mother is practicing the ancient Chinese art of *feng shui* (pronounced "fung shway"). Translated literally as "wind" and "water," *feng shui* is alluded to only once in the book as An-mei Hsu's balance of "the right amount of wind and water" (122). Although the term "*feng shui*" is never used overtly in conjunction with Ying-ying St. Clair, its tenets are fundamental to her worldview.

Stephen Skinner defines *feng shui* as "the art of living in harmony with the land, and deriving the greatest benefit, peace and prosperity from being in the right place at the right time" (4). The precepts of *feng shui* were system-atized by two different schools in China over a thousand years ago. The Form School, or intuitive approach, was developed by Yang Yün-Sung (c. 840–888 A.D.) and flourished in Kiangsi and Anhui provinces. Practitioners focus on the visible form of the landscape, especially the shapes of mountains and the direction of watercourses. The Compass School, or analytical approach, was developed by Wang Chih in the Sung dynasty (960 A.D.) and spread throughout Fukien and Chekiang provinces as well as Hong Kong and Tai-wan (Skinner 26). The analytic approach is concerned with directional ori-entation in conjunction with Chinese astrology. As Walters notes, Compass School scholars have traditionally "placed greater emphasis on the impor-tance of precise mathematical calculations, and compiled elaborate formulae and schematic diagrams" (10). Geomancers using this approach employ an elaborate compass called the *lo p'an,* astrological charts and horoscopes, nu-merological data, and special rulers.

According to Susan Hornik, the beliefs encompassed by *feng shui* date back 3,000 years to the first practice of selecting auspicious sites for burial tombs in order to "bring good fortune to heirs" (73). As Skinner explains, "Ancestors are linked with the site of their tombs. As they also have a direct effect on the lives of their descendants, it follows logically that if their tombs are located favourably on the site of a strong concentration of earth energy or *ch'i,* not only will they be happy but they will also derive the power to aid their descendants, from the accumulated *ch'i* of the site" (11). By the Han dy-nasty (206 B.C.), the use of *feng shui* was extended to the selection of dwell-ings for the living (Hornik 73). The basic idea is to attract and channel *ch'i,* or beneficial energy, and "accumulate it without allowing it to go stagnant" (Skinner 21). Since *ch'i* encourages growth and prosperity, a wise person will consider how to manipulate it to best effect through *feng shui,* the study of placement with respect to both natural and man-made environments. As a form of geomancy *feng shui* is "the exact complement of astrology, which is divination by signs in the Heavens" (Walters 12), but it is based on a differ-ent presupposition. Whereas the course of the stars and planets is fixed, the earthly environment can be altered by human intervention through *feng shui.* The practice of *feng shui* offers yet another variation of the belief that people have the power to affect their destiny.

Thus Ying-ying St. Clair's seemingly idiosyncratic actions and their non-sensical explanations in "The Voice from the Wall" are grounded in a coherent system of beliefs and practices concerned with balancing the environment. Since Ying-ying feels her surroundings are out of balance, she does everything she can to correct them. For instance, she moves "a large round mirror from the wall facing the front door to a wall by the sofa" (108). *Ch'i* is believed to en-ter a dwelling through the front door, but a mirror hung opposite the entrance may deflect it back outside again. Mirrors require careful placement so as to encourage the flow of *ch'i* around a room. Furniture, too, must be positioned according to guidelines that allow beneficial currents of *ch'i* to circulate without stagnating. Through properly placed furniture "every opportunity can be taken to correct whatever defects may exist, and to enhance whatever positive qualities there are" (Walters 46). Hence, Ying-ying rearranges the sofa, chairs, and end tables, seeking the best possible grouping. Even a "Chinese scroll of goldfish" is moved. When large-scale changes are impossible, *feng shui* practitioners frequently turn to symbolic solutions. Strategically placed aquariums containing goldfish are often prescribed for structural problems that cannot be altered, in part because aquariums symbolically bring all Five Elements together into balance (Collins 21). In Ying-ying's case, a picture is substituted for live goldfish, which represent life and growth.

Ying-ying's attempt to balance the living room follows a *feng shui* tradition: "If beneficial *ch'i* are lacking from the heart of the house, the family will soon drift apart" (Walters 42). But Ying-ying is also compensating for negative environmental and structural features that she cannot modify. The apartment in the new neighborhood is built on a steep hill, a poor site, she explains, because "a bad wind from the top blows all your strength back down the hill. So you can never get ahead. You are always rolling backward" (109). In ancient China the ideal location for a building was in the shelter of hills that would protect it from bitter northerly winds. However, a house at the very base of a sloping road would be vulnerable to torrential rains, mudslides, and crashes caused by runaway carts. Ying-ying's concern with psychic rather than physical danger is consistent with modern applications of *feng shui*, but her notion of an ill wind sweeping downhill is based on traditional lore. In addition to the unfortunate location of the apartment building, its lobby is musty, a sign that it does not favor the circulation of *ch'i*. The door to the St. Clairs' apartment is narrow, "like a neck that has been strangled" (109), further restricting the entrance of beneficial energy. Moreover, as Ying-ying tells Lena, the kitchen faces the toilet room, "so all your worth is flushed away." According to the Bagua map derived from the *I Ching*, the ancient Chinese book of divination, every building and every room has eight positions that correspond to various aspects of life: wealth and prosperity; fame and reputation; love and marriage; creativity and children; helpful people and travel; career; knowledge and self-cultivation; and health and family (Collins 61–62). Heidi Swillinger explains the problem of a dwelling where the bathroom is located in the wealth area: "Because the bathroom is a place where water enters and leaves, and because water is a symbol of wealth, residents in such a home might find that money tends to symbolically go down the drain or be flushed away."[5] Even if the St. Clairs' bathroom is not actually in the wealth area, *feng shui* guidelines dictate that it should not be placed next to the kitchen in order to avoid a clash between two of the symbolic Elements, Fire and Water.

In light of the bad *feng shui* of the apartment, Ying-ying's unhappiness with it is logical. Once she finishes altering the living room, she rearranges Lena's bedroom. The immediate effect of the new configuration is that "the nighttime life" of Lena's imagination changes (109). With her bed against the wall, she begins to listen to the private world of the family next door and to use what she hears as a basis for comparison with her own family. It is not clear whether Lena's bed has been moved to the "children" area of the room, which would enhance her *ch'i*, but certainly the new position is more in keeping with the principles of good *feng shui,* which indicate a bed should be placed against a wall, not a window (Walters 53).From this standpoint, Ying-ying's inauspicious positioning of the crib against the window appears to be inconsistent with her other efforts. Lena notes, "My mother began to bump into things, into table edges as if she forgot her stomach contained a baby, as if she were headed for trouble instead" (109). Since according to *feng shui* theory protruding corners are threatening (Collins 47), Ying-ying's peculiar neglect toward sharp table edges along with her placement of the crib suggest that her efforts at generating good *feng shui* are suspended with regard to her unborn baby.

When the baby dies at birth, apparently from a severe case of hydrocephalus and spina bifida, Ying-ying blames herself: "My fault, my fault. I knew this before it happened. I did nothing to prevent it" (111). To Western ears her self-accusation sounds odd, for birth defects such as spina bifida are congenital, and nothing Ying-ying could have done would have prevented the inevitable. However, her Eastern world-view dictates that fate can be manipulated in order to bring about good effects and to ward off bad ones. Ying-ying believes that her violation of good *feng shui* principles constitutes negligence, causing the baby to die. She is accusing herself not merely of passivity but of deliberate complicity with a malignant fate.

The burden of guilt Ying-ying carries over an abortion from her first marriage is the root of her disturbed mental state during her pregnancy. Her bumping into table edges may even be a form of self-punishment. In any case, whether she has subconsciously tried to harm the fetus or has merely failed to fend off disaster through the use of *feng shui,* in blaming herself for the baby's death Ying-ying is clearly wrestling with her responsibility for the death of her first son. In her mind the two events are connected: "I knew he [the baby] could see everything inside me. How I had given no thought to killing my other son! How I had given no thought to having this baby" (112). Instead of finding any resolution after the baby dies, Ying-ying becomes increasingly withdrawn. She cries unaccountably in the middle of cooking dinner and frequently retreats to her bed to "rest."

The presence of *feng shui* in the story suggests that however displaced, demoralized, and severely depressed Ying-ying may be, she is not "crazy," as

Lena fears. Ying-ying's compulsion to rearrange furniture does not presage a psychotic break with reality but rather signals that, transplanted to a foreign country where she must function according to new rules and expectations, Ying-ying relies on familiar practices such as *feng shui* and astrology to interpret and order the world around her, especially when that world is in crisis. Lena, of course, is locked into a ten-year-old's perspective and an American frame of reference. She shares Jing-mei Woo's problem of being able to understand her mother's Chinese words but not their meanings. Whereas Clifford St. Clair's usual practice of "putting words" in his wife's mouth stems from his knowing "only a few canned Chinese expressions" (106), Lena's faulty translation of her mother's distracted speech after the baby dies reflects a lack of sufficient personal and cultural knowledge to make sense of Ying-ying's references to guilt.

Ying-ying's story, "Waiting Between the Trees," traces the origins of her decline to a much earlier time. At sixteen Ying-ying is married to a man who impregnates her, then abandons her for an opera singer. Out of grief and anger, she induces an abortion. However, after this defiant act she loses her strength, becoming "like the ladies of the lake" her mother had warned her about, floating like "a dead leaf on the water" (248–49). Unfortunately, Ying-ying's Tiger characteristic of "waiting patiently for things to come" (248) turns from easy acceptance of whatever is offered into listlessness and acquiescence over a period of fourteen years: "I became pale, ill, and more thin. I let myself become a wounded animal" (251). She confesses, "I willingly gave up my *chi*, the spirit that caused me so much pain" (251). Giving up her vital energy is tantamount to giving up her identity. By the time Clifford St. Clair takes her to America, she has already become "an unseen spirit," with no trace of her former passion and energy. Nevertheless, she retains her ability to see things before they happen. Her prescience stems from her trust in portents, which constitutes another facet of her belief system. When she is young, a flower that falls from its stalk tells her she will marry her first husband. Later on, Clifford St. Clair's appearance in her life is a sign that her "black side" will soon go away. Her husband's death signals that she can marry St. Clair.

Years later, Ying-ying can still see portents of the future. She knows Lena's is "a house that will break into pieces" (243). Ying-ying also continues to think in terms of *feng shui*. She complains that the guest room in Lena's house has sloping walls, a fact which implies the presence of sharp angles that can harbor *sha*, malignant energy signifying death and decay. With walls that close in like a coffin, the room is no place to put a baby, Ying-ying observes. But it is not until Ying-ying sees her daughter's unhappy marriage that she accepts responsibility for the fact that Lena has no *ch'i* and determines to regain her own fierce spirit in order to pass it on to her daughter. Ying-ying knows she must face the pain of her past and communicate it to her daughter so as to supply Lena with the personal and cultural knowledge of her mother's life that she has always lacked. By recounting her life's pain, Ying-ying will in essence reconstruct her lost identity. To set things in motion, she decides to topple the spindly-legged marble table in the guest room so that Lena will come to see what is wrong. In this instance Ying-ying manipulates her environment in a literal as well as a symbolic sense, drawing on her traditional Chinese worldview once more in order to effect the best outcome for her daughter's life.

Unlike her mother, Lena has no consistent belief system of her own. She inherits Ying-ying's ability to see bad things before they happen but does not possess the power to anticipate good things, which suggests that Lena has merely internalized "the unspoken terrors" that plague Ying-ying (103). According to Philip Langdon, "second- or third-generation Chinese-Americans are much less likely to embrace *feng shui* than are those who were born in Asia" (148). Not only is Lena a second-generation Chinese-American, she is half Caucasian, which makes her Chinese heritage even more remote. Nonetheless, Lena is profoundly affected by Ying-ying's way of perceiving the world. As a child Lena is obsessed with knowing the worst possible thing that can happen, but unlike her mother, she has no sense of being able to manipulate fate. Thus, she is terrified when she cannot stop what she supposes to be the nightly "killing" of the girl next door, which she hears through her bedroom wall. Only after Lena realizes that she has been wrong about the neighbor family does she find ways to change the "bad things" in her mind.

Lena's muddled notions of causality and responsibility persist into adulthood. In "Rice Husband," she still views herself as guilty for the death of Arnold Reisman, a former neighbor boy, because she "let one thing result from another" (152). She believes there is a relation between her not having cleaned her plate at meals when she was young and Arnold's development of a rare and fatal complication of measles. She wants to dismiss the link as ridiculous, but she is plagued by doubt because she has no philosophical or religious scheme by which to interpret events and establish parameters for her personal responsibility: "The thought that I could have caused Arnold's death is not so ridiculous. Perhaps he was destined to be my husband. Because I think to myself, even today, how can the world in all its chaos come up with so many coincidences, so many similarities and exact opposites?" (154). Whereas Ying-ying's belief system affords her a sense of certainty about how the world operates, Lena's lack of such a system leaves her in confusion.

It is Lena's uncertainty about causality together with her failure to take purposive action that leads Ying-ying to believe her daughter has no *ch'i*. Lena tells herself, "When I want something to happen or not happen—I begin to look at all events and all things as relevant, an opportunity to take or avoid" (152). But Ying-ying challenges her, asking why, if Lena knew the marble table was going to fall down, she did not stop it. By analogy she is asking Lena why she does not resolve to save her marriage. Lena muses, "And it's such a simple question" (165). It is unclear whether Lena has already decided not to rescue the marriage or whether she is simply confused about her capacity to act on her own behalf. But the fact that Lena cannot answer her mother's question quietly privileges Ying-ying's perspective on the situation, much as An-mei's viewpoint of Rose's predicament is validated in "Without Wood."

Marina Heung has pointed out that among works which focus on mother-daughter relations, *The Joy Luck Club* is "remarkable for foregrounding the voices of mothers as well as of daughters" (599). However, Tan goes further than "foregrounding" the mothers; she subtly endorses their worldview at strategic points in the text. Whereas Rose, Lena, and Jing-mei are paralyzed and unable to move forward in their relationships and careers and Waverly is haunted by a lingering fear of her mother's disapproval, Suyuan, Lindo, An-mei, and even Ying-ying demonstrate a resilient belief in their power to act despite having suffered the ravages of war and the painful loss of parents, spouses, and children. Out of the vast range of Chinese religious, philosophical, and folkloric beliefs, many of which stress self-effacement and passivity, Tan focuses on practices that allow her characters to make adjustments to their destinies and thereby preserve and perpetuate their identities. Suyuan Woo is most striking in this regard. She goes outside of conventional Chinese beliefs to make up her own means of dealing with fate. Suyuan invents "Joy Luck," whereby she and her friends in Kweilin "choose [their] own happiness" at their weekly mah jong parties instead of passively waiting for their own deaths (25). Joy Luck for them consists of forgetting past wrongs, avoiding bad thoughts, feasting, laughing, playing games, telling stories, and most importantly, hoping to be lucky. The ritualistic set of attitudes and actions that Suyuan and her friends observe keep them from succumbing to despair. When the war is over, Suyuan holds on to the main tenet of her belief system—that "hope was our only joy"—by refusing to assume a passive role in the aftermath of tragedy. She never gives up hope that by persistence she may be able to locate the infant daughters she left in China. When Suyuan says to Jing-mei, "You don't even know little percent of me!" (27), she is referring to the complex interplay among the events of her life, her native culture and language, and her exercise of her mind and will. These things constitute an identity that Jing-mei has only an elusive and fragmentary knowledge of.

The references in *The Joy Luck Club* to traditional beliefs and practices such as astrology, *wu-hsing*, and *feng shui* emphasize the distance between the Chinese mothers and their American-born daughters. Tan hints through the stories of Lindo and Waverly Jong that a degree of reconciliation and understanding is attainable between mothers and daughters, and she indicates through Jing-mei Woo's journey that cultural gaps can be narrowed. In fact, Jing-mei Woo starts "becoming Chinese" as soon as she crosses the border into China (267). But overall, Tan's portrayal of first-generation immigrants attempting to transmit their native culture to their offspring is full of situations where "meanings" are untranslatable. The breakdown in communication between mothers and daughters is poignantly encapsulated in "American Translation," the vignette that introduces the third group of stories in the book. A mother tells her daughter not to put a mirror at the foot of her bed: "'All your marriage happiness will bounce back and turn the opposite way'" (147). Walters notes that mirrors are "regarded as symbols of a long and happy marriage" but also that "care has to be taken that they are not so placed that they are likely to alarm the soul of a sleeper when it rises for nocturnal wanderings" (55). According to *feng shui* principles, a mirror "acts as a constant energy reflector and will be sending [a] stream of intensified power into the space over and around [the] bed, day and night. It will be a perpetual cause of disturbance" during sleep (Lam 105). The daughter in the vignette is "irritated that her mother s[ees] bad omens in everything. She had heard these warnings all her life." Lacking an understanding of the cosmological system to which her mother's omens belong, the daughter simply views them as evidence that her mother has a negative outlook on life.

When the woman offers a second mirror to hang above the headboard of the bed in order to remedy the problem, she is seeking to properly channel the flow of *ch'i* around the room. The mother comments, "this mirror see that mirror—*haule!*—multiply your peach-blossom luck." The daughter, however, does not understand her mother's allusion to peach-blossom luck, which "refers to those who are particularly attractive to the opposite sex" (Rossbach 48). By way of explanation, the mother, "mischief in her eyes," has her daughter look in the mirror to see her future grandchild. She is acting in accordance to the ancient Chinese belief that the "mysterious power of reflection" of mirrors, which reveal "a parallel world beyond the surface," is magical (Walters 55). The daughter, unfortunately, can only grasp literal meanings: "The daughter looked—and *haule!* There it was: her own reflection looking back at her." The mother is incapable of translating her worldview into "perfect American English," so the daughter's comprehension remains flawed, partial, incomplete. Whether or not she apprehends, from her literal reflection, that she herself is the symbol of her mother's own peach-blossom luck is ambiguous. In the same way, the uneasy relations between the older and younger women in *The Joy Luck Club* suggest that the daughters understand only dimly, if at all, that they are the long-cherished expression of their mothers' Joy Luck.

NOTES

1. For a discussion of existential unrepeatability and the role of memory in *The Joy Luck Club*, see Ben Xu, "Memory and the Ethnic Self: Reading Amy Tan's *The Joy Luck Club*," *MELUS* 19.1 (1994): 3–18. An interesting treatment of language, storytelling, and maternal subjectivity in Tan's novel can be found in Marina Heung, "Daughter-Text / Mother-Text: Matrilineage in Amy Tan's *Joy Luck Club*," *Feminist Studies* 19.3 (1993): 597–616.

2. Jing-mei Woo thinks her mother's "telltale Chinese behaviors" are expressly intended to embarrass her, including Suyuan's predilection for yellow, pink, and bright orange (143, 267). When Jing-mei arrives in China, she notices "little children wearing pink and yellow, red and peach," the only spots of bright color amidst drab grays and olive greens (271). Tan seems to suggest through this detail that Suyuan's color preferences reflect not only her personal taste but Chinese patterns and traditions. According to Sarah Rossbach, yellow stands for power, pink represents "love and pure feelings," and orange suggests "happiness and power" (46–47). In this light, Lindo Jong's criticism of Suyuan's red sweater in "Best Quality" is ironic since it is Lindo who provides evidence that red is regarded by the Chinese as an auspicious color connoting "happiness, warmth or fire, strength, and fame" (Rossbach 45). In "The Red Candle" Lindo mentions not only her mother's jade necklace and her mother-in-law's pillars, tables, and chairs but also her own wedding banners, palanquin, dress, scarf, special eggs, and marriage candle as being red.

3. Jing-mei Woo, born in the same year as Waverly (37), is a Metal Rabbit, and like Waverly, she exhibits a "Rabbit-like" sensitivity to criticism, especially when it comes from her mother.

4. The Chinese system of astrology has Buddhist origins, while the theory of the Five Elements derives from Taoist thought. Holmes Welch observes that "there was little distinction—and the most intimate connections—between early Buddhism and Taoism" (119).

5. Similar reasoning obtains in "Rice Husband" when Ying-ying tells Lena that a bank will have all its money drained away after a plumbing and bathroom fixtures store opens across the street from it (149). Lena comments that "one month later, an officer of the bank was arrested for embezzlement."

WORKS CITED

Collins, Terah Kathryn. *The Western Guide to Feng Shui*. Carlsbad, CA: Hay House, 1996.

Govert, Johndennis. *Feng Shui: Art and Harmony of Place*. Phoenix: Daikakuji, 1993.

Heung, Marina. "Daughter-Text / Mother-Text: Matrilineage in Amy Tan's *Joy Luck Club*." *Feminist Studies* 19.3 (1993): 597–616.

Hornik, Susan. "How to Get that Extra Edge on Health and Wealth." *Smithsonian* Aug. 1993: 70–75.

Jackson, Dallas. "Chinese Astrology." *Los Angeles Times* 20 Feb. 1991, Orange County ed.: E2. *News*. Online. Lexis-Nexis. 15 Mar. 1997.

Lam, Kam Chuen. *Feng Shui Handbook*. New York: Henry Holt, 1996.

Langdon, Philip. "Lucky Houses." *Atlantic* Nov. 1991: 146+.

Maspero, Henri. *Taoism and Chinese Religion*. Trans. Frank A. Kierman, Jr. Amherst: University of Massachusetts Press, 1981.

Rossbach, Sarah. *Living Color: Master Lin Yun's Guide to Feng Shui and the Art of Color*. New York: Kodansha, 1994.

Scott, Ann. "Chinese New Year: The Year of the Tiger." *United Press International* 5 Feb. 1986, International sec. *News*. Online. Lexis-Nexis. 15 Mar. 1997.

Skinner, Stephen. *The Living Earth Manual of Feng-Shui*. London: Routledge, 1982.

Swillinger, Heidi. "Feng Shui: A Blueprint for Balance." *San Francisco Chronicle* 8 Sept. 1993: Z1. *News*. Online. Lexis-Nexis. 15 Mar. 1997.

Tan, Amy. *The Joy Luck Club*. New York: G.P. Putnam, 1989.

Walters, Derek. *Feng Shui: The Chinese Art of Designing a Harmonious Environment*. New York: Simon & Schuster, 1988.

Welch, Holmes. *Taoism: The Parting of the Way*. Revised ed. Boston: Beacon, 1966.

Xu, Ben. "Memory and the Ethnic Self: Reading Amy Tan's *The Joy Luck Club*." *MELUS* 19.1 (1994): 3–18.

Youngblood, Ruth. "Baby-Poor Singapore Looks to Dragon for Help." *Los Angeles Times* 29 Nov. 1987, sec. 1: 41. *News*. Online. Lexis-Nexis. 15 Mar. 1997.

YUAN YUAN

The Semiotics of China Narratives in the Con/texts of Kingston and Tan

"How 'Chinese' is *The Woman Warrior?*" Sau-ling Cynthia Wong asks in her essay "Kingston's Handling of Traditional Chinese Sources" (27). The native-ness of ethnic American literature is a complex issue that deserves serious consideration and intelligent discussion. I have noticed that to date it is not the nativeness of our ethnic narratives that has escaped critical attention but the narrative reconfiguration of nativeness in literary representation. That is to say, the whole issue of nativeness in literary texts requires careful examination in the context of cultural differences and in relation to subject positions. In this essay, I explore the theoretical implications of that "native" issue by inquiring into the semiotics of "China experiences" in terms of "China narratives" within the contexts of Maxine Hong Kingston's *The Woman Warrior* and *China Men* and Amy Tan's *The Joy Luck Club* and *The Kitchen God's Wife*.

The "China experiences" presented by Kingston and Tan emerge as narratives of recollection—which means that in their novels they have reconstructed various narratives of experiences in China against the background of American society and within the context of American culture. Their China narratives emerge in the "other" cultural context informed by a complex process of translation, translocation, and transfiguration of the original experiences in China. In fact, China experiences are generally transfigured into "China

Critique: Studies in Contemporary Fiction, Volume 40, Number 3 (Spring 1999): pp. 292–303. Copyright © 1999 Heldref Publications and the Helen Dwight Erid Educational Foundation.

141

narratives" only after they have lost their reference to China; thus they are related more to the present American situation than to their original context in Chinese society. The present American context provides meaning and determines the content of the China narrative. Only under such circumstances as loss of origin can China experiences emerge as a China narrative—a text reconfigured within other contexts. "China narrative," therefore, differs from China experiences and signifies a specific kind of self-reflexive discourse that is reinscribed within another cultural context to serve specific purposes: self-affirmation or self-negation, remembrance or repression. Eventually, in the novels of both Kingston and Tan, China as a geographical location is transliterated into a semiotic space of recollection; China as personal experiences is translated into a cultural repository for reproduction; and, as a text, China is reconfigured into a variety of discourses: myth, legend, history, fantasy, films, and talk-stories.

The China narrative in both Kingston and Tan serves as an undercurrent but central text that structures the present relationship between mothers and daughters because of the specific position it occupies in their lives. Therefore, the cross-cultural hermeneutics of China is conducted within that domestic space, between two generations in general and between the Chinese mothers and their American-born daughters in specific. As products of different cultures and histories, mothers and daughters abide by different cultural values and possess different modes of interpretation. In fact, they speak entirely different languages whenever they talk about China. "My mother and I spoke two different languages, which we did," Jing-Mei Woo says in *The Joy Luck Club*, "I talked to her in English, she answered back in Chinese" (23). The bilingual conversation turns into a game of translation; and in that translation, meaning is transfigured, displaced, and occasionally, lost. As Jing-Mei Woo says: "We translated each other's meanings and I seemed to hear less than what was said, while my mother heard more" (27).

Both mothers and daughters constantly have to re-evaluate their respective China narratives that are grounded in entirely different cultural contexts, with different historical references and subject positions. For the mothers, China narratives inform a process of recollection (history or loss of it) whereas for the daughters, who have never been there, China narratives become a text of culture. In other words, China experiences as semiotic texts are reconstituted through a choice of two modes of discourse: history or culture. Eventually, China becomes a semiotic site where culture and identity are fought over, negotiated, displaced, and transformed. Instead of being a static ontological presence of a unitary category, China becomes a hermeneutic space for articulating identity and difference, a process that governs the cultural and historical reconstitution of the subjects.

Mother's Loss Narrative: Recollecting and Repositioning

In Tan's *The Joy Luck Club* and *The Kitchen God's Wife,* loss functions as the dominant metaphor for the mothers' China narratives and the central code to decipher their existence. Each mother's story of her China experiences eventually develops into a semiotics of loss. Hence, moving to America means to them loss of identity and the reality of existence—being reduced to ghosts in alien territory. Even though mothers and daughters interpret China with different codes and from different positions, they are all over-shadowed by a prevalent sense of loss. To quote Ying-Ying St. Clair in *The Joy Luck Club:* "We are lost" (64). The daughters seem to be lost between cultures whereas the mothers appear to have lost everything. Later in the same novel, Jing-Mei Woo says of her mother: "She had come here in 1949 after losing everything in China: her mother and father, her family home, her first husband, and two daughters, twin baby girls" (141).

In *The Kitchen God's Wife,* the China narrative is based on Winnie's painful experiences in China. In fact, the pain and suffering that are central to Winnie's recollection invite repression rather than recall. Her China narrative is subject to constant postponement and erasure to conceal the unspeakable experience and repressed memory. As Winnie says: "Now I can forget my tragedies, put all my secrets behind a door that will never be opened, never seen by American eyes" (81). Memory for Winnie embodies loss or pain; her China narrative essentially requires concealing instead of unfolding. Remembering inevitably entails pain and, eventually, desire for repression transforms into a necessity of repression. Winnie's experience of China is transfigured into a discourse of repression and her recollection of China experiences is translated into a loss narrative.

Within the American context, mothers' recollections of China experiences demonstrate more loss of memory than recall of the past. Forgetting, paradoxically, becomes the key to recollection. In *The Joy Luck Club,* Jing-Mei Woo complained of her mother's repeating the same Kweilin story to her in various versions. She said: "I never thought my mother's Kweilin story was anything but a Chinese fairy tale. The endings always changed. [. . .] The story always grew and grew" (12). In *The Kitchen God's Wife,* Winnie, failing to recall her mother, provides us contradictory versions of her mother's image, believing her to be pretty, strong, educated, and coming from a good family. But later she admits that "maybe my mother was not pretty at all, and I only want to believe that she was" (120). That is why Winnie keeps repeating to herself: "Now I no longer know which story is the truth, what was the real reason why she left. They are all the same, all true, all false. So much pain in everyone. I tried to tell myself, the past is gone, nothing to be done, just forget it. That's what I tried to believe" (130). Because of memory loss, there is simply no prior text present to initiate recollection in the first place. Hence, recollection radically alters itself in a creative process. "Loss narrative" becomes the central feature that characterizes the mother's China narrative. In short, China lies at an absolute distance from present remembrance, irretrievably lost beyond recall, made present only through a narrative that invites forgetting instead of remembering.

Ironically, China, lost or otherwise, functions as the locus that defines the mother's sense of reality. American experience, on the other hand, only characterizes her marginal existence and alien position. Mothers tend to have their home and identity centered elsewhere—in China. In *The Woman Warrior*, Kingston writes: "Whenever my parents said 'home,' they suspended America" (99). Life in America, for her mother, is too disappointing to be real. The China experience, at least, can be transliterated into a body of ideas and vocabulary that gives her a unique sense of reality and presence. Hence, China narrative, which is both defining and defined by the mothers, becomes an imaginary text of China with a displaced mentality and exile consciousness, conditioned by both repression and nostalgia.

Therefore, recollection reveals a process of negotiation with the past, constantly translating and revising the past into a narrative that grants reality to present situations. In a displaced context, the mothers have constructed China narratives for themselves and for each other. One mother, Helen, who figures in *The Kitchen God's Wife*, comments on the past to Winnie: "She and I have changed the past many times, for many reasons. And sometimes she changes it for me and does not even know what she has done" (69). It is indeed ironical that at the end of the novel both of them are compelled to tell truths that they no longer remember, and continue to recount them only after they have lost memory. That is why Pearl, Winnie's daughter, complains: "I am laughing, confused, caught in endless circles of lies" (524). The past, paradoxically, is lost in the process of recollection.

China is, so to speak, a "mother land," a repository of history with haunting memories and extraordinary experiences—a repository for reproduction. The mothers constantly revise their China narratives in terms of their present conscious needs and unconscious desires, asserting them in the context of American culture for self-empowerment.

China experiences, or the past in general, even though forgotten to a certain extent, have always been reconstituted by the mothers into narratives that carry out special missions: to control the fate of their "American-made" daughters. Thus, the loss narrative is transformed into an authoritative discourse. In *The Kitchen God's Wife*, Winnie says to her daughter: "In China back then, you were always responsible to somebody else. It's not like here in the United States—freedom, independence, individual thinking, do what you want, disobey your mother. No such thing" (162). In that case, she has transformed an absent text into a powerful narrative for the purpose of domination. She is using China narrative to establish and reinforce her present authoritative position in America.

Lacking ontological stability and lost in constant recollection, China narrative is fabricated and manipulated in various forms. Ironically, the power of China narrative resides precisely in its "loss of reality." In *The Joy Luck Club*, the mothers, who assume the absolute authority on China, transform China into a semiotic space wherein they can continue to exercise the power that they have lost in the other context—the Chinese society. Collectively, they have constructed another cultural territory, actually an extra-territory within American society. Eventually, China experiences in the mothers' narratives are translated into a mode of discourse, a style of domineering, a tongue for control, and a gesture for having authority over the daughters' lives and molding their subjectivity. In that case, China becomes less a geographical location than a cultural extra-territory that the mothers have created in order to construct the subjectivity of their "American-made" daughters.

China experiences become a repository of potential power from which the mothers draw excessive narratives that support their exercise of control. Sometimes, they turn their China experiences into a disciplinary lesson that reinforces restrictive cultural values (Brave Orchid's story of the dead aunt); sometimes they translate their personal memory into a fantastic tale with powerful seduction (Suyun Woo's Kweilin story); and sometimes they transliterate China into a secret text from which daughters are excluded and only the mothers themselves have direct access (Winnie's story). As Lena St. Clair in *The Joy Luck Club* says: "When we were alone, my mother would speak in Chinese, saying things my father could not possibly imagine. I could understand the words perfectly, but not the meaning" (109). That is, only the mother possesses the key to decode the meaning of China narrative. Hence, Chinese, a secondary language to the daughters, becomes the mothers' primary discourse strategy to manipulate their daughters. The mother in *The Joy Luck Club*, reminds her daughter that because *The Book of Twenty-Six Malignant Gates* is written in Chinese "You cannot understand it. That is why you must listen to me" (87). Daughters, on the other hand, resist their mothers' China narratives by reminding them that their stories are out of context because, as Jing-Mei Woo asserts, "this wasn't China" (152).

In *The Joy Luck Club*, Jing-Mei Woo says of her mother: "Over the years, she told me the same story, except for the ending, which grew darker, casting long shadows into her life, and eventually into mine" (7). Apparently, the mothers are using their narrative powers to construct their daughter's identities, as if to continue the "remarkable" China experiences and to extend Chinese history and culture through their daughters' existence. Although transfigured into authoritative discourses that dominate the daughters, China narratives are in effect grounded on the semiotics of loss. Hence, China narrative is but a ghost story: an absence resides at the very center of the text that determines its ultimate signification.

Daughter's Translation: Father's Silence and Mother's Talk-Stories

In Kingston's *The Woman Warrior* and *China Men,* the daughter's experience of China as a semiotic space is structured in a polarized position between her mother's complicated talk-stories on the one hand and her father's impenetrable silence on the other. That intertextual relationship between presence and absence determines the semiotic function of China narrative for Kingston. She has to decode her father's silence and her mother's speech, a process involving more than simply attempting to locate her mother in *The Woman Warrior* or seeking her father in *China Men.* In both novels, Kingston finds herself by negotiating her relation to her parents, to a semiotic space defined as China narrative, and to the Chinese culture.

Kingston's *China Men* is composed against the background of her father's silence. Kingston writes to her father: "You say with the few words and the silences: No Stories. No past. No China" (14). For her, China is a country she made up within an American context, along with her history and her family mythology in *China Men.* She dramatizes her ancestors' memory in a grand style by transliterating the "oral history" into a cultural epic.

As a daughter, Kingston feels both compelled and obligated to speak on her father's behalf, to decipher his silence of the past, to hear his China narrative. Kingston writes: "You kept up a silence for weeks and months. We invented the terrible things you were thinking" (14). Similarly, she invents a China narrative for her father and writes into American history the contributions of the Chinese laborers by reconstructing a legendary text for the "people without history." Kingston writes: "I'll tell you what I suppose from your silences and few words, and you can tell me that I'm mistaken. You just have to speak up with the real stories if I've got you wrong" (15). She wants to know "the Chinese stories"; she wants to go back to China to see her "ancestral village"; and she wants to meet "the people with fabulous imaginations." Kingston writes: "I want to discern what it is that makes people go West and turn into Americans. I want to compare China, a country I made up, with what country is really out there" (87).

Thus, in *China Men,* Kingston formulates father land or China in an imaginary space wherein she offered various versions of her father's origin. However, root-seeking always ends up elsewhere. She has to speak truth by creating legends, making a legendary history for her father, reconstructing a China narrative for him in his absence. In short, she creates myth out of silence and legend out of absence. The China narrative in *China Men* is entirely created by the daughter who dedicates a history to the father.

In *The Woman Warrior*, Kingston is asking: "Chinese-American, when you try to understand what things in you are Chinese, how do you separate what is peculiar to childhood, to poverty, insanities, one family, your mother who marked your growing with stories, from what is Chinese? What is Chinese tradition and what is the movies?" (5–6). Kingston confronts the perplexing issue of China narrative within the context of her mother's talk-stories and her own fantasy, forbidden tales and her own dreams. About "a great power, my mother talking-story" (19–20), Kingston observes: "I couldn't tell where the stories left off and the dreams began, her voice and the voice of the heroines in my sleep" (19). "Real" China seems to lie at the distance of the inevitable loss.

China narrative in *The Woman Warrior* is, first of all, translated from personal experience into a narrative of recollection. Her mother's China narrative, based on the recollection of her direct experience of China, is transfigured into a "historical" text. That text is further reconfigured in the American context into her daughter's bicultural text that consists of recapitulation of her mother's talk-stories. Evidently, Kingston's knowledge of China is based on her (m)other's narratives and, eventually, Kingston's China narrative becomes a translation of a translation—in fact, a cultural reconstruction. That accounts for Kingston's reconstitution of her dead aunt's sexual identity according to Western code and American culture. In that instance, historical and cultural reconstruction of China is divided along bicultural views and bifocal perspectives.

The daughter's China narrative, based on the primary text of her mother's recollection, by way of myths, legends, talk-stories, informs the operation of a second order linguistic system. That is to say, the daughter's cognition of China seems always to be structured, mediated, and overdetermined by the semiotics of the (m)other tongue that serves as the first order symbolic signification. Therefore, the daughter's reconstruction of the China narrative is based on the signifier of the first linguistic order (her mother's narrative) that assumes a historical reference to China. The mother's narrative functions as the ultimate interpretative frame of the daughter's reconceptualization of China, actually, the absolute horizon of the daughter's cognition of China. Put more precisely, her mother's China narrative itself constitutes the absolute horizon of Kingston's recognition of China experiences.

In her mother's talk-stories, China resides in a domain of memory based on personal experience of social reality. For Kingston, China is a territory of dream and fantasy. In her dreams, she has revenged her family, fantasizing her China experiences as compensation for "disappointing American life." But, of course, those China experiences are entirely based on the tales of and from China by way of her mother's talk-stories that have already been translated in a new cultural context and with reference to their American experiences. In

"Boundaries of the Self: Gender, Culture, Fiction," Roberta Rubenstein points out: "Their offspring born in America inherit this split between cultures without ever having seen their ancestral land, except imaginatively, through their elders' eyes" (166). And this is exactly Kingston's vision—filtered through her mother's eyes and her mother's tongue. Her mother's stories radically shape her vision of China and the Chinese—the place of her ancestral origin. From that displaced context and removed memory, she invents a China in a fantasy space, reconfiguring the ghost of China to inscribe her present subject position. Growing up in America, she has to distinguish what is supernatural and what is real, what are ghosts and what are people.

Individuation from the (M)other: Ghost or Otherwise

In Kingston's *The Woman Warrior*, the boundaries between self and the other are not clearly defined until the daughter confronts and reinscribes the past, the China experience. The daughter is forced to negotiate her position between conflicting sets of discourses: of family, ethnicity, culture, history, and nationality. To reach a reconciliation, Kingston must come to terms with herself in relation to the historical situation she inherits from her mother and then must choose her own subject position. She has to extricate herself from the identity fabricated by her mother's China narrative and assert her own subject position by reconfiguring bicultural discourse.

Both mother and daughter develop multiple discourses to encode their existences. Both attempt to carve out a personal space in an alien culture that has limited and marginalized their lives, their heritage, and their language. Kingston, however, living on the edges of two communities, has to choose between her mother's home culture and the alien culture. *The Woman Warrior* dramatizes Kingston's growing up among contradictions and confusions between cultures and languages. Wendy Ho remarks: "Like her mother, the daughter negotiates the preservation and the subversion of aspects of traditional Chinese culture against the pressures of the mainstream of Western society. However, she is in a precarious position of her own: she is not Chinese enough for her mother, father and ethnic community and not American-feminine enough to find a home among the white 'ghost'" (227).

Kingston writes: "They would not tell us children because we had been born among ghosts, were taught by ghosts, and were ourselves ghost-like. They called us a kind of ghosts" (183). Ghost represents tension and problems of language and cultural system. However, Kingston refuses to be reduced to simply a ghost in "an alien culture." Instead, she positively re-creates a unique identity separate from the ghost position. In *The Woman Warrior*, she has to confront all the ghosts from China with which her mother has haunted her childhood: Fa Mu Lan, her mother, Brave Orchid, the dead aunt, Moon

Orchid, and herself. She has to transcend that ghost terrain to enter "a ghost-free country."

Ghosts in her narrative possess multiple perspectives. They are signifiers with diverse meanings, especially when configured in a multicultural context. In "*The Woman Warrior* as a Search for Ghost," Gayle K. Fujita Sato remarks: "'Ghosts' define two antithetical worlds that threaten the narrator's sense of a unified self. How is she to articulate her own location, which is 'Chinese American,' when history, tradition, and family have formulated 'China' and 'America' as reciprocally alien territories?" (139).

Kingston refuses to live a hyphenated experience and remain a victim to her mother's China narrative. She manages to go beyond her mother's talk-stories by subverting the designated position defined by her mother's past experience. Self-production depends upon both preservation and progression. On the one hand, by resisting her mother's codification of her identity as a Chinese slave-girl, Kingston disrupts the "slave narrative"; on the other hand, she rejects the ex-centric self, discontent with being reduced to an unnamable ghost in an alien culture. In effect, Kingston transcends the boundaries of both cultures by rewriting the China narrative once authorized by her mother and rejecting the displaced China experience in American society.

In *The Woman Warrior*, Kingston is refuting not simply China, Chinese culture, or the (m)other tongue, but the "Chineseness" that is specifically produced under the new historical and cultural circumstances. She resists the victimization of stereotypification by establishing a separate identity aside from the "Chineseness" forged in America—the artificial construct of the Chinese that diminishes her status and delimits her power. Therefore, her separation from the mother signifies the process of individuation from both mother's land and mother's tongue and results in her finding her own reality and space in existence and creating her own language and authority. Kingston is determined that she has to "leave home to see the world logically." She says: "I continue to sort out what's just my childhood, just my imagination, just my family, just the village, just movies, just living.[. . .] Soon I want to go to China and find out who's lying[. . .]" (205).

Translating the In-Between Position: Re-creation

Each ethnic group constructs a unique self-image that reflects its response to the impact of the dominant culture. Their reactions vary according to their different positions, to the social environments, and to the dominant value systems. The self that emerges can be defensive, aiming to preserve the original cultural values and keeping its alienation and marginality. Or the self can be extensive, losing marginality by mediating between two cultures. Thus, multicultural environments force each ethnic group to balance a duality and negotiate the distance.

In *The Woman Warrior*, Kingston is both part of and apart from the two separate worlds; she positions herself across languages and across cultures. The double perspective of the home culture and the other culture can be both disabling and enabling, delimiting and empowering. I would argue that the self, instead of dangling as a double-alienated outsider, can succeed in bridging the two cultures and merging the duality.

The in-between situation, I believe, does not necessarily inform a split duality of inherent contradiction. It signifies not so much a fissure as a bridge that both divides and connects. Kingston acknowledges the influence of both cultures that exist not as an antithesis that excludes each other but as an integration that combines both. She is at home in this duality. She does not want to build a wall that divides but to create a bridge that connects.

For instance, Kingston does not simply question the traditional mythology of China but also incorporates it into her writing. Thus she revives part, the useful part, of the mythology instead of repressing it. Kingston appropriates Fa Mu Lan by configuring it into a new cultural context. Thus it emerges as a paradox: She uses the power of Chinese mythology to reinforce her American identity, thereby transcending the customary ways of defining the self and defying the village mentality of Chinatown. In this case, ethnicity no longer hampers her ways of thinking but enriches her imagination, which is feasting on diverse traditions and cultures.

I would argue that this in-between position, instead of producing a "feeling of being between worlds, totally at home nowhere" (Ling, *Between Worlds* 105), is not inherently a negative one. It can be positively employed. Kingston's novels demonstrate the phenomenon of multicultural texts. In *The Woman Warrior*, Kingston says: "I learned to make my mind large, as the universe is large, so that there is room for paradoxes" (29). That is why Kingston asks her mother: "Does it make sense to you that if we're no longer attached to one piece of land, we belong to the planet?" (107). Evidently, she creates a paradoxical self in *The Woman Warrior* that reflects the diversity of American culture.

I entirely agree with what Amy Ling says in *Between Worlds: Woman Writers of Chinese Ancestry* about the second generation immigrant experiences:

> The very condition [of the between-world] itself carries both negative and positive charges. On the one hand, being between worlds can be interpreted to mean occupying the space or gulf between two banks; one is thus in a state of suspension, accepted by neither side and therefore truly belonging nowhere. [. . .] On the other hand, viewed from a different perspective, being between worlds may be considered as having footholds on both banks and therefore belonging to two worlds at once. One does

not have less; one has more [. . .], the person between worlds is
in the indispensable position of being a bridge. (177)

Kingston's use of China narrative transcends its original contexts. Her
translocation of Chinese mythology signifies cultural replacement and re-
position that help her form a distinctive identity of her own. She creates her
own mythology within the myth of Fa Mu Lan. That paradoxical borrowing emerges as a border issue of bridging instead of separating. She has to
separate herself from her ancestral village and its traditions and enter the
complex multicultural reality of her American experiences. Paradoxically,
her fantasy of China has saved her from a totally depressing fate in America.
The Chinese mythology functions as a semiotic empowerment in the process of identity formation.

   Moreover, what is the American identity if not paradoxical? Historically, American identity has always been defined in relation to the other: other
places, other cultures, and other times. That double perspective is a uniquely
American phenomenon. In fact, Kingston's perplexity over identity touches
on an issue essential to American culture. Hence, her search for identity reveals those complex cultural transactions: her American identity is reinforced
by Chinese mythology that, even though somewhat relegated to the "other"
category, nevertheless functions as the ideological basis of her self construction. She is not simply repeating what has been taught to her, but is adapting
Chinese mythology to her present situation with an imaginative creativity.
Still, as Sau-Ling Cynthia Wong allows: "Whether her alterations to traditional material constitute creative adaptation or willful exploitation, realistic
reflection or second-generation cultural disorientation or irresponsible per-
version of a precious heritage, is a question teachers must work through with
their students" (35).

   Robert G. Lee also agrees that "for Kingston, myths, necessarily rebuilt,
have a strategic value in helping to analyze contemporary events. She recognizes that the power of myth resides in its capacity to be recontextualized and
inscribed with new meanings" (59). Apparently, the new historical circumstances may actually require that Kingston refabricate the mythical texture
of her narrative. She herself argues in her essay "Cultural Mis-Readings by
American Reviewers" that the Chinese mythology in *The Woman Warrior* is
"but one transformed by America" (57). She reminds us again of what many
people fail to recognize: that the "Chinese myths have been transmuted by
America" (58). She observes in her "Personal Statement" that myths and
lives maintain a dialogic interrelation and "the myths transform lives and are
themselves changed" (24). "Sinologists have criticized me for not knowing
myths and for distorting them.[. . .] They don't understand that myths have
to change, be useful or be forgotten. Like the people who carry them across

oceans, the myths become American. The Myths I write are new, American" (24). Instead of being controlled by Chinese mythology, Kingston rewrites it to create her own American myth.

In "'Emerging Canons' of Asian American Literature and Art," Amy Ling asks: "Must the multicultural writer/artist be totally and exclusively answerable to his or her ethnic community, be the spokesperson of that community, tell the community's stories and tell them accurately? Or can she or he claim the right to express an individual vision and personal concerns, and to modify the myths and legends of a group to his or her own artistic purpose?" (195–196). I believe that that question involves the issue of subject position for both Kingston and Tan. That is, who is writing, a Chinese or an American?

Writing, for Kingston and Tan, means a process of confrontation, discovery, and creation of their cultural identities. Both present themselves as American novelists of Chinese descent, resisting the hyphenated experience embodied by the so-called "mestiza consciousness." Accordingly, their novels represent American people and contribute to American literature. Therefore, their writings mark a transition from the position of separation and alienation to that of accommodation and re-position, initiating a positive self-invention instead of a denial of ethnic origin. Apparently, they go beyond mere justification of ethnic identity but are related to the issue of re-creation and re-placement. The creative negotiation between self and the other can effectively reinforce the ethnic subject—the assertion of the repressed subject within a multicultural context.

Both Kingston and Tan write to reconstitute the American experience through the strategy of difference, highlighting the importance of difference within American cultures by challenging the status quo of American identity. Both argue for participating in cultural construction instead of remaining in a stereotypical position as temporary sojourners—alienated and displaced personalities. I believe that gesture challenges the very constitution of the Americanness of American culture and identity.

In an interview with Paula Rabinowitz, Kingston remarked: "Actually, I think my books are much more American than they are Chinese. I felt that I was building, creating, myself and these people as American people, to make everyone realize that they are American people.[. . .] Also, I am creating part of American literature, and I was very aware of doing that, of adding to American literature" (177–178). In "Cultural Mis-Readings by American Reviewers," she reasserts her position as an American writer: "I am an American. I am an American writer, who, like other American writers, wants to write the great American novel. *The Woman Warrior* is an American book" (57–58). Interestingly enough, the issue of China narrative in the novels of Kingston and Tan ends up somewhere in American literature.

Works Cited

Ho, Wendy. "Mother/Daughter Writing and the Politics of Race and Sex in Maxine Hong Kingston's *The Woman Warrior.*" Hune, 225–238.

Hune, Shirley, Hyung-Cha Kim, Stephen S. Fugita, Amy Ling, eds. *Asian Americans: Comparative and Global Perspectives.* Pullman: Washington State University Press, 1991.

Kingston, Maxine Hong. *China Men.* New York: Knopf, 1980.

———. "Cultural Mis-Readings by American Reviewers." *Asian and Western Writers in Dialogue: New Cultural Identities.* Ed. Guy Amirthanayagam. London: Macmillan, 1982. 55–64.

———. "Interviewing Maxine Hong Kingston with Paula Rabinowitz." *Michigan Quarterly Review.* 26 (Winter 1987): 177–187.

———. "Personal Statement" *Lira,* 223–225.

———. *The Woman Warrior: Memoirs of a Girlhood among Ghosts.* New York: Random, 1975.

Lee, Robert G. "*The Woman Warrior* as an Inversion in Asian American Historiography." Lim, 52–63.

Lim, Shirley Geok-Lin, ed. *Approaches to Teaching Kingston's* The Woman Warrior. New York: MLA, 1991.

Ling, Amy. *Between Worlds: Woman Writers of Chinese Ancestry.* New York: Pergamon, 1990.

———. "'Emerging Canons' of Asian American Literature and Art." Hune, 191–198.

Rubenstein, Roberta. *Boundaries of the Self: Gender, Culture, Fiction.* Chicago: University of Illinois Press, 1987.

Sato. Gayle K. Fujita. "*The Woman Warrior* as a Search for Ghosts." Lim, 138–147.

Tan, Amy. *The Joy Luck Club.* New York: Ballantine, 1989.

———. *The Kitchen God's Wife.* New York: Ballantine, 1991.

Wong, Sau-Ling Cynthia. "Kingston's Handling of Traditional Chinese Sources." *Lira,* 26–36.

SHENG-MEI MA

"Chinese and Dogs" in Amy Tan's
The Hundred Secret Senses:
Ethnicizing the Primitive à la New Age

New Age

Marianna Torgovnick's Gone Primitive: Savage Intellects, Modern Lives (1990) takes the pulse of the contemporary world in such a way that it sheds light on Amy Tan:

> [A]n essential fact of urban life in the last decades of the twentieth century: its polyglot, syncretic nature, its hodgepodge of the indigenous and imported, the native and the foreign. In the deflationary era of postmodernism, the primitive often frankly loses any particular identity and even its sense of being "out there"; it merges into a generalized, marketable thing—a grab-bag primitive in which urban and rural, modern and traditional Africa and South America and Asia and the Middle East merge into a common locale called the third world which exports garments and accessories, music, ideologies, and styles for Western, and especially urban Western, consumption. (37)

MELUS, Volume 26, Number 1 (Spring 2001): pp. 29–44. Copyright © 2001 MELUS.

Reified and atomized in economies of advanced technology, the "Western" self feels drained, in need of recharging or healing in a spiritual sense, for which purpose the "primitive" third-world cultures are deployed. Simultaneously marked by its bestial savagery and spiritual transcendence, the primitive other is made to coalesce the physical with the metaphysical. In *The Hundred Secret Senses* (1995), imbued with such an ethos, the ethnic other's faculties of sight, hearing, taste, smell, and touch, as well as the capacity to feel, are intensified by fusions with animal senses and instincts in order to, paradoxically, invoke the hidden, essentialist, and extra-sensory human soul. Tan's version of primitivism views rationality as an obstacle to the union of the body and the mind. To make sense of the chaotic, damaged modern life, Tan routinely bypasses reason and descends to basic sensations, which, however, never take leave of the realm of nonsense entirely. Into this strange equation, Amy Tan interjects a third variable: ethnicity. Writing in the post-civil rights era, influenced by the multicultural milieu of the United States, Tan realigns the animalistic and the spiritual with the ethnic. The Chinese ancestry of her protagonists in *Secret* allows them to access the magical realm à la New Age, to be reborn as whole and wholesome human beings.

Tan's ethnicizing of the primitive contributes significantly to her success among white, middle-class, "mainstream" readers living in the climate of the New Age. As Torgovnick remarks in *Primitive Passions* (1997), "the New Age seems to be everywhere but continues to elude definition" (172). Resembling its hotbed of late capitalism, the New Age remains barely perceptible because of its omnivorous appetite of absorbing and commodifying alien cultural elements. That the New Age escapes precise definition should not, however, discourage us from contextualizing a writer like Amy Tan in the New Age. Indeed, it is only through such a close reading of specific cultural practices that one comes to discern what has alarmingly been naturalized as a mode of life.

In consonance with the consumerist social reality, Tan features San Francisco yuppies with New Age preoccupations with the self. Tan's breezy style is at its best as she depicts the protagonists, the Bishops, "busy" with their advertising business. Furthermore, the precise real estate lingoes of the Bishops during house-hunting make possible the reader's identification with the protagonists through the shared frustrations of an urban lifestyle. Interior decoration proves to be Olivia Bishop's forte as well. She expertly deciphers the layers of paint she removes from the wall of her newly purchased co-op: "a yuppie skin of Chardonnay-colored latex . . . followed by flaky crusts of the preceding decades—eighties money green, seventies psychedelic orange, sixties hippie black, fifties baby pastels" (119). Olivia is the homeowner of, so to speak, the social history of the United States, a history which constructs the American identity.

With respect to the multicultural nature of this capitalist society, the mixed-blood Bishops embody the cultural hybridization of a minority like

Asian Americans. Tan's fascination with interracial characters predates *Secret*, for instance, Lena St. Clair in *The Joy Luck Club* (1989), and Jimmy Louie and his granddaughters, Tessa and Cleo, in *The Kitchen God's Wife* (1991). In *Secret*, the multiracial lineage crystallized in Olivia's search for a proper last name in the eve of her divorce. She does not wish to revert back to her stepfather's name of Laguni, a fabricated Italian name for orphans. Nor does she want "Yee," the name and identity Olivia's father usurps in order to come to the U.S. "Bishop" is a name she intends to rid herself of but retains in the end. The ethnic impulse, nevertheless, is preserved as she names her new-born baby "Li" after her late half-sister Kwan. Arguably, one can read in this obsessive whitening of characters throughout Tan's career a reflection of her assimilation.

The portrayal of the yuppie's here and now entails, strangely, a New Age overreaching into the exotic/ethnic, or the "Chinese and dogs," as if the self would remain unfulfilled unless garbed in primitive attire. It is important to note that the effort is not to efface the self but to embellish it. Wouter J. Hanegraaff has long asserted that the New Age revisionism is a grab-bag where "Oriental ideas and concepts have, almost without exception, been adopted only insofar as they could be assimilated into already-existing western frameworks" (517). Hanegraaff is echoed by Torgovnick, who finds New Agers to invariably put diverse rituals and symbols from other cultures "in the service of a thoroughly modern world view that takes the self as a thing to be owned, cultivated, and coddled—the veritable hub of the universe" (*Primitive Passions* 176), oblivious to the erasure of self in Buddhism and many other traditions.

Accordingly, Tan integrates 1990s realism with Orientalist discourse. Tan's vivid, richly-textured description of the lifestyle of the professional class, of their house-hunting saga, and even of the avalanche which threatens to demolish their life contrasts sharply with the fuzziness of Changmian, China. The idyllic preindustrial countryside exists for the express purpose of touristic impressions and narcissistic wish-fulfillment. The Bishops' "former life" or previous incarnation at Changmian during the Taiping rebellion is similarly packaged in a set of tropes to ease the Western reader's entry into the Orient. American missionaries, Chinese bandits, and the Hakkas of the Taiping Rebellion led by the Christian convert Hong Xiuquan in the year of *"Yi-ba-liu-si"* (1864) are arrayed to manage the alienness. And it is here that Tan's kinship with the New Age ethos is blatantly exposed: she kneads together cultural elements as mutually exclusive as Christian linearity and Buddhist cyclic reincarnation, or the 1990s yuppies and the 1860s Hakkas, to advance her plot.

Tan sets part of her story at the time of the Taiping Rebellion (1851–1864) during the Ching dynasty, a turmoil which exacted 30 million lives and, according to Rudolf G. Wagner, was "the most important rebellion of the nineteenth century . . . with its decisive break with many traditional ideas such as footbinding, Confucianism, and its idea of selective adoption of Western technology and institutions" (1–2). Wagner attributes the cause for this "best documented rebellion in Chinese imperial history" to "the friendly contact sought by many missionaries and by the Taiping's themselves," resulting in "an unusually large, if far from complete, body of original Taiping documents" (2). The Taiping uprising is best documented for Westerners like Amy Tan, whose interest is aroused no less by the missionary mediation.

Moreover, the leader, Hong Xiuquan, was clearly influenced by the revivalist tradition of "England and Scotland, the United States, Germany, and Sweden in the first decades of the last century" (Wagner 11). The Taiping Rebellion was guided by a vision obtained in Hong's illness; in a state of delirious ecstasy, he revealed that he was the younger brother of Jesus, and son of God, mandated to eradicate the devils of Manchus and Confucianism. Much of this history is extracted by Tan, whose tale unfolds in the environs of the Thistle Mountain (Zijing Shan), the Tainping stronghold in Guangxi (41).

In a similar vein, Tan borrows from the historical Hakka and the Buddhist notion of reincarnation. Hong Xiuquan and most of his followers are Hakkanese. The feuding between the Hakka ("guest people") and Punti ("local Cantonese") leads to the eruption of the Taiping Rebellion, which serves to construct "Hakka identity through history" (29). Hakka's Christian belief, however fragmentary in Hong's interpretation, assuredly contradicts the motif of reincarnation in *Secret*. Progressing on a linear course toward heaven or eternal damnation, Christian theology is incompatible with the cyclic framework of Buddhism.

The heavy psychoanalytic bent of the New Age no doubt encourages Tan to view reincarnation in the Jungian sense as the accumulated result of *karma* or "psychic heredity." Tan's emplotment of *karma* at times betrays the casual attitude verging on unwitting mockery that New Agers take toward other traditions. The evil General Cape repays his debt to Miss Banner, Olivia's former self, by becoming Olivia's pet dog, hence neutralizing evil in a pseudo-Buddhist way. On the other hand, *karma* compels the interracial and cross-cultural Yiban ("Half-man") to be reborn as the mixed-race Simon Bishop. The adopted Elza instinctively reacts to Auschwitz because of her allegedly Polish Jewish ancestry. At the heart of Tan's arrogance in the cosmic reshuffling of history and religion lies her affinity to the New Age movement.

Closely related to the 1960s counterculture, the New Age obsession with the self reflects the disillusionment with the sixties utopian vision, which "turn[ed] into the narcissistic Me Generation of the 1970s and the ambitious, self-involved young professionals of the 1980s. . . . [Despite the apparent differences, they are children of the sixties in] the search for self-fulfillment in the here and now" (Dickstein 18). The title of Stephen A Kent's essay crystallizes the evolution nicely: "Slogan Chanters to Mantra Chanters: A Deviance

Analysis of Youth Religious Conversion in the Early 1970s." Tan in the 1990s continues the legacy of focusing narrowly on self-realization, even at the expense of coupling Chinese with dogs.

"Chinese and Dogs"

The celebration of Chinese-ness in Tan must be traced back to the American-ness of the author and her readers. The embrace of ethnic origin presupposes a source culture eager to be embraced, or one that is malleable enough for the author's fancy. This supposition leads Tan to conclude all three of her novels on the same note: the rediscovery of Chinese-ness beneath the protagonist's American veneer. Jing-mei June Woo's "Chinese genes" are felt to be activated once her feet land on Chinese soil at the end of *The Joy Luck Club*. In *The Kitchen God's Wife*, Pearl's apprehension that she might be the daughter of the sadistic, demonic Wen Fu is dispelled by her mother who weighs traditional Chinese principles of yin and yang over "genetics, blood type, paternity tests" (511), procedures that mark modern Western science. *Secret* likewise reveals the mixed-race Olivia coming to terms with her former life as a missionary in China. Beholding the beautiful landscape of Changmian, China, Olivia "feel[s] as if the membrane separating the two halves of my life has finally been shed" (205). For such a fantastic, potentially unflattering formula to strike a chord with "mainstream" American readers and create what Sau-ling Cynthia Wong calls the "Sugar Sisterhood" and the "Amy Tan Phenomenon," one suspects that Tan somehow validates the melting pot, the salad bowl, or a number of ethnocentric theories of American identity. Indeed, Tan's vision of multicultural America comes with trappings of Orientalism, upgraded by New Age chic, presented by hip San Francisco yuppies.

Tan's success hinges on her ability to revive Orientalist tropes as if she rejects them. To illustrate, one turns to the loaded phrase of "Chinese and dogs" in the context of nineteenth-century colonies like Hong Kong and foreign concessions. Imperialist history is enacted in Bruce Lee's *The Chinese Connection* (1972) when the sign outside a public park in Shanghai bars "Chinese and dogs" from entering. An outraged Lee then leaps into the air and kicks the sign to smithereens. The historical humiliation appears to metamorphose into an ethnic hubris in Tan since, initially at least, *only* "Chinese and dogs" gain entry into her New Age mystical fallacy. Following the modernist primitivism in the West, Tan celebrates the exotic Chinese other in the image of animals with supernatural instincts. Because the protagonists, Olivia and Simon Bishop, are both Amerasians, Western readers, by a strange but long-established Orientalist logic, could deduce that the noble savage is part of themselves as well. However, by no means is this part considered the core of Western identity. In fact, that tie with primitivism can be shed like a piece of clothing, like the New Age guru Yanni's shifting sets of the Taj Mahal and the Forbidden City in a single telecast performance.

By exploiting the thin line between the incomprehensible and the irrational, between the inspired and the insane, between the profound and the pathetic, between "secret senses" and nonsense, Tan is able to hold in double vision the comic Chinese sidekick Kwan, Olivia's half-sister. At once a seer with "yin eyes" (3) and a specimen of superstitious gibberish, Kwan at one point of the novel attempts to explain "secret senses" to Olivia:

> "Ah! I already tell you so many time! You don't listen? Secret sense not really secret. We just call secret because everyone has, only forgotten. Same kind of sense like an ant feet, elephant trunk, dog nose, cat whisker, whale ear, bat wing, clam shell, snake tongue, little hair on flower. Many things, but mix up together."
> "You mean instinct."
> "Stink? Maybe sometimes stinky—a"
> "Not stink, *instinct*. It's a kind of knowledge you're born with. Like . . . well, like Bubba, the way he digs in the dirt."
> "Yes! Why you let dog do that! This not sense, this nonsense, mess up your flower pot!"
> "I was just making a—ah, forget it. What's a secret sense?"
> "How I can say? Memory, seeing, hearing, feeling, all come together, then you know something true in your heart." (102)

Although endowed with mystical power, Kwan comes with the age-old baggage of Orientalism, evidenced in her pidgin English and her ludicrous ideas.

Through Kwan, Tan bestows the human body with mysterious power. To draw from the resources available to all, Kwan tells the Secret that is the Body that is the Soul: the inner spirit accessed through human physical sensations equated with the animal's senses. The elaboration of the various animals' keenest sensory organs intends to bring out the magical nature of the secret sense. The choice of animal senses, however, exposes the author's scientific knowledge rather than Kwan's preindustrial training. Whereas "ant feet," "elephant trunk," "dog nose," "cat whisker," "bat wing," and "snake tongue" may be metaphors for mental sharpness in a number of old civilizations, "little hair on flower," "clam shell," and "whale ear," are pieces of information most likely accrued by students of modern science. It is fairly difficult to envision a Kwan sitting through PBS's *Nature* or *Nova* to obtain scientific knowledge. At least, the novel does not depict such scenes.

Nevertheless, the refrain of animal senses proceeds in pidgin English, entirely without the proper possessive unit, hence the achieving a nonsensical quality to it, one that recalls Charlie Chan's aphorisms. Despite Kwan's seemingly random speech pattern, Tan uses pidgin English with great precision and calculation, illustrated by the word play on "stink" and "*instinct*". Further borrowing from Orientalist practices emerges in Olivia's frustration with Kwan's explanation of secret senses, a frustration that echoes the reader's inability to understand Kwan. Olivia's "I was just making a—ah, forget it" eerily resembles the concluding line of Roman Polanski's *Chinatown* (1974): "Forget it, Jake! It's Chinatown!" Chinatown comes to exemplify an evil and unjust world, totally beyond human comprehension; the private detective played by Jack Nicholson is therefore urged to forgo the pursuit of criminals amidst or outside Chinatown.

The deliberate pidginization of Kwan's dialogue comes into sharp focus when, half a dozen pages later, Tan has Olivia retell the same animal kinship with secret senses. During Kwan's séance with Simon's late girlfriend, Elza, Olivia believes that she in fact feels Elza's spirit:

> [Elza] wasn't like the ghosts I saw in my childhood. She was a billion sparks containing every thought and emotion she'd ever had. She was a cyclone of static, dancing around the room, pleading with Simon to hear her. I knew all this with my one hundred secret senses. With a snake's tongue, I felt the heat of her desire to be seen. With the wing of the bat, I knew where she fluttered, hovering near Simon, avoiding me. With my tingly skin, I felt every tear she wept as a lightning bolt against my heart. With the single hair of a flower, I felt her tremble, as she waited for Simon to hear her. Except I was the one who heard her—not with my ears but with the tingly spot on top of my brain, where you know something is true but still you don't want to believe it. (107).

A strategic retreat from Kwan's exclusively animal imageries, Olivia marshals New Age electromagnetic, biochemical terminologies. The ghost becomes gyrating "sparks," "a cyclone of static, dancing around the room." Olivia's pseudo-scientific language diminishes the distance of the protagonist from the middle-class reader, whom Kwan's jabbering serves only to alienate. Even when the same kind of elemental, primordial references to animal senses are raised, they are accomplished through parallelism and in perfect English, with the proper grammatical structure restored: "a snake's tongue," "the wing of a bat," "my tingly skin," and "the single hair of a flower." Olivia's "translation" of Kwan's remarks is crucial to link the ethnic other with the modern reader. The reinterpretation helps sustain the tension between Oriental stupidity and mystery.

Granted, this shift from pidgin to standard English seems justified by the two speakers' varying proficiencies in the English language. And Tan has

indeed matured stylistically in *Secret* by eschewing the artificial divisions between four pairs of mothers and daughters in *Joy* and the privileging of the
mother's Chinese tales in *Kitchen*. In her third novel, Tan has learned to do
three different voices exceptionally well and, moreover, to interweave them
seamlessly: the hip, fluent English of the American-born Bishops; the simple,
stilted English taken to be literal translation of Kwan's stories in Chinese;
and Kwan's pidgin which mangles English for comical effect. Yet, to attribute
Kwan's pidgin to her non-native-speaker status obfuscates the crux of the
problem: the novelist's white gaze at Kwan.

Tan inscribes Kwan with a linguistic exoticism that could only stem from
an outsider's ears, a fact painfully clean if one compares Kwan's English with
Louis Chu's language in *Eat a Bowl of Tea* (1961). Representing the ghettoized
community in post-war Chinatown, Chu develops a vulgar, abusive, and vivid
language that befits disgruntled bachelors. The Chinese men endlessly exchange insults, such as "many-mouthed bird, go sell your ass"; "you dead boy";
"shut up your mouth [not simply 'shut up']"; "wow your mother"; "where are
you going to die?" Marlon K. Hom in his review of the novel commends
Chu for translating "the Chinese speech faithfully into lively English" and
for "retain[ing] the source language's original figurative and picturesque idiomatic expression." Chu accomplishes this because he takes an insider's position vis-à-vis his characters' dialogues, eschewing "the literal translation of
Chinese speech into the servile, stilted English" or a transliteration of "Chinese sounds" followed by "appended English explanations" (98). However, the
subtleties of Chu's conversations, for example, "shut up your mouth," would
only be captured by a bilingual reader. To an English-speaking reader, Chu's
language seems far less inviting than Kwan's fortune cookie "spitch," to bor-
row Frank Chin's phrase in *The Year of the Dragon*.

In addition to meshing together the three Englishes (fluent, stilted, and
pidgin), Tan even attends to the possibility of a fourth linguistic scenario: the
failure of Olivia's English in China. On the airplane to China, Olivia, para-
noic about crashes, does not know how to order, in Chinese, "gin and tonic" to
calm her nerves. And Kwan seems to take special delight in Olivia's difficulty.
Olivia once again comes up short when she tries to win over a cow herder
who, having heard her tense and lengthy explanation, replies "in perfectly
enunciated English, . . . Assholes" (294). That cow herder turns out to be another Asian American tourist.[1] Tan exhibits with this episode her grasp of the
changing demographics of Asian Americans and the forces of globalization.
In view of her meticulous depiction of the multiplicity of Asian American
subjectivity, it becomes even more disconcerting to see how Tan clings to
nineteenth-century stereotypes of the Orient and the Oriental, albeit with a
New Age twist.

Put bluntly, for Kwan the Chinese "familiar" is a dog, serving doggedly the Chinese-American master, Olivia. Kwan's "dogged-ness" comes through in the determined pursuit of Olivia through reincarnations, in the loyalty to and solicitations of Olivia, despite utter humiliation, and in the obtuseness one is forced to conclude from her bad English and superstitions. Ever since her debut in the narrative, Kwan is in fact accompanied by animals and insects. Upon her arrival in the United States, Kwan offers Olivia a gift of grasshopper, which sends Olivia bawling in the airport. Tan adopts the microscopic, anatomical description of the cricket to demonstrate the alienation and instinctive rejection Olivia feels toward Kwan, her newly-arrived Chinese past. A common plaything for Chinese children, the grasshopper is defamiliarized as "a six-legged monster, fresh-grass green, with saw-blade jaws, bulging eyes, and whips for eyebrows" (10). Once again, the first thing Kwan undertakes upon return to China is to release a snow owl. The strategy of defamiliarization continues to function in that the owl is originally destined for the Chinese dining table, a barbaric practice to the affluent first world. Not just Kwan but all Chinese are animal-related. Miss Banner, Olivia's previous incarnation, calls her Hakka companion, Kwan's former self, "Miss Moo," after the sound of a cow.

The proximity to animals highlights the keen senses of the Chinese and sinophile characters. Miss Moo "felt a twist in my stomach, a burning in my chest, an ache in my bones" (174), in the wake of Miss Banner's elopement with General Cape and hence abandonment of her friends. The elopement may well be brought about by, Miss Moo regrets, her own praying for Miss Banner's happiness, a terribly irony which "shriveled my [Miss Moo's] scalp" (63). The searing human feelings of these characters are often narrated in awkward English to achieve an Orientalist effect, to defamiliarize universal emotions as exotic, somehow deeper, ones. Describing Miss Banner's misfortune, Miss Moo says that "she grew many kinds of sadness in her heart" (47), an unidiomatic and somewhat poetic expression that suggests at once foreignness and aestheticism. Note that Miss Moo's refrains of the body, be it "stomach," "chest," "bones," "scalp," or "heart," bring forth the physical coordinate in the New Age attempt at spiritual healing. Tan uses these deep pains in sensory terms as springboards for extra-sensory or trans-material leaps across the "karmic circle" (91).

The call of the primordial/spiritual is so strong that even the interracial yuppie Olivia cannot ignore it. In other words, Olivia's body "doggedly" feels the pull of her former life in China, just as her Americanized mind dismisses it. Whenever traumatic events in her life flash through the story, Olivia resorts to pidgin identical to Miss Moo's or Kwan's: the memory of electroshock treatments administered on Kwan "hurt my [Olivia's] teeth" (16). Olivia's dreams based on her violent death at the hands of the Ching dynasty soldiers are saturated with sensory impressions: "I've tasted cold ash falling"; "I've seen a thousand spears flashing like flames"; "I've touched the tiny grains of a stone wall"; "I've smelled my own musky fear"; and so forth. Such impressionistic snippets echo other intense moments in Olivia's life, such as the witnessing of Elza's ghost and the book's finale in the valley of the soul when Olivia smells the "dank, fusty odor . . . an olfactory version of déja vu—deja senti . . . like the way animals know" (310).

Before the knowing arrives, however, un-knowing, or the un-learning of rationality, has to occur. In exotic China, presumably their place of origin, Olivia and, to a lesser degree, Simon abandon control and become the Chinese other which is, in Tan's logic, the "essence" of the self. The key moment for this identity transformation comes while Olivia photographs the almost ritualistic killing of a chicken for a feast welcoming her and other American guests (264). Olivia acts simultaneously as an ethnographer documenting some primitive initiation rite and as an accomplice "shooting" the chicken whose blood is slowly being drained. Unlike Simon who passes judgement ("That was fucking barbaric. I don't know how you could keep shooting" [264]), Olivia submits herself to China, "where I have no control, where everything is unpredictable, totally insane" (261), leading her "instincts [to] take over" for photography. Tan, however, tries to deflate this sublime instant in the same way that Kwan's prophecy sounds also like idiocy. When Olivia inquires after the procedure of the killing, the old woman responds that she prolongs the chicken's death throes "for your photos" (265).

Subsequently, Olivia and Simon join in the uncivilized and hence the supra-civilized as they follow the lead of Kwan "at a half-crouch" to squat around to partake the chicken dinner (266). With such postures increasingly found only in the third world, they plunge deeper into the land of oblivion by consuming the local brew, "pickle-mouse wine. . . . Very famous in Guilin."[2] At the bottom of the wine bottle lurks "something gray. With a tail." In response, the Bishops' brains tell them to "retch," but they burst out "laughing" instead (268). Guilin itself does not produce any world-renowned liquor, whereas the province of Guizhou adjacent to Guilin geographically and close in pronunciation boasts of the wine of *mao-t'ai. Mao-t'ai*, of course, bears no resemblance at all to the sensational "pickle-mouse." It is fairly difficult to conceive of the Chinese, including the Hakkanese who are alleged to inhabit Changmian, naming their wine after the mouse, a pest as much detested in China as it is in the West. Even though the local characters may have concocted the name to poke fun at the Bishops, the ultimate creator of the phrase is Amy Tan. Revealingly, Tan's brand of spirits is christened in accordance with her New Age primitivism. With the function of "brain[s]" or reason suspended, a revolting sight turns into the threshold of an epiphany.

In the same breath as the mis-naming of wine, Tan misinterprets the site of the story as well. The fabricated site of Changmian is taken to pun, in mandarin, both "sing silk" and "long sleep." Equally poetic, both translations of the village name accentuate the gist of the novel. The protagonist Olivia's past life and the buried mementoes in Changmian are to be excavated in this present life by means of her secret senses, windows to one's soul. The two halves of the self are separated and linked, metaphorically, by a long hibernation in the image of Hakka's "never-ending" folk songs like silky threads. However, "mian" means "cotton" rather than "silk" (275). It may not simply be Tan's inadequate understanding of the Chinese language which results in this error. Tan is likely to be romanticizing the Orient in the stock images of silk, jade, porcelain, and so forth, whereas cotton readily evokes the American South and slavery, associations entirely inappropriate in the context. Granted that "silky" is more romantic than "cotton-like," granted that "pickle-mouse" is more revolting than the meaningless *mao-t'ai*, Tan's consistent mis-management of the Chinese language and culture is calculated to bring forth a fictional universe at once aesthetic and abominable, at once uplifting and degrading, in the exact Orientalist formula.

Initiated by ritual killing and sharing, of Bacchus-like intoxication, this dislocation of the Bishop's reasoning faculty is helped along by the renaming of objects and places. Willfully and unabashedly, Tan manipulates the representation of the other for her own ends as in the whole elaborate scheme of the Bishops' home-coming across continents and reincarnations. Put another way, the Bishops' previous lives as unrequited lovers in mid-nineteenth century China serves principally to silhouette their present crisis in marriage and to provide the means for a happy resolution. As such, the ceremony of wine and food concludes on a marriage bed. The inebriated couple makes love on a traditional marriage bed, after months of separation. Tan's New Age appeal lies ultimately in such facile usage of the primitive other. A marital dilemma or identity crisis with which modern readers readily identify is resolved by a revisiting of some magical fountain of youth, which blends animalistic, spiritual, and ethnic components.

The New Age obsession with healing never fails to loom behind the trope of China. Each and every one of Tan's female characters suffers from one illness or another. The Chinese matrons are often so strong-willed and "negative-thinking" (*Kitchen* 152; as opposed to the New Age precursor of "Positive Thinking") that they are taken to be mentally unstable, their malaise deriving from excessive repression of the past. The Chinese-American daughters are likewise caught in the emotional quandary of loving and hating their mothers. Tan's women are constantly plagued by the loss of their children, siblings, or parents. Specifically in *Kitchen*, the protagonist Pearl is afflicted with multiple sclerosis, Aunt Helen with a brain tumor, and Pearl's mother with too much pain and abuse from her first husband.

More appealingly, dog-like Chinese companions often have to be sacrificed in this spiritual convalescence for Chinese Americans. At the end of *Secret,* Kwan vanishes into Changmian's labyrinth of caves in exchange for, in a manner of speaking, Simon's return. The bittersweet, melodramatic reunion of the Bishops entails Kwan's disappearance. Of course, the melodramatic plot culminates in the birth of the Bishops' Samantha Li, who is given Kwan's last name in part because she is supposed to be Kwan's reincarnation. As James Moy diagnoses, "only through its [Asia's] death, or representational self-effacement, does Asia become real for Western audiences" (356). "Real" in the sense of "functional" or an irreplaceable ingredient in the Orientalist discourse, Kwan is preceded by Giacomo Puccini's Madame Butterfly, and in Tan's *Joy,* by Suyuan Woo, Jing-mei June Woo's mother, who dies to make possible the emotional return to China of the American-born June. To a lesser extent, Grand Auntie Du in *Kitchen* dies in the opening chapter to pave the way for the protagonists' disclosures of their secrets. Tan's melodrama of ethnicity hinges on the coexistence of the tragic demise of the Chinese characters and the rebirth of the Chinese-American ones. One cannot help recalling the episode in Tan's *Kitchen* revolving around the Shanghai prostitute Min. Min performs masochistic illusions of being tortured to death for the entertainment of mostly foreign clientele at Shanghai's Great World in the French concession. While the author purports to criticize foreign encroachment of China via Min's torn limbs, it is ironic that Tan's imagination invariably involves the death of Chinese sidekicks for the recovery or self-discovery of Chinese American protagonists.

In closing, I find it hard to resist a silly word play: "dog" spelled backwards becomes "god."[3] To Amy Tan, "Chinese dogs" and "Chinese gods" are one and the same, dogs deified, gods mongrelized. With both qualities instilled into "Chinese-ness," Tan's true motive is the construction of the American self which engineers and marionettes New Age ethnicity and primitivism. By rendering the Chinese simultaneously animalistic and divine, Tan in effect becomes an invisible creator, whose creatures reenact the Orientalist fantasies of her massive "mainstream" following."[4]

NOTES

1. Amy Tan feels that what she takes to be the cow herder can be, in San Francisco, "a doctoral student, a university lecturer, a depressed poet-activist" (293), hence highlighting the complexity of the Asian and Asian American differences. What appears to be a native of the rural Changmian in China turns out to be a fellow Asian American.

2. The liquor or "local brew" introduced to the Bishops by the two Chinese women reminds one of the witches' brew in Shakespeare's *Macbeth*.

3. Both James Joyce in *Finnegans Wake* and Samuel Beckett in *Waiting for Godot* give variations of this word game.

4. This article originally appeared as chapter 6 of Ma's *The Deathly Embrace*.

Works Cited

The Chinese Connection. Dir. Lo Wei. Perf. Bruce Lee. Golden Harvest, 1972.

Chu, Louis. *Eat a Bowl of Tea*. 1961. New York: Lyle Stuart, 1990.

Constable, Nicole. *Christian Souls and Chinese Spirits: A Hakka Community in Hong Kong*. Berkeley: University of California Press, 1994.

Dickstein, Morris. "After Utopia: The 1960s Today." *Sights on the Sixties*. Ed. Barbara L. Tischler. New Brunswick: Rutgers University Press, 1992. 13–23.

Hanegraaff, Wouter J. *New Age Religion and Western Culture: Esotericism in the Mirror of Secular Thought*. New York: E. J. Brill, 1996.

Hom, Marlon K. Review of *Eat a Bowl of Tea*. *Amerasia Journal* 6.2 (1979): 95–98.

Jung, C. G. *Psychology and Religion: West and East*. Trans. R. F. C. Hull. New York: Pantheon, 1958.

Kent, Stephen A. "Slogan Chanters to Mantra Chanters: A Deviance Analysis of Youth Religious Conversion in the Early 1970s." *Sights on the Sixties*. Ed. Barbara L. Tischler. New Brunswick: Rutgers University Press, 1992: 121–133.

Ma, Sheng-mei. *The Deathly Embrace: Orientalism and Asian American Identity*. Minneapolis: University of Minnesota Press, 2000.

Moy, James. "The Death of Asia on the American Field of Representation." *Reading the Literatures of Asian America*. Ed. Shirley Geok-lin Lim and Amy Ling. Philadelphia: Temple University Press, 1992: 349–357.

Prebish, Charles. "*Karma* and Rebirth in The Land of the Earth-Eaters." *Karma and Rebirth: Post Classical Developments*. Ed. Ronald W. Neufeldt. Albany: State University of New York Press, 1986: 325–338.

Shih, Vincent Y. C. *The Taiping Ideology: Its Sources, Interpretations, and Influences*. Seattle: University of Washington Press, 1967.

Tan, Amy. *The Hundred Secret Senses*. New York: Putnam, 1995.

———. *The Joy Luck Club*. New York: Putnam, 1989.

———. *The Kitchen God's Wife*. New York: Putnam, 1991.

Torgovnick, Marianna. *Gone Primitive: Savage Intellects, Modern Lives*. Chicago: University of Chicago Press, 1990.

———. *Primitive Passions*. New York: Knopf, 1997.

Wagner, Rudolf G. *Reenacting the Heavenly Vision: The Role of Religion in the Taiping Rebellion*. (China Research Monograph 25.) Berkeley: University of California Press, 1982.

Weller, Robert P. *Resistance, Chaos and Control in China: Taiping Rebels, Taiwanese Ghosts and Tiananmen*. Seattle: University of Washington Press, 1994.

Wong, Sau-ling Cynthia. "'Sugar Sisterhood': Situating the Amy Tan Phenomenon," *The Ethnic Canon*. Ed. David Palumbo-Liu. Minneapolis: University of Minnesota Press, 1995. 172–210.

LISA M. S. DUNICK

The Silencing Effect of Canonicity: Authorship and the Written Word in Amy Tan's Novels

In the past twenty years, novels such as Maxine Hong Kingston's *Woman Warrior*, Leslie Marmon Silko's *Ceremony*, and works by an array of African American women writers have become relatively common occurrences on university syllabi. The inclusion of these female authored texts is often a function of their difference from the grand narratives of "traditional" American literature. University instructors and literary critics alike have tended to highlight traditionally oral forms of narration, especially women's oral story-telling, found in many of these ethnic women's texts as equal to the traditional grand narratives of Western literature. While the attention given to these authors has broadened our definitions and understanding of what we consider literary, it has at the same time highlighted these authors' difference to such an extent that they remain always in some respect outside of or in opposition to a traditional conception of the canon. In some cases, the effect of this limitation have been to valorize texts that fit into the neat models of what writing by ethnic American authors should do and has relegated writers who do not fit into these models to the outskirts of our critical interest. Thus, certain writers become naturalized as intrinsically important, while others are relegated to the realm of the popular.[1]

In the realm of Asian American women's literature, we can see this exclusionary effect in discussions about Amy Tan's works. The criticism about

MELUS, Volume 31, Number 2 (Summer 2006): pp. 3–20. Copyright © 2006 MELUS.

169

Tan's works centers on the way that the dialogic nature of talk-story functions either to create or to bridge gaps between bi-cultural, bilingual immigrant mothers and their Americanized second-generation daughters.[2] In particular, since Maxine Hong Kingston's *Woman Warrior* underscored the Chinese tradition of "talk-story" as a major trope in Chinese American women's narratives, focus on this specific oral tradition has become the center of much of the critical work being done about Chinese American women writers. However, in the case of Tan's texts, this critical focus on the importance of talk-story serves to limit the interpretive work to be done on these texts. Studies of Amy Tan's first three novels, *The Joy Luck Club* (1989), *The Kitchen God's Wife* (1991), and *The Hundred Secret Senses* (1995), have correctly identified patterns of tension in her texts that result from the conflict between the oral storytelling of Chinese mothers (what has been identified as talk-story) and their American daughters' initial resistance to and eventual acceptance of that mode of narration.[3] Critical work on Tan's texts has largely ignored aspects of that corpus which separates it from the work of writers like Kingston—the importance of written texts and the literacy of Chinese mothers.[4] Consequently, by failing to recognize that Tan highlights the crafting of written texts as important, critics also have failed to appreciate fully Tan's representation of her Chinese mothers[5] and the work that these texts do within a broader context of literature.

This critical shortcoming may be recognized and perhaps rectified with a reassessment of her work through the lens of *The Bonesetter's Daughter* (2001). This novel's intense focus on the literary quality of women's writing may allow us to recognize that literary quality of women's writing may allow us to recognize that literacy in the form of writing and written texts represents an important and often more effective means of transmitting cultural memories and cultural identity across generational lines than talk-story. Furthermore, *The Bonesetter's Daughter* is not a completely new development in or deviation from Tan's previous themes, but represents a more fully developed reworking of issues about identity and language than we can find in many of her works.[6] Through an analysis of the importance of written texts, this study will demonstrate the ways that Tan's works present literacy and writing in order to reveal the critical problems with identifying non-Western narratives only through an understanding of oral traditions. The misreading of authorship in *The Bonesetter's Daughter* mirrors the mechanisms of inclusion and exclusion necessary in both forming and reacting to the literary canon and the silencing function that imposes limits on the possibilities of recognizing literary value.

Throughout Tan's novels, talk-story promotes multiple levels of misunderstanding between both Chinese-speaking mothers and English-speaking daughters and between persons who speak different Chinese dialects. As a linguistic strategy, talk-story in Tan's novels often fails to convey clearly the speaker's message to her audience. Some critics have attempted to complicate the use of talk-story in their analysis of Tan's work, but they never see literacy and written narrative as an alternative. Judith Caesar indicates that while Tan's use of a multi-voiced talk-story narrative is noteworthy, even more significant is who speaks in the texts. Following the usual line of argument that privileges orality, Caesar specifically argues that by privileging the accented and fragmented speech of Chinese immigrants, Tan gives their voices validity in the same way that African American writers have validated the vernacular speech of black communities (170). Caesar's arguments demonstrate the way that literary critics have found value in Tan's work through an interpretation of Chinese speech as a rhetorical device. Chandra Tyler Mountain recognizes that the memory fueling these stories "becomes the agent involved in redeeming cultures; it becomes a political struggle against the negation of cultures" (42). Consequently, many critics have recognized talk-story as a source of agency for Asian American women writers because it allows them a mode of discourse not constricted to the confines of traditional Western narratives.

In her article "The Semiotics of China Narratives in the Con/Texts of Kingston and Tan," Yuan Yuan comes closest to recognizing the limits of talk-story in Tan's novels by arguing that they embody a distinct aspect of loss. Throughout her novels, Tan's characters emphasize that their immigration to the United States after World War II caused an erosion or loss of their cultural memories. Throughout her texts, Chinese-born mothers attempt to perpetuate these cultural memories in the stories told to their American-born daughters, but often with mixed results. For the daughters, these talk-stories do not represent a stable text but depend solely on the mothers' memories. Thus, the mothers' continual revision of their stories often signals an erasure or loss of China as referent for the American-born listeners. As Yuan argues, "In short, China lies at an absolute distance from the present remembrance, irretrievably lost beyond recall, made present only through a narrative that invites forgetting instead of remembering" (293). Using China as the missing "prior text," Yuan calls attention to the inability of oral talk-story in Tan's novels to establish and maintain an intergenerational cultural memory of China as a cultural homeland, but she does not attempt to find alternative contexts within Tan's work.

The problems caused by talk-story, or oral communication in general, occupy a major place in Tan's first novel, *The Joy Luck Club*, when Jing-Mei describes not understanding her mother's story about the time her mother spent in Kweilin during World War II. Jing-Mei states that she never saw the story as anything more than a "Chinese fairy tale" because "the endings always changed" (25). Her mother's constant revision of the story's ending did not provide a narrative that Jing-Mei was able to recognize and claim as her own. Jing-Mei understands what her mother was attempting to tell her only after

Suyuan finishes the story for the last time. Gasping with the stunned realization that the story had always been true, Jing-Mei asks her mother what happened to the babies in the story. Suyuan "didn't even pause to think. She simply said in a way that made it clear there was no more to the story: 'Your father is not my first husband. You are not those babies'" (26). Jing-Mei can only begin to understand the story's significance when her mother gives it a recognizable ending and imposes on it a narrative structure that Jing-Mei recognizes.

The misinterpretations and misunderstandings of Suyuan's story are representative of those throughout the body of Tan's work. In part, these miscommunications are a result of faulty translation. Translation, as Ken-fan Lee points out, "suggests not only literal transformation but also cultural and psychological interaction" (107). A successful translation entails more than a desire to understand; a successful translation also entails ability and cultural knowledge.[7] Throughout Tan's novels, these failed attempts at communication are in part produced by a tension between persons who have different understandings of how stories, culture, and language are supposed to work.

Far from being complete failures, the tensions produced by competing forms of narration are somewhat alleviated through Tan's portrayal of the didactic nature of the mothers' voices. Winnie Louie's narrative, which comprises the bulk of Tan's second novel, *The Kitchen God's Wife,* provides a specific example of a mother who must teach her daughter how to listen and understand her stories as she speaks. In this text, Winnie narrates secret pasts and truths "too complicated" to tell her American daughter, but can only speak in English she has not wholly mastered. Winnie says that she will tell her daughter "not what happened, but why it happened, how it could not be any other way" (100). In the narrative that follows, Winnie uses talk-story to narrate her own history, but as she talks she must help her daughter understand both her broken English and what remains untranslatable. While the story chronicles the life of a young Winnie from orphan to abused wife, the narration consciously draws attention to the language that it uses.

Though Winnie speaks to her daughter in English, she must attempt to teach her Chinese words that *when spoken* have no translation. When Winnie is in urgent need of money from her dowry account, she sends a telegram to her cousin Peanut that reads "Hurry, we are soon *taonan*" (259). She continues with her explanation of the necessity for funds, but is cut off with a question about what the word means from her listening daughter. Winnie tries to answer her daughter by explaining the significance of the word since she cannot translate its literal meaning. She says,

> This word, *taonan?* Oh, there is no American word I can think of
> that means the same thing. But in China, we have lots of different
> words to describe all kinds of troubles. No 'refugee' is not the

meaning, not exactly. Refugee is what you are after you have been *taonan* and are still alive. And if you are alive, you would never want to talk about what made you *taonan*. (260).

This passage demonstrates the voice that Tan develops for her Chinese mothers by balancing the simplicity of dictation with vivid imagery to illustrate the narrative. It also demonstrates the confusion and misunderstanding common in exchanges between Tan's mothers and daughters. However, once she has explained and developed the idea of *taonan,* she can use the word throughout the rest of her narrative in place of a less specific English translation. Later, when she tells her daughter how fear can change a person, she says "you don't know such a person exists inside of you until you become *taonan*" (270). While the true significance of the word is always missing from the narrative, her daughter can begin to understand the importance of the word through her mother's instruction. Therefore, talk-story cannot be read as a complete failure, not should it be ignored in Tan's texts. However, talk-story cannot function properly for these Chinese mothers and American daughters without a source of mediation.

In Tan's novels, often the source of that mediation comes through the vehicle of the written text. For instance, in *The Joy Luck Club* the differences between Chinese dialects become evident when Lindo Jong cannot communicate with her future husband, Tin, because of his Cantonese dialect. Although they are both in a class to learn English, even that mode of communication is not wholly available because they can only speak the "teacher's English," which consists of simple declarative sentences about cats and rats. During English class, the two must use written Chinese characters to communicate with each other. Lindo sees those written notes as an important conduit for their relationship. She tells the reader, "at least we had that, a piece of paper to hold us together" (263). Though Lindo and Tin cannot understand the Chinese dialects that each one *speaks* they can understand the Chinese characters written on paper. While the two may be unable to speak to one another, the universality of a written Chinese character allows them to communicate clearly across the boundaries of speech.

This use of written texts reoccurs in the relationship between Lindo and Tin as they use written texts to facilitate their courtship. An-mei tells Lindo that in the movies, people use notes passed in class to "fall into trouble," so they devise a plan to "pass a note" to Tin (263). Because they work in a fortune cookie factory and can control the fortunes, the women decide to arrange a marriage proposal by putting the message in a cookie. Earlier, these fortunes were seen as both powerful and foolish by Lindo and An-mei, but appropriated for their own use, the fortunes become a valuable form of written communication. Sorting though the many Americanized fortunes, they settle on "A house is not a home when a spouse is not at home" to cross the boundaries of both translation and propriety (264). Because it breaks with Chinese custom for a woman to initiate a marriage proposal, Lindo uses the fortune cookie to "ask" Tin to marry her in a language and a custom that is not her own. The English writing must be translated (because Tin does not know the meaning of "spouse"), but the physicality of the text allows Tin to take the message and translate its meaning outside of the immediacy of speech. The use of a text, in this case an English text, allows Lindo to determine her future using the silence of the writing at a point when the vehicle of talk-story could not work, even with another Chinese-speaking person.

Lindo's use of the fortune cookie is an example of how we can find small, but important places where the tensions and misunderstandings between speakers must be alleviated through writing or written texts. Like Lindo Jong, Winnie Louie in *The Kitchen God's Wife* is highly aware of the importance of writing and authorship. Winnie demonstrates her ability to create meaning through writing the banners that she designs for her floral business. As Pearl tells the reader, the red banners she includes with each floral arrangement did not contain typical congratulatory sayings. Instead, "all the sayings, written in gold Chinese Characters, are of her own inspiration, her thoughts about life and death, luck and hope" (19). These inspirational banners with their creative sayings like "Money Smells Good in Your New Restaurant Business" and "First-Class Life for your First Baby" represent more than a creative outlet. For Winnie Louie, their authorship is the very reason for her business's success and an expression of her identity.

Winnie continually stresses the importance of her literacy and that of her mother. As a child on a trip to the market with her mother, Winnie tells the reader that she could not read and therefore could not tell what the paper her mother purchased was. Unable to read, she misses vital information about events that will eventually change her life. However, by the end of her narrative, her ability to write letters to her future husband enables her to escape from China before the Communists take power. In a society where the "traditional way" (121) deems that "the girl's eyes should never be used for reading, only for sewing" (121), the fact that Winnie's mother was both highly educated and bilingual represents an important difference. Winnie's ability to write in both Chinese and English indicates that her use of oral narrative was a conscious choice rather than the result of some limitation. That Winnie can choose between the two languages and modes of expression demonstrates that talk-story works only in selective situations and that it is not the only choice Chinese women have authentic self expression. Instead, literacy—the ability to both read and write—marks Tan's mother figures as powerful forces in her texts.

Though Tan asserts the voice of Chinese immigrant women through her own writing, the written texts that appear throughout her works endow Chinese and Chinese-immigrant women the agency to write *themselves*, an agency that critics have not yet recognized in the over-emphasis on talk-story. Tan has intentionally fashioned a complexity of voice for her Chinese mother figures. In her essay, "Mother Tongue," Tan emphasizes her conscious desire to give validity to the voice of those who speak "broken" or non-standardized Englishes in her novels. She tells her reader that she writes her stories with all of the Englishes she has used throughout her life. Most importantly, she says that she "wanted to capture what language ability tests can never reveal: her [mother's] intent, her passion, her imagery, the rhythms of her speech and the nature of her thoughts" (7). Tan attempts to capture what no language ability test would reveal: the fundamental literacy of her Chinese mothers. In addition, she also captures their literary ability. Tan's emphasis on the aesthetic power of non-native speakers emphasizes the art inherent in their narrative. Instead of representing the reclamation of voice, as some studies have suggested, Tan's portrayal of Chinese women's use of written texts demonstrates a less marginalized presentation of Chinese mothers than the critical focus on talk-story would indicate.

In *The Bonesetter's Daughter* Tan focuses her attention even more closely on the possibilities for communication in written texts. In his article on *The Joy Luck Club,* Stephen Souris argues that the Chinese mothers in that text speak into a void and that "no actual communication between mothers and daughters occurs" (107). He goes on to suggest that it becomes the reader who establishes the connections between the dialogic voices of the text and in whom the prospect for reception of the stories resides. In *The Bonesetter's Daughter,* Tan creates the possibility for the reception of cultural and personal memory in the American daughter because the daughter, in effect, becomes the reader of her mother's text.

The Bonesetter's Daughter focuses intently on the permanence of written texts and writing's most basic materiality through the recognition of ink's physicality. The connections between the physical nature of ink, the process of writing, and the lasting nature of text resonate throughout the narrative. Pan, LuLing's teacher and father figure, recognizes that writing preserves the moment in a way that cannot easily be retracted or erased and through this recognition stresses the effect of permanence in written texts. He believes that written texts become artifacts, and so he emphasizes the importance of writing one's "true purpose" when he reminds LuLing that "once you put ink to paper, it becomes unforgiving" (295).

Precious Auntie also specifically connects the act of writing with the quality of the text produced. She teaches her daughter, LuLing, that when you use the modern bottled ink,

You simply write what is swimming on the top of your brain.
And the top is nothing but pond scum, dead leaves, and mosquito
spawn. But when you push an inkstick along an inkstone, you take
the first step to cleansing your mind and your heart. You push and
you ask yourself, What are my intentions? What is in my heart
that matches my mind? (225)

Precious Auntie thus stresses the physical process of writing by drawing
attention to the amount of work entailed in preparing an inkstone for writing. She believes that the use of an inkstone, a more physical process of
writing, forces the writer to be conscious of her true purpose, rather than the
immediate feeling of the moment. Through repetition of this idea, the novel
emphasizes the importance of intent in writing and indicates that the type
of writing important to the characters in the novel is not the unthinking
act of recording immediate thoughts but the conscious and deliberate act of
preserving and communicating specifically selected messages.

Consequently, the writing and texts in *The Bonesetter's Daughter* are
represented as having power and importance *because* they are conscious and
deliberate rather than haphazard. Precious Auntie teaches LuLing that when
writing "a person must think about her intentions," and LuLing recognized
that when Precious Auntie wrote, "her *ch'i* flowed from her body into her arm,
through the brush, and into the stroke" (269). Each stroke, then, becomes
representative of the energy and character of the writer, and the words on the
page can signify more than the ideas that the shapes represent; they come
to signify the intent and character of the author. The marks on the paper
do more than represent words because they also somehow embody the life
and person of the writer. The autobiography that LuLing writes so precisely
does more than tell her life story; the perfection of the vertical rows and
complete absence of mistakes alerts Ruth to the clearly evident care taken
with its creation and the text's consequent importance. Although Ruth cannot understand the meaning of the manuscript's Chinese characters, she can
understand that they are important through their presentation.

Ruth could only understand this deeper significance because she had
developed a respect for writing's importance as a child through her sand writing and her diary. The young Ruth recognized that she "had never experienced such power with words," as she wrote "messages" from Precious Auntie
to give her mother instructions (85). As a child Ruth used words to gain
power over her mother by pretending to write the words she said Precious
Auntie's ghost told her. Her "ghost writing" had the power to move her family
and upset her mother's daily life, even though the words were only her own.
A similar power was also available to Ruth when she wrote out the hate she
felt for her mother in her diary because she knew that her mother would read

the diary and she knew that the words would affect her mother in a specific way. As she wrote the words in her diary, she was conscious of her intent and recognized that

> what she was writing was risky. It felt like pure evil. And the descending mantle of guilt made her toss it off with even more bravado. What she wrote next was even worse, such terrible words, which later—too late—she had crossed out. [. . .] 'You talk about killing yourself, so why don't you ever do it? I wish you would. Just do it, do it, do it!' (159)

When Ruth discovers the next day that her mother has fallen out of a window, her worst fears about the power of her writing make her believe that she has killed her mother. She comes to believe that words and writing have importance because of their potential power, a belief that will affect her throughout her life.

As an adult, Ruth states that her childhood guilt and fear has prevailed over her desire to write her own words. She knows that by writing a novel in the high style of writers like Jane Austen, she could "revise her life and become someone else. She could be somewhere else" (31). But the possibility of erasing those parts of her life she does not like through revision frightens her, and her fear of imagining her life differently through the vehicle of a novel stops her from writing her own texts and restricts her to writing texts for others as a ghost writer. Even as an adult, she believes that "writing what you wished was the most dangerous form of wishful thinking" (31). The fear that revising her mother out of her fictional life may erase her from reality hinders Ruth from claiming any sense of agency she might find though original authorship. Ruth's career as a ghost writer allows her to mold the words of others without the possibility of affecting her own life. Her fear also emphasizes other characters' perception of writing's power in this text. She has no personal investment when writing the words of others; they remain "safe" for Ruth.

Ruth eventually comes to recognize the importance of original authorship through the discovery of her mother's autobiography. Just as Precious Auntie saved LuLing through writing her autobiography, LuLing's writing replicates that rescue through her autobiography's effect on Ruth. By the end of the text, Ruth will continue the tradition started by Precious Auntie and begin to write her own stories. These Chinese women use written autobiographies to reveal and establish lasting conceptions of their individual identities. The text reveals Precious Auntie's identity to the reader through the autobiography that LuLing writes for Ruth, even though LuLing never actually reveals this secret to her daughter. Thus, Tan's palimpsest-like layering of written autobiographies in *The Bonesetter's Daughter* highlights the specific connection between authorship and the articulation of self and the importance of written text over oral narrative.

The written nature of these autobiographies illuminates each woman's sense of identity, while it also emphasizes the stability and power of written narratives over the oral. For LuLing, writing has a cultural and an ancestral importance. By replicating her own mother's autobiographical writing, she displays reverence for the importance and power of literacy. However, writing also has a practical importance for LuLing because she understands that her memory—and thus her ability to orally narrate those memories—is failing. She begins her narrative with the statement "These are the things I must not forget" (173). This opening line of her autobiography indicates that through her writing she will be able to preserve the past beyond her own memory of it. LuLing's narrative achieves a physical permanence like that of an artifact that the constant revisions and indeterminacies of talk-story lack. Although her speech (like that of Tan's other mothers) often results in misunderstandings and an estranged relationship with her daughter, her written narrative allows Ruth finally to understand her story.

Unlike the oral narratives told by the Joy Luck mothers, Winnie Louie, and Kwan Li in Tan's first three novels, LuLing's written narrative allows Ruth to be prepared to consciously understand and internalize the cultural importance of the story. Because LuLing's stories are written, they retain a possibility for translation beyond the immediacy of a mother-daughter exchange; the text's materiality allows LuLing's memory to be uncovered and read at a point when her dementia prohibits her from orally passing on her story and memories to her daughter. The written text also differs from oral narratives in that it allows for later translation and mediation—the only way that Ruth is able to understand the text—while an oral narrative's immediacy creates a transitory moment in which the story must be understood. Ruth's inability to read Chinese highlights a specific form of illiteracy and makes tangible the necessity for the specific knowledge necessary to translate meaning between mothers and daughters, a need that parallels that of the other daughter figures in Tan's work. The written text's permanence and physicality allow Ruth to give the manuscript to someone who has access to both English and Chinese for translation.

This translation comes through Mr. Tang, who is only able to recreate LuLing's voice in her text because he understands both the Chinese and English language systems. Using a photograph of LuLing when she was younger, Mr. Tang uses all of his senses to interpret LuLing's manuscript. He tells Ruth that "seeing her would help [him] say her words in English the way she has expressed them in Chinese" (341). Telling Ruth that he will need two months to translate the narrative completely, Mr. Tang declares "I don't like to just transliterate word for word. I want to phrase it more naturally, yet insure these are your mother's words, a record for you and your children for generations to come. They must be just right" (342). His declaration that he does not "transliterate" LuLing's writing signifies a move beyond a strict inter-lingual translation to an incorporation of textual mediation.[8] It also should remind us both of Precious Auntie's earlier statements about writing and of Tan's own position as a writer who translates Chinese and Chinese American culture for a larger audience. Mr. Tang recognizes the importance of giving Ruth access to her mother's words through the embedded signals inscribed in the process of writing. Mr. Tang's desire to capture LuLing's "essence" in the text is a recognition of writing's ability to preserve a moment, an intent, and the character of both. Mr. Tang recognizes that LuLing's text is more than a simple historical account, but can contain evidence of LuLing's entire self. This recognition leads him to emphasize the preservation of both the mean-ing of the text and of LuLing's aesthetic voice in the process of translation.

Tan clearly succeeds at giving a legitimate voice to the Chinese im-migrant mothers in her texts through the representation of their storytelling, both oral and written. Her articulation of women's authorship and the em-phasis on the power and importance of written words throughout her novels should signal that Tan works from an aesthetic tradition broader than that of talk-story or even of oral narrative; she works also from a literary tradi-tion. In the conclusion of *The Bonesetter's Daughter*, the image of Ruth using her recognition of Chinese identity by actively engaging in the act of writ-ing emphasizes the importance of the literary tradition in Tan's own work. "Ruth remembers this [her mother's story] as she writes a story. It is for her grandmother, for herself, for the little girl who became her mother" (403). The production of an *écriture feminine*—of women writing women and of woman writing herself—becomes repeated and amplified through the written auto-biographies of Precious Auntie, LuLing, and eventually Ruth by means of the writings of another American daughter, Tan herself.

As I have already argued, *The Bonesetter's Daughter* does not represent a divergence from an earlier pattern, but the amplification of an often ig-nored pattern in Tan's work. The misunderstanding of these patterns may have oversimplified analyses of Tan's works. For instance, if we recognize LuLing's narrative as a written text because it lacks the verbal markers of other narratives, perhaps the reading of *The Joy Luck Club* as an experiment in talk-story and the voices as actual *oral* voices does not take fully into ac-count the possibility that each voice has in effect authored its own written text. In the mothers' sections of *The Joy Luck Club*, we do not see the same stylized representation of speech that we find in Tan's texts when someone hears a Chinese immigrant speak. The mothers' voices do not seem to speak directly to their American daughters, as Winnie Louie's or Kwan Li's voices do, but instead seem to create texts that their daughters do not read. In certain sections of those texts, the voice of each mother becomes the narrative voice, and each woman effectively authors her own autobiography. Although it is Tan who actually writes these autobiographies, the narrative voices are highly literate and highly literary in their use of highly stylized and manipulated language. The importance of inscribing one's self on paper resonates most powerfully in *The Bonesetter's Daughter*, but it is speech's failure and the appearance of texts throughout Tan's other novels that should serve to suggest new ways to interpret written representations of Chinese immigrant women.

Tan's Chinese mothers not only verbally convey their stories but also use writing to assert their identity. Their understanding of literacy, the power facilitated by the permanency of writing, and their active engagement with and use of written texts demonstrate that Tan's mothers do more than talk-story. Scholarship about Chinese American literature became more recognized and integrated into the university curriculum after the highly successful *Woman Warrior* by Maxine Hong Kingston, but imposing the same critical paradigms on the works of Amy Tan (and perhaps other Chinese American writers) has confined and distorted the discussion of Tan's texts. The lack of critical recognition of Tan's Chinese mothers' literacy has produced studies and analyses that depended on an assumption of marginalization or silence. Many critics have assumed that the mothers' fragmented English represents their only means to impart a specifically Chinese cultural memory and identity to their American daughters. These studies have been important in opening the discussion of Tan's work, but they have missed the complexity of the representations of Chinese American immigrant women available in Tan's work. Amy Tan's novels do not demonstrate the inability of Chinese mothers to communicate with their American daughters but the artistic complexity of these interactions. Tan has created a literary tradition apart from Kingston. Not dependent on speech alone, Tan's mothers are able to move between speech and writing, voice and silence, through their literacy rather than their limitations.

More importantly perhaps, the misreading of authorship within these texts serves as a potent metaphor for the misreading of Tan's own authorship. In fact, the relative lack of favorable critical attention that Tan's work has received as compared to Maxine Hong Kingston's displays the effects of canon formation and canon critique. In his chapter "Material Choices," Robert Dale Parker argues that arguments critiquing the canon often rest on the notion of representation, and it is because of this reliance on the idea of representation that they ultimately fail. The idea of representation assumes that "there is a stable and coherent entity to be represented" and that "there can be an equation or one-to-one relation between signifier and signified, and that the signified (e.g., identity) somehow rests independently of and underneath the process (e.g., a novel) of signifying it" (171). Thus, the critical inclination to recognize oral narratives, like talk-story, assumes a certain identity politics—by representing one voice in the canon, we represent a constitutive identity (a good and noble endeavor, certainly).[9] But if the canon is expanded or obliterated to make room for, based on some notion of difference from a master narrative (i.e., representative of a majority identity), then there exists the risk of limiting based on the very exoticism of that difference. The terms of the discussion have not changed to be more inclusive, but instead use difference as a new policing mechanism.

Twenty-five years after Lyotard introduced a critique of grand narratives in *The Postmodern Condition*, the syllabi of university courses has expanded to include women's writing and the writing of women of color, but as this analysis of Tan's work demonstrates, this inclusion often comes at the cost of silencing the multiplicity of voices that challenge notions of identity representation on which critiques of the canon have been based. The focus on and near-fetishization of oral narratives, or other "non-traditional" narrative strategies, can produce the same limiting effect that those attempting to expand or abandon the canon critique. The failure to recognize what should be considered a major theme running throughout Tan's work and the pervasive focus on oral narrative demonstrate the way that critical practice informs reception and eventual recognition of texts. If, as John Guillory argues, the canon—composed of those works that appear on syllabi—serves as an ideological tool to teach the masses, we must also understand that this tool, which so many have used to represent the minority or ethnic voice, at the same time keeps it safely confined.

Notes

1. Guillory argues that "the distinction between serious and popular writing is a condition of canonicity; it belongs to the history of literacy, of systematic regulation of reading and writing, as the adaptation of that system's regulatory procedures to social conditions in which the practice of writing is no longer confined to a scribal class" (23–24).

2. For studies that focus on the dialogic in Tan's work see especially Souris, Wang, and Braendlin.

3. For critics who focus on oral narratives between mothers and daughters in Tan's work, see Chen, Reid, Shear, and Xu. For more general discussions of talk-story in Tan's work see Foster, Unali, and Reid.

4. Tan's work is often overlooked for other reasons besides the use or lack of talk-story. What has been perceived s a relative simplicity or the popularity of her novels has also had an effect on the academic reputation of her works. In a review of *The Bonesetter's Daughter* in *The Houston Chronicle*, Gibson writes, "Amy Tan has become the Rodney Dangerfield of contemporary novelists: Too often she doesn't get the critical respect she deserves because her books are such tremendous best sellers. If her writing is that popular, some critics conclude, it must be less serious

than that of lesser-known artists like Maxine Hong Kingston, whose *Woman Warrior* is taught at many universities" (21).

5. I do not mean to argue that critics have ignored or overlooked the Chinese mothers in Tan's work. Many critics have productively analyzed the mothers in Tan's novels. See especially Gately, Braendlin, and Shen. However, this study seeks to add to the current discussion by bringing to light an ignored element of the presentation of Chinese mothers: literacy.

6. While *The Hundred Secret Senses* does not focus on written texts as much as her other novels, the literacy of the mother figure remains important. In *The Hundred Secret Senses*, Olivia Laguni also becomes acutely aware of the limitations of illiteracy when she travels to China. As she drives through a Chinese village with her Chinese half-sister, she realizes that she cannot read the signs and requires Kwan, the text's mother-figure, to translate for her. While Olivia's illiteracy makes her relatively helpless, Kwan's ability to move between Chinese and English in both spoken and written language aligns her with the pattern of highly literate and *literary* mother-figures who have no need to negotiate between a Chinese and American self.

7. For more information on translation in Tan, see Yuan, Hamilton, Chen, and Lee.

8. For more information on the differences between intralingual, interlingual, and intersemiotic translation, see the use of Jakobson in Dan.

9. Guillory has more thoroughly explained the problem with a liberal pluralism as applied to canon formation.

Works Cited

Braendlin, Bonnie. "Mother/Daughter Dialog(ic)s in, around and about Amy Tan's *The Joy Luck Club.*" *Private Voices, Public Lives: Women Speak on the Literary Life.* Ed. Nancy Owen Nelson. Denton TX: University of North Texas Press. 1995. 111–124.

Caesar, Judith. "Patriarchy, Imperialism, and Knowledge in *The Kitchen God's Wife.*" *North Dakota Quarterly* 62.4 (1994): 164–174.

Chen, Victoria. "Chinese American Women, Language, and Moving Subjectivity." *Women and Language* 18.1 (1995): 3–7.

Dan, Shen. "Misreadings and Translation." *Cultural Dialogue and Misreading.* Ed. Mabel Lee and Meng Hua. Sydney, Australia: Wild Peony, 1997. 183–192.

Foster, M. Marie Booth. "Voice, Mind, Self: Mother-Daughter Relationships in Amy Tan's *The Joy Luck Club* and *The Kitchen God's Wife.*" *Women of Color: Mother-Daughter Relationships in 20th-Century Literature.* Ed. Elizabeth Brown-Guillory. Austin: University of Texas Press, 1996. 208–227.

Gately, Patricia. "Ten Thousand Different Ways: Inventing Mothers, Inventing Hope." *Paintbrush* 22 (1995): 51–55.

Gibson, Sharan. "Cheekiness of Tan: How Dare a Best-Selling Novelist Continue to Write Good Books?" *Houston Chronicle* 18 Feb. 2001: 21.

Guillory, John. *Cultural Capital: The Problem of Literary Canon Formation.* Chicago: University of Chicago Press, 1993.

Hamilton, Patricia L. "Feng Shui, Astrology, and the Five Elements: Traditional Chinese Belief in Amy Tan's *The Joy Luck Club.*" *MELUS* 24.2 (1995): 125–145.

Lee, Ken-fan. "Cultural Translation and the Exorcist: A Reading of Kingston's and Tan's Ghost Stories." *MELUS* 29.2 (2004): 105–127.

Leonard, George J. "Characters: The Asian Ideogram Systems—An Invitation for Beginning Students." *The Asian Pacific Heritage: A Companion to Literature and Arts*. Ed. George J. Leonard. New York: Garland, 1999. 15–28.

Lyotard, Jean François. *The Postmodern Condition: A Report on Knowledge*. Trans. Geoff Bennington and Brian Massumi. Minneapolis: University of Minnesota Press, 1984.

Mountain, Chandra Tyler. "'The Struggle of Memory Against Forgetting': Cultural Survival in Amy Tan's *The Joy Luck Club*." *Paintbrush* 22 (1995): 39–50.

Parker, Robert Dale. *The Invention of Native American Literature*. Ithaca NY: Cornell University Press, 2003.

Reid, E. Shelley. "'Our Two Faces': Balancing Mothers and Daughters in *The Joy Luck Club* and *The Kitchen God's Wife*." *Paintbrush* 22 (1995): 20–38.

Shear, Walter. "Generation Differences and the Diaspora in *The Joy Luck Club*." *Critique* 34.3 (1993): 193–199.

Shen, Gloria. "Born a Stranger: Mother-Daughter Relationships and Storytelling in Amy Tan's *The Joy Luck Club*." *International Women's Writing: New Landscapes of Identity*. Ed. Anne E. Brown and Marjanne E. Goozé. Westport CT: Greenwood, 1995. 233–244.

Souris, Stephen. "'Only Two Kinds of Daughters': Inter-Monologue Dialogicity in *The Joy Luck Club*." *MELUS* 19.2 (1994): 99–123.

Tan, Amy. "Mother Tongue." *The Threepenny Review* 43 (1990): 7.

———. *The Bonesetter's Daughter*. New York: Ballentine, 2001.

———. *The Hundred Secret Senses*. New York: Vintage, 1995.

———. *The Joy Luck Club*. New York: Vintage, 1991.

———. *The Kitchen God's Wife*. New York: Ivy, 1991.

Unali, Linda. "Americanization and Hybridization in *The Hundred Secret Senses*." *Hitting Critical Mass* 4.1 (1996): 135–144.

Wang, Qun. "The Dialogic Richness of *The Joy Luck Club*." *Paintbrush* 22 (1995): 76–84.

Xu, Wenying. "Amy Tan." *Asian American Novelists: A Bio-Bibliographical Critical Sourcebook*. Ed. Emmanuel S. Nelson. Westport, CT: Greenwood, 2000. 365–373.

Yuan, Yuan. "The Semiotics of China Narratives in the Con/Texts of Kingston and Tan." *Critique* 40.3 (1999): 292–303.

Chronology

1952	Amy Ruth Tan born on February 19 in Oakland, California, to John Yueh-han, a Baptist minister and Beijing-educated electrical engineer, and Daisy (Tu Ching) Tan, a vocational nurse and member of a Joy Luck Club whose stories about her life in China have been an inspiration in many of Tan's works; her mother died of Alzheimer's disease in late 1999.
1960	First published work, "What the Library Means to Me," appears in the Santa Rosa *Press Democrat*.
1967	Tan's older brother, Peter, dies of a brain tumor; seven months later, her father dies of a brain tumor; shortly afterward, doctors discover that her mother has a benign brain tumor. Mother confesses that she had been married to an abusive man in China and has three daughters whom she lost track of after the Communists came to power. After deaths of brother and father, mother takes Amy and her younger brother, John Jr., to live in Switzerland.
1970	Mother sends Amy to Baptist college in Oregon; Amy defies her, abandons pre-med studies to pursue study of English linguistics; follows her boyfriend to San Jose City College.
1973	Receives a B.A. in English and linguistics from San Jose State University. Jobs include bartender, switchboard operator, carhop, horoscope writer, and pizza maker.
1974	Receives an M.A. from San Jose State University; marries her boyfriend, Louis M. DeMattei, a tax attorney, on April 6.

185

1974–1976   Enrolled in doctoral program at University of California, Santa Cruz, and later, at Berkeley, through 1976. Leaves doctoral studies to pursue interest in working with the developmentally disabled as a language development consultant to the Alameda County Association for Retarded Citizens.

1976–1981   Language consultant to programs for disabled children, Alameda County Association for Retarded Citizens, Oakland.

1980–1981   Project director MORE Project, San Francisco. Freelance business writer for IBM, Apple, and AT&T.

1981–1983   Reporter, managing editor, and associate publisher for *Emergency Room Reports*.

1985   Short story, "Endgame," published in *Seventeen* magazine. Publishing agent asks her to write a book outline.

1983–1987   Freelance technical writer; begins writing fiction and taking jazz piano lessons as a form of therapy to engage her "workaholic" energies. In 1987, Tan accompanies her mother to China for a reunion with the three other daughters. Publishing agent asks her to write a book from the 1985 outline. Tan quits business writing to finish the work, completed in four months, which becomes *The Joy Luck Club*.

1989   *The Joy Luck Club* published; receives Commonwealth Club gold award for fiction, Bay Area Book Reviewers award for best fiction, American Library Association's best book for young adults award, nomination for National Book Critics Circle award for best novel, and nomination for *Los Angeles Times* book award; on *New York Times* bestseller list for eight months. A short story, "Two Kinds," published in *Atlantic*.

1990   Critical essays "The Language of Discretion," and "Mother Tongue" published.

1991   *The Kitchen God's Wife* published; designated 1991 Booklist editor's choice and nominated for Bay Area Book Reviewers award. Receives Best American Essays award; awarded honorary LHD, Dominican College. A short story, "Peanut's Fortune," published in *Grand Street*.

1992   *The Moon Lady*, a children's book, published (illustrated by Gretchen Schields).

1993   Writes screenplay, with Ronald Bass, for *The Joy Luck Club*.

1994   *Sagwa, the Chinese Siamese Cat*, a children's book, published (illustrated by Gretchen Schields).

1995   Novels, *The Hundred Secret Senses* and *The Year of No F* published.

1999	Tan is guest editor of *The Best American Short Stories, 1999.*
2001	*The Bonesetter's Daughter* is published.
2003	*The Opposite of Fate: A Book of Musings* is published.
2005	*Saving Fish from Drowning* is published.
2008	Operatic version of *The Bonesetter's Daughter* opens at San Francisco Opera.

Amy Tan lives in San Francisco and New York City.

Contributors

HAROLD BLOOM is Sterling Professor of the Humanities at Yale University. He is the author of 30 books, including *Shelley's Mythmaking* (1959), *The Visionary Company* (1961), *Blake's Apocalypse* (1963), *Yeats* (1970), *A Map of Misreading* (1975), *Kabbalah and Criticism* (1975), *Agon: Toward a Theory of Revisionism* (1982), *The American Religion* (1992), *The Western Canon* (1994), and *Omens of Millennium: The Gnosis of Angels, Dreams, and Resurrection* (1996). *The Anxiety of Influence* (1973) sets forth Professor Bloom's provocative theory of the literary relationships between the great writers and their predecessors. His most recent books include *Shakespeare: The Invention of the Human* (1998), a 1998 National Book Award finalist, *How to Read and Why* (2000), *Genius: A Mosaic of One Hundred Exemplary Creative Minds* (2002), *Hamlet: Poem Unlimited* (2003), *Where Shall Wisdom Be Found?* (2004), and *Jesus and Yahweh: The Names Divine* (2005). In 1999, Professor Bloom received the prestigious American Academy of Arts and Letters Gold Medal for Criticism. He has also received the International Prize of Catalonia, the Alfonso Reyes Prize of Mexico, and the Hans Christian Andersen Bicentennial Prize of Denmark.

MELANIE McALISTER is associate professor of American studies and international affairs at the Elliott School of International Affairs, George Washington University. She is the author of *Epic Encounters: Culture, Media, and U.S. Interests in the Middle East since 1945* (rev. ed. 2005).

MARINA HEUNG is associate professor of English at Baruch College, City University of New York. In addition to her study of Amy Tan, she has written articles about cinema.

JUDITH CAESAR is an associate professor of English at the American University of Sharjah in the United Arab Emirates. She has written two books about living and teaching literature in the Middle East: *Crossing Borders* (1999) and *Writing Off the Beaten Track* (2002), in additional to several articles on contemporary literature.

SAU-LING CYNTHIA WONG is associate professor of Asian American studies at the University of California, Berkeley. She has published many essays on Asian-American literature as well as her book, *Reading Asian American Literature: From Necessity to Extravagance* (1993).

WENYING XU teaches creative writing at Florida Atlantic University. She won the *Prairie Schooner* Reader's Choice Award in 1991.

M. MARIE BOOTH FOSTER is professor of English and vice president of instruction at Central Florida Community College. Her *Bibliography of Southern Black Creative Writers, 1829-1953* was published in 1988.

LINA UNALI teaches at the University of Rome Tor Vergata. Her English-language books are *Talk-Story in Chinatown and Away: Essays on Chinese American Literature and on US-China Relationships* (1998) and *Winter in Pearl Street* (2006).

PATRICIA L. HAMILTON is associate professor of English at Union University in Jackson, Tennessee. She has written articles about Daniel Defoe and Frances Burney.

YUAN YUAN has written articles on Samuel Beckett, J. M Coetzee, Maxine Hong Kingston, and postmodern literature.

SHENG-MEI MA is professor of English at Michigan State University. He has written *Immigrant Subjectivities in Asian American and Asian Diaspora Literatures* (1998), *The Deathly Embrace: Orientalism and Asian American Identity* (2000), and *East-West Montage: Reflections on Asian Bodies in Diaspora* (2007).

LISA M. S. DUNICK is a graduate teaching assistant at the University of Illinois, Urbana-Champaign.

Bibliography

Angier, Carole. "*The Joy Luck Club*," *New Statesman & Society* (30 June 1989): p. 35.

Baker, John F., and Calvin Reid. "Fresh Voices, New Audiences," *Publishers Weekly* (9 August 1993): p. 32.

Beard, Carla. *Amy Tan's* The Joy Luck Club (Piscataway, N.J.: Research and Education Association, 1996).

Bellafonte, Gina. "People," *Time* (14 September 1992): p. 79.

Braendlin, Bonnie. "Mother/Daughter Dialog(ic)s in, around, and about Amy Tan's *The Joy Luck Club*," in *Private Voices, Public Lives: Women Speak on the Literary Life*, edited by Nancy Owen Nelson (Denton: University of North Texas Press, 1995), pp. 111–124.

Caesar, Judith. "Patriarchy, Imperialism, and Knowledge in *The Kitchen God's Wife*," *North Dakota Quarterly*, Volume 62, Number 4 (1994–1995): pp. 164–174.

Chen, Victoria. "Chinese American Women, Language, and Moving Subjectivity," *Women and Language*, Volume 28, Number 1 (1995): pp. 3–7.

Colker, David. "Learn a Little of Her Story," *Los Angeles Times* (22 December 1995): E3.

Davis, Rocío G. "Identity in Community in Ethnic Short Story Cycles: Amy Tan's *The Joy Luck Club*, Louise Erdrich's *Love Medicine*, Gloria Naylor's *The Women of Brewster Place*," in *Ethnicity and the American Short Story*, edited by Julie Brown (New York: Garland, 1997), pp. 3–23.

———. "Wisdom (Un)heeded: Chinese Mothers and American Daughters in Amy Tan's *The Joy Luck Club*," *Cuadernos de Investigacion Filologica*, Volumes 19–20 (1993–1994): pp. 89–100.

Dew, Rob Forman. "*The Kitchen God's Wife*," *New York Times Book Review* (16 June 1991): p. 9.

Drolet, Anne McCart. "Telling Her Stories to Change the Con(text) of Identity: Four Novels by Contemporary American Women Authors of Color," *DAI*, Volume 54, Number 8 (February 1994): pp. 940–954.

Duke, Michael. "Red Ivy, and Green Earth Mother," *World Literature Today*, Volume 65, Number 2 (Spring 1991): p. 361.

Feldman, Gayle. "*The Joy Luck Club:* Chinese Magic, American Blessings, and a Publishing Fairy Tale," *Publishers Weekly* (7 July 1989): p. 24.

Foster, M. Marie Booth. "Voice, Mind, Self: Mother-Daughter Relationships in Amy Tan's *The Joy Luck Club* and *The Kitchen God's Wife*," in *Women of Color: Mother-Daughter Relationships in 20th-Century Literature*, edited by Elizabeth Brown-Guilory (Austin: University of Texas Press, 1996): pp. 208–227.

Greenlaw, Lavina. "The Owl's Story," *Times Literary Supplement* (16 February 1996): B13.

Hamilton, Patricia L. "Feng Shui, Astrology, and the Five Elements: Traditional Chinese Belief in Amy Tan's *The Joy Luck Club*," *MELUS*, Volume 24, Number 2 (1999): pp. 125–145.

Heung, Marina. "Daughter-Text/Mother-Text: Matrilineage in Amy Tan's *Joy Luck Club*," *Feminist Studies*, Volume 19 (Fall 1993): pp. 597–616.

Ho, Wendy. "In Her Mother's House: The Politics of Asian-American Mother-Daughter Writing," in *Critical Perspectives on Asian Pacific Americans* (Walnut Creek, Calif.: AltaMira, 1999).

Hubbard, Kim. "The Joy Luck Club Has Brought Writer Amy Tan a Bit of Both," *People*, Volume 31 (10 April 1989): pp. 149–150.

Huntley, E. D. *Amy Tan: A Critical Companion* (Westport, Conn.: Greenwood Press, 1998).

Kakutani, Michiko. "Sisters Looking for Ghosts in China," *New York Times* (17 November 1995): B13.

Koenig, Rhoda. "Nanking Pluck," *New York* (17 June 1991): p. 83.

Kramer, Barbara. *Amy Tan, Author of* The Joy Luck Club (Springfield, N.J.: Enslow, 1996).

Ling, Amy. *Between Worlds: Women Writers of Chinese Ancestry* (New York: Pergamon, 1990), pp. 14, 105, 130, 132, 134, 136–138, 141.

Lipson, Eden Ross. "The Wicked English-Speaking Daughter," *New York Times Book Review* (19 March 1989): p. 3.

Lowe, Lisa. "Heterogeneity, Hybridity, Multiplicity: Marking Asian American Differences," *Diaspora: A Journal of Transnational Studies*, Volume 1, Number 1 (1991): pp. 24–44.

Lyall, Sarah. "In the Country of the Spirits: At Home with Writer Amy Tan," *New York Times* (28 December 1995): B1.

————. A Writer Knows that Spirits Dwell Beyond Her Pages," *New York Times* (29 December 1995): B1.

Ma, Sheng-Mei. "'Chinese and Dogs' in Amy Tan's *The Hundred Secret Senses:* Ethnicizing the Primitive à La New Age," *MELUS*, Volume 26, Number 1 (2001): pp. 29–44.

McAlister, Melanie. "(Mis) Reading *The Joy Luck Club*," *Asian America: Journal of Culture and the Arts*, Volume 1 (1992): pp. 102–118.

Merina, Anita. "Joy, Luck, Literature," *NEA Today*, Volume 10, Number 3 (October 1991): p. 9.

Messud, Claire. "Ghost Story," *New York Times Book Review* (29 October 1995): p 11.

Michael, Magali Cornier. *New Visions of Community in Contemporary American Fiction: Tan, Kingsolver, Castillo, Morrison* (Iowa City: University of Iowa Press, 2006).

Mistri, Zenobia. "Discovering the Ethnic Name and the Genealogical Tie in Amy Tan's *The Joy Luck Club*," *Studies in Short Fiction*, Volume 35 (1998): pp. 251–257.

Mitchell, David Thomas. "Conjured Communities: The Multiperspectival Novels of Amy Tan, Toni Morrison, Julia Alvares, Louise Erdrich, and Christina Garcia," *DAI*, Volume 54, Number 1 (May 1994): pp. 940–968.

Nurse, Donna. "House of the Spirits," *MacLean's* (6 November 1995): p. 85.

Ong, Caroline. "Re-Writing the Old Wives Tales," *Times Literary Supplement* (5 July 1991): p. 20.

————. "Roots Relations," *Times Literary Supplement* (29 December 1989): p. 14–47.

Pavey, Ruth. "Spirit Levels," *New Statesman & Society* (16 February 1996): p. 38.

Peter, Nelson, and Peter Freundlich. "Women We Love: Nine Who Knock Us Out," *Esquire* (August 1989): p. 86.

Pollard, D. E. "Much Ado About Identity," *Far Eastern Economic Review* (27 July 1989): p. 41.

Reid, E. Shelley. "The Compound I: Narrative and Identity in the Novels of Toni Morrison, Louise Erdrich, and Amy Tan," *DAI*, Volume 55, Number 11 (May 1995): pp. 950–948.

————. "'Our Two Faces': Balancing Mothers and Daughters in *The Joy Luck Club* and *The Kitchen God's Wife*," *Paintbrush*, Volume 22 (1995): pp. 20–38.

Roback, Diane, and Shannon Maughan. "All 1992 Children's Books," *Publishers Weekly* (20 July 1992): p. 35.

Ryan, Marya Mae. "Gender and Community: Womanist and Feminist Perspectives in the Fiction of Toni Morrison, Amy Tan, Sandra Cisneros, and Louise Erdrich," *DAI*, Volume 56, Number 9 (March 1996): 954–971.

Schecter, Ellen. "The Moon Lady," *New York Times Book Review* (8 November 1992): p. 31.

Schueller, Malini Johar. "Theorizing Ethnicity and Subjectivity: Maxine Hong Kingston's *Tripmaster Monkey* and Amy Tan's *The Joy Luck Club*," *Genders*, Volume 15 (Winter 1992): pp. 72–85.

Scott, Margaret. "California Chinoiserie," *Far Eastern Economic Review* (30 May 1996): p. 37.

Shapiro, Laura. "The Generation Gap in Chinatown," *Newsweek* (27 September 1993): p. 70.

———. "Ghost Story," *Newsweek* (27 September 1993): p. 70.

———. "*The Kitchen God's Wife*," *Newsweek* (24 June 1991): p. 63.

Shear, Walter. "Generational Differences and the Diaspora in *The Joy Luck Club*," *Critique*, Volume 34 (Spring 1993): pp. 193–199.

Shen, Gloria. "Born of a Stranger: Mother-Daughter Relationships and Storytelling in Amy Tan's *The Joy Luck Club*," in *International Women's Writing: New Landscapes of Identity*, edited by Anne E. Brown and Marjanne E. Gooze (Westport, Conn.: Greenwood Press, 1995): pp. 233–244.

Simpson, Janice C., and Pico Iyer. "Fresh Voices Above the Noisy Din: New Works by Four Chinese–American Writers Splendidly Illustrate the Frustrations, Humor, and Eternal Wonder of the Immigrant's Life," *Time* (3 June 1991): p. 66.

Skow, John. "Tiger Ladies," *Time* (27 March 1989): p. 98.

Smorada, Claudia Kovach. "Side-Stepping Death: Ethnic Identity, Contradiction, and the Mother(land) in Amy Tan's Novels," *Fu Jen Studies: Literature & Linguistics*, Volume 24 (1991): pp. 31–45.

Snodgrass, Mary Ellen. *Amy Tan: A Literary Companion* (Jefferson, N.C.: McFarland, 2004).

Somogyi, Barbara and David Stanton, "Interview with Amy Tan," *Poets & Writers*, Volume 19 (September–October 1991): pp. 24–32.

Souris, Stephen. "'Only Two Kinds of Daughters': Inter-Monologue Dialogicity in *The Joy Luck Club*," *MELUS*, Volume 19, Number 2 (1994): pp. 99–123.

Sterritt, David. "*The Joy Luck Club*," *Christian Science Monitor* (16 September 1993): p. 11.

Tan, Amy. "Amy Tan," in *Writers Dreaming*, edited by Naomi Epel (New York: Carol Southern Books, 1993).

———. "Angst and the Second Novel," *Publishers Weekly* (5 April 1991): p. 4.

———. "Lost Lives of Women," *Life*, Volume 14, Number 4 (1 April 1991): pp. 90–91.

"Tan, Amy," *Current Biography*, Volume 53, Number 2 (February 1992): p. 55.

Unali, Lina. "Americanization and Hybridization in *The Hundred Secret Senses* by Amy Tan," *Hitting Critical Mass*, Volume 4, Number 1 (1996): pp. 135–144.

Wang, Qun. "The Dialogic Richness of *The Joy Luck Club*," *Paintbrush*, Volume 22 (1995): pp. 76–84.

Wong, Sau-Ling Cynthia. "'Sugar Sisterhood': Situating the Amy Tan Phenomenon," in *The Ethnic Canon: Histories, Institutions, and Interventions*, edited by David Palumbo-Liu (Minneapolis: University of Minnesota Press, 1995): pp. 174–210.

Xu, Ben. "Memory and the Ethnic Self: Reading Amy Tan's *The Joy Luck Club*," in *Memory, Narrative, and Identity: New Essays in Ethnic American Literatures*, edited by Amritjit Singh, Joseph T. Skerrett Jr., and Robert E. Hogan (Boston: Northeastern University Press, 1994): pp. 261–277.

Xu, Wenying. "A Womanist Production of Truths: The Use of Myths in Amy Tan," *Paintbrush*, Volume 22 (1995): pp. 56-66.

Young, Pamela. "Other with a Past: The Family Album Inspires a Gifted Writer," *MacLean's* (15 July 1991): p. 47.

Yuan Yuan. "The Semiotics of China Narratives in the Con/texts of Kingston and Tan," *Critique*, Volume 40, Number 3 (1999): pp. 292–303.

Acknowledgments

Melanie McAlister. "(Mis) Reading *The Joy Luck Club*," *Asian America: Journal of Culture and the Arts*, Volume 1 (1992): pp. 102–118. © 1992 Melanie McAlister. Reprinted with permission of the author.

Marina Heung. "Daughter-Text/Mother-Text: Matrilineage in Amy Tan's *Joy Luck Club*," was originally published in *Feminist Studies*, Volume 19, Number 3 (Fall 1993): pp. 597–616. © 1993 Feminist Studies. Inc. Reprinted with permission of the publisher.

Judith Caesar. "Patriarchy, Imperialism, and Knowledge in *The Kitchen God's Wife*" first appeared in *North Dakota Quarterly*, Volume 64, Number 2 (1994–1995): pp. 164–174. © 1994 North Dakota Quarterly. Reprinted with permission of the publisher.

Sau-Ling Cynthia Wong. "'Sugar Sisterhood': Situating the Amy Tan Phenomenon," was originally published in *The Ethnic Canon: Histories, Institutions, and Inverventions*, edited by David Palumbo-Liu (Minneapolis: University of Minnesota Press, 1995): pp. 174–210. © 1995 University of Minnesota Press. Reprinted with permission of the publisher.

Wenying Xu. "A Womanist Production of Truths: The Use of Myths in Amy Tan," *Paintbrush*, Volume 22 (Autumn 1995): pp. 56–66. © 1995 Wenying Xu. Reprinted with permission of the author.

M. Marie Booth Foster. "Voice, Mind, Self: Mother-Daugher Relationships in Amy Tan's *The Joy Luck Club* and *The Kitchen God's Wife*," from *Women of color: Mother-Daughter Relationships in 20ᵗʰ Century Literature*, edited by Elizabeth Guilory-Brown. © 1996 University of Texas Press. Reprinted with permission of the publisher.

Lina Unali. "Americanization and Hybridization in *The Hundred Secret Senses* by Amy Tan," *Hitting Critical Mass: A Journal of Asian American Cultural Criticisms*, Volume 4, Number 1 (1996): pp. 135–144. © 1996 Lina Unali. Reprinted with permission of the author.

Patricia L. Hamilton. "Feng Shui, Astrology, and the Five Elements: Traditional Chinese Belief in Amy Tan's *The Joy Luck Club*," *MELUS: The Journal of the Society for the Study of the Multi-Ethnic Literature of the United States*, Volume 24, Number 2 (Summer 1999): pp. 125–145. © 1999 MELUS. Reprinted with permission of the publisher.

Yuan Yuan. "The Semiotics of China Narratives in the Con/texts of Kingston and Tan," *Critique*, Volume 40, Number 3 (Spring 1999): pp. 292–303. Published by Heldref Publications, 1319 Eighteenth St., NW, Washington, DC 20036-1802. © 1999 Heldref Publications. Reprinted with permission of the Helen Dwight Reid Educational Foundation.

Sheng-Mei Ma. "'Chinese and Dogs' in Amy Tan's *The Hundred Secret Senses:* Ethnicizing the Primitive à la New Age," *MELUS: The Journal of the Society for the Study of the Multi-Ethnic Literature of the United States*, Volume 26, Number 1 (Spring 2001): pp. 29–44. © 2001 MELUS. Reprinted with permission of the publisher.

Lisa M. S. Dunick. "The Silencing Effect of Canonicity: Authorship and the Written Word in Amy Tan's Novels," *MELUS: The Journal of the Society for the Study of the Multi-Ethnic Literature of the United States*, Volume 31, Number 2 (Summer 2006): pp. 3–20. © 2006 MELUS. Reprinted with permission of the publisher.

Index